Statistics
on
Social Work Education
in the United States: 2000

By

Todd M. Lennon

COUNCIL ON SOCIAL WORK EDUCATION
ALEXANDRIA, VIRGINIA

Council on Social Work Education
1725 Duke Street, Suite 500
Alexandria, VA 22314
Phone: (703) 683-8080
Fax: (703) 683-8099
E-mail: info@cswe.org
WWW: http://www.cswe.org

Frank R. Baskind, President
Donald W. Beless, Executive Director

CSWE Archives 2002-410-01

ISBN 0-87293-093-9

FOREWORD

Statistics on Social Work Education in the United States is published annually by the Council on Social Work Education. Data are provided by CSWE accredited baccalaureate and master's degree programs of social work education. Data on the number of students receiving degrees cover the academic year 1999-2000. All other data are referenced to November 1, 2000.

Special appreciation is extended to Todd Lennon who compiled and analyzed the data and wrote this report and to Stephanie Dunn for her assistance. I also would like to express my appreciation to the program deans, directors, faculty, and staff for their cooperation in completing the survey instruments.

June 15, 2002

Donald W. Beless
Executive Director

GREYSCALE

BIN TRAVELER FORM

Cut By _Eric R_ Qty _45_ Date _10/2/24_

Scanned By _Kimlyn_ Qty _____ Date _10/2/24_

Scanned Batch IDs

_____   _____   _____

Notes / Exception

_____

_____

_____

_____

_____

TABLE OF CONTENTS

LIST OF TEXT TABLES

INTRODUCTION

This report contains the results of a survey of all baccalaureate and master's degree programs in social work accredited by the Council on Social Work Education in September 2000. In October 2000, one survey for faculty and program data and one to three surveys for student data were sent to all accredited programs, depending upon the administration and accreditation status of the program. The surveys used were as follows:

Schedule I - Social Work Education Programs and Faculty
Schedule II - Statistics on Baccalaureate Social Work Education Programs
Schedule III - Statistics on Master of Social Work Education Programs
Schedule IV - Statistics on Doctoral Social Work Education Programs
Schedule V - Statistics on Social Work Education Programs in Candidacy

Response rates to the schedules varied (see Table 1). Schedule I was sent to all social work programs, regardless of their accreditation status. Jointly administered baccalaureate/master's programs were sent one copy of Schedule I. Of the 501 programs sent Schedule I, 446 (89.0%) returned it. Despite an extended period of accepting responses and appeals for returns again this year, there has not been a 100% response from programs since 1982. These facts should be taken into consideration when comparing the aggregated data in this report with those in previous years.

TABLE 1

Number of Responses to 2000 Survey Schedules I - V

Schedule Sent	Number Sent	Number Received	Percent Received
Schedule I	501	446	89.0
Schedule II	420	372	88.6
Schedule III	139	126	90.6
Schedule IV	67	53	79.1
Schedule V	51	45	88.2

Many factors have influenced the presentation of this report. Due to rounding decimals to one or two places, percent totals or sub-totals within tables may not reflect the exact sum of the numbers preceding them. Also, totals in all tables may not correspond with one another due to the variation in response rates. In some cases, programs chose not to respond to a particular item in the survey, or incorrect data were received and requests for corrections went unanswered. Lists of accredited baccalaureate and graduate social work degree programs may be found in Appendices B and C.

SOCIAL WORK EDUCATION PROGRAMS

Geographic Distribution

The geographic distribution of social work education programs and faculty (see Table 2) remains virtually unchanged from year to year. The Midwestern states (Region 5) have the highest concentration of social work education programs and faculty. The majority of programs are located in the eastern half of the nation (Regions 1-5, 69.7% of programs responding). When looking at the number of faculty reported in these tables, one should remember that programs were asked to respond with information about all faculty in their program, regardless of position (e.g., full-time, part-time, adjunct, tenure).

TABLE 2

Social Work Education Programs and Faculty, by Geographic Region and Level of Program*

Region	Level of Program							
	Graduate Only		Joint		Baccalaureate Only		Total	
	Programs	Faculty	Programs	Faculty	Programs	Faculty	Programs	Faculty
1	5	325	6	123	20	121	31	569
2	6	234	8	487	32	196	46	917
3	5	212	11	405	40	201	56	818
4	5	225	20	537	53	275	78	1,037
5	6	201	21	776	73	415	100	1,392
6	3	139	14	353	30	160	47	652
7	4	100	10	268	23	100	37	468
8	2	91	4	67	10	56	16	214
9	5	112	8	227	10	55	23	394
10	1	47	4	119	7	36	12	202
Total	42	1,686	106	3,362	298	1,615	446	6,663

* Column totals may not correspond among tables within this report due to variance in response rates.

Region 1 - Connecticut, Maine, Massachusetts, New Hampshire, Rhode Island, Vermont
Region 2 - New Jersey, New York, Puerto Rico, Virgin Islands
Region 3 - Delaware, District of Columbia, Maryland, Pennsylvania, Virginia, West Virginia
Region 4 - Alabama, Florida, Georgia, Kentucky, Mississippi, North Carolina, South Carolina, Tennessee
Region 5 - Illinois, Indiana, Michigan, Minnesota, Ohio, Wisconsin
Region 6 - Arkansas, Louisiana, New Mexico, Oklahoma, Texas
Region 7 - Iowa, Kansas, Missouri, Nebraska
Region 8 - Colorado, Montana, North Dakota, South Dakota, Utah, Wyoming
Region 9 - Arizona, California, Hawaii, Nevada, Guam
Region 10 - Alaska, Idaho, Oregon, Washington

Institutional Characteristics

Table 3 shows that the majority of social work education programs are located in state institutions. State institutions also employ 63.2% of all social work faculty. It is evident from this table that stand-alone baccalaureate programs have very small faculties compared with graduate or joint programs. The frequency distribution of the institutional auspices has remained consistent from year to year.

TABLE 3

Social Work Education Programs and Faculty, by Institutional Auspices and Level of Program*

Institutional Auspices	Level of Program							
	Graduate Only		Joint		Baccalaureate Only		Total	
	Programs	Faculty	Programs	Faculty	Programs	Faculty	Programs	Faculty
Public								
State	22	747	82	2,555	134	906	238	4,208
Other	1	49	3	27	4	36	8	112
Private								
Church-related	5	161	11	322	125	532	141	1,015
Other	13	724	10	458	35	141	58	1,323
Combined	1	5	0	0	0	0	1	5
Total	42	1,686	106	3,362	298	1,615	446	6,663

* Column totals may not correspond among tables within this report due to variance in response rates.

As noted in Table 4, graduate and joint programs are most likely to be found in institutions with 10,000 or more full-time students. Conversely, stand-alone baccalaureate programs are most often found in institutions with full-time enrollments of less than 5,000. The distribution of programs across institutions of various sizes has not varied much from year to year.

TABLE 4

Social Work Education Programs, by Size of College/University Enrollment and Level of Program*

Full-time Enrollment	Level of Program			
	Graduate Only	Joint	Baccalaureate Only	Total
Under 2,000	3	4	89	96
2,000 - 4,999	6	15	94	115
5,000 - 9,999	7	16	64	87
10,000 - 19,999	10	31	46	87
20,000 and over	15	40	5	60
Total	41	106	298	445

* Column totals may not correspond among tables within this report due to variance in response rates.

The predominant ethnic/gender institutional identification among respondents was "non-ethnic, coeducational" (88.3%). Social work education programs in "black, coeducational" institutions make up 5.8% of all programs responding, while "non-ethnic, women's" institutions make up 3.6%, and "other ethnic, coeducational" make up 2.2%.

Number of Faculty

Stand-alone baccalaureate programs typically have faculties numbering fewer than 10 (259 of 291 in Table 5). There are no stand-alone baccalaureate programs with 30 or more faculty members. Larger faculties are characteristic of joint master's/baccalaureate and stand-alone graduate programs. The mean number of faculty members in graduate and joint programs is 34.11, a decrease of 2.90 from last year. The mean number of faculty members in stand-alone baccalaureate programs is 5.42, a slight decrease.

TABLE 5

Social Work Education Programs, by Number of Faculty and Level of Program*

Number of Faculty	Level of Program			
	Graduate Only	Joint	Baccalaureate Only	Total
Fewer than 10	6	7	259	272
10 - 19	8	34	29	71
20 - 29	2	20	3	25
30 - 39	4	18	0	22
40 - 49	6	7	0	13
50 - 59	4	6	0	10
60 and over	12	13	0	25
Total	42	105	291	438

* Column totals may not correspond among tables within this report due to variance in response rates.

SOCIAL WORK FACULTY

Every responding program reported faculty data on Schedule I. As previously mentioned, programs were asked to report every faculty member regardless of their position or time spent in the program. Although programs reported on 6,590 faculty members, the data received on many faculty members were incomplete or inaccurate. These faulty cases were not included in the following tables, so none of the tables will show information on all of the faculty members reported by programs. Care should be taken when comparing the data among tables because of the various response rates.

One part of the survey asked programs to report the percentage of a full-time equivalent (FTE) each faculty member spent in social work education and other institutional responsibilities. For this report, "full-time" refers to those faculty members who spend 50% or more of an FTE in social work education. This distinction should be kept in mind while reviewing Tables 6 and 8 and Tables 18 through 24.

Time in Social Work Education

Of all social work faculty, 59.8% spend 100% of an FTE in social work education. An additional 9.3% of full-time social work faculty spend 50 - 99% of an FTE in social work education. Table 6 shows that a greater percentage of faculty in baccalaureate programs hold full-time appointments in social work than do their colleagues in graduate and joint programs. This indicates that graduate programs are more likely to use part-time faculty than are baccalaureate programs. Part-time social work faculty most frequently also have a part-time university appointment.

TABLE 6

Faculty, by Type of College/University Appointment, Level of Program,
and Percent of Time in Social Work Education*

Percent of Time in Social Work Education	Type of College/University Appointment	Level of Program							
		Graduate Only		Joint		Baccalaureate Only		Total	
		#	%	#	%	#	%	#	%
100%	Full-time	875	56.1	1,823	58.9	1,034	65.2	3,732	59.8
50 - 99%	Full-time	132	8.5	292	9.4	156	9.8	580	9.3
25 - 49%	Full-time	4	0.2	11	0.4	28	1.8	43	0.7
	Part-time	197	12.6	472	15.3	213	13.4	882	14.1
Less than 25%	Full-time	9	0.6	6	0.2	24	1.5	39	0.6
	Part-time	343	22.0	490	15.8	132	8.3	965	15.5
Total		1,560	100.0	3,094	100.0	1,587	100.0	6,241	100.0

* Column totals may not correspond among tables within this report due to variance in response rates.

Table 7 displays the distribution of time faculty members are assigned to the baccalaureate and graduate levels in jointly administered social work programs. This table indicates that faculty in joint programs devote proportionately more time to the graduate program than to the baccalaureate program. Just over half of the faculty members in such programs spend all of their time in the graduate program.

TABLE 7

Faculty in Jointly Administered Programs,
by Time Assigned to Graduate and Baccalaureate Social Work Education 1999-2000*

Time Assigned to Graduate and Baccalaureate Social Work Education	1999		2000		% Change
	#	%	#	%	
All to Graduate	1,422	54.4	1,583	53.5	-0.9
Most to Graduate	368	14.1	414	14.0	-0.1
Equal to Both	302	11.6	346	11.7	0.1
Most to Baccalaureate	138	5.3	159	5.4	0.1
All to Baccalaureate	383	14.7	455	15.4	0.7
Total	2,613	100.0	2,957	100.0	

* Column totals may not correspond among tables within this report due to variance in response rates.

Sixty-seven of the graduate programs also offer a doctoral program. Table 8 shows how much time faculty members in the programs responding to the survey spend in the doctoral program. Only 5.4% of graduate faculty spend more than half an FTE in the doctoral program, while seven of ten spend none.

TABLE 8

Full-time Faculty in Programs Offering Doctoral Social Work Education,
by Percentage of Time Assigned to Doctoral Level*

Percent of Time Assigned to Doctoral Level	#	%
None	1,415	70.5
1 - 24%	306	15.3
25 - 49%	176	8.8
50% and over	109	5.4
Total	2,006	100.0

* Column totals may not correspond among tables within this report due to variance in response rates.

Demographic Characteristics

The following tables display various demographic characteristics of social work faculty, including age, gender, ethnicity, highest earned degree, rank, primary responsibility within the social work program, tenure, and salary. To maintain continuity with previous years' statistics, data for faculty assigned to jointly administered master's/baccalaureate programs have been aggregated with those of stand-alone master's program faculty.

Age, Gender, and Ethnicity

The distribution of male and female faculty members by age groups is displayed in Table 9. The modal age group at both levels and for both genders is 45-54 again this year. Males are more likely to be older than females at each level. The mean ages for males are 52.0 (graduate/joint) and 50.8 (baccalaureate). The mean graduate/joint female faculty member's age is 49.4, while the mean baccalaureate female faculty member's age is 47.8. On average, baccalaureate faculty members are 1.5 years younger than their counterparts at the graduate/joint level. These means have not varied much from year to year, but do appear to be increasing. Almost two-thirds of social work faculty are women, a statistic that has remained relatively consistent over the years.

TABLE 9

Faculty, by Age, Gender, and Level of Program*

Level of Program	Age	Gender					
		Male		Female		Total	
		#	%	#	%	#	%
Graduate and Joint	Under 35	59	3.6	156	5.8	215	5.0
	35 - 44	282	17.4	599	22.0	881	20.3
	45 - 54	658	40.6	1,181	43.6	1,839	42.5
	55 and Older	622	38.4	774	28.6	1,396	32.2
	Total	1,621	100.0	2,710	100.0	4,331	100.0
Baccalaureate	Under 35	24	4.7	71	7.5	95	6.5
	35 - 44	94	18.4	230	24.4	324	22.3
	45 - 54	211	41.4	435	46.1	646	44.5
	55 and Older	181	35.5	207	22.0	388	26.7
	Total	510	100.0	943	100.0	1,453	100.0

* Column totals may not correspond among tables within this report due to variance in response rates.

Table 10 displays the ethnicity of male and female social work education faculty members. The ethnic categories used in the survey were based on previous years' surveys and the membership categories of the Council. "Foreign" faculty are those faculty who are in the United States without a resident visa. The percentage of ethnic minority faculty at the graduate/joint level remained virtually the same as last year. An increase of 1.2 was found at the baccalaureate level. Tables 51 and 52 show that the percentages of minority faculty in baccalaureate and graduate/joint programs are the highest they have been in five years. African Americans continue to be the largest minority group, comprising 59.7% of all minorities at the graduate/joint level and 62.4% at the baccalaureate level. The percentage of male graduate/joint faculty members who are ethnic minorities is very similar to that of the women, although slightly higher. However, 4.0 percentage points separate male and female minority faculty members at the baccalaureate level with the percentage of women being higher.

TABLE 10

Faculty, by Ethnicity, Gender, and Level of Program*

Level of Program	Ethnicity	Gender					
		Male		Female		Total	
		#	%	#	%	#	%
Graduate and Joint	African American	223	12.3	449	14.5	672	13.7
	Asian American	54	3.0	78	2.5	132	2.7
	Chicano/Mexican American	63	3.5	60	1.9	123	2.5
	American Indian	18	1.0	27	0.9	45	0.9
	Puerto Rican	30	1.6	58	1.9	88	1.8
	Other	32	1.8	34	1.1	66	1.3
	Total Minorities	420	23.2	706	22.8	1,126	23.0
	Foreign	4	0.2	6	0.2	10	0.2
	White	1,388	76.6	2,380	77.0	3,768	76.8
	Total	1,812	100.0	3,092	100.0	4,904	100.0
Baccalaureate	African American	84	14.4	190	17.8	274	16.6
	Asian American	14	2.4	14	1.3	28	1.7
	Chicano/Mexican American	15	2.6	26	2.4	41	2.5
	American Indian	10	1.7	16	1.5	26	1.6
	Puerto Rican	9	1.5	42	3.9	51	3.1
	Other	8	1.4	11	1.0	19	1.1
	Total Minorities	140	23.9	299	27.9	439	26.5
	Foreign	3	0.5	2	0.2	5	0.3
	White	442	75.6	769	71.9	1,211	73.2
	Total	585	100.0	1,070	100.0	1,655	100.0

* Column totals may not correspond among tables within this report due to variance in response rates.

The educational attainment of male and female social work education faculty members is displayed in Table 11. The proportions displayed in this table do not change significantly from year to year. Graduate/joint faculty are more likely to hold doctorates than are their baccalaureate-level counterparts. Over twice as many baccalaureate faculty members hold a master's in social work as their highest degree than hold a doctorate in social work. The master's degree in social work is the highest earned degree for almost six out of ten baccalaureate faculty. At both levels, men are more likely than women to hold a doctorate. Of all faculty who hold doctorates, those holding doctorates in social work are in the majority. Very small proportions of social work faculty hold degrees in medicine or law or degree categories other than master's or doctorates. Likewise, very few social work faculty hold master's degrees in fields other than social work as their highest earned degree.

TABLE 11

Faculty, by Highest Earned Degree, Gender, and Level of Program*

Level of Program	Highest Earned Degree	Gender					
		Male		Female		Total	
		#	%	#	%	#	%
Graduate and Joint	Master's						
	Social Work	632	36.0	1,543	51.2	2,175	45.6
	Other	28	1.6	55	1.8	83	1.7
	Doctorate						
	Social Work	752	42.8	1,060	35.2	1,812	38.0
	Other	320	18.2	320	10.6	640	13.4
	Medicine or Law	19	1.1	33	1.1	52	1.1
	Other	6	0.3	4	0.1	10	0.2
	Total	1,757	100.0	3,015	100.0	4,772	100.0
Baccalaureate	Master's						
	Social Work	294	50.5	677	63.8	971	59.1
	Other	13	2.2	20	1.9	33	2.0
	Doctorate						
	Social Work	171	29.4	232	21.9	403	24.5
	Other	94	16.2	120	11.3	214	13.0
	Medicine or Law	8	1.4	8	0.8	16	1.0
	Other	2	0.3	4	0.3	6	0.4
	Total	582	100.0	1,061	100.0	1,643	100.0

* Column totals may not correspond among tables within this report due to variance in response rates.

Table 12 displays the educational attainment of social work education faculty members by ethnic categories. The most reliable percentages displayed here are under the African American and White categories—the other minority categories have relatively few cases counted and should be interpreted with caution.

TABLE 12

Faculty, by Highest Earned Degree, Ethnicity, and Level of Program*

Level of Program	Highest Earned Degree	Ethnicity						
		African Am.	Asian Am.	Chicano/ Mex. Am.	Am. Indian	Puerto Rican	Other & Foreign	White
Graduate and Joint	Master's							
	Social Work	45.2	28.8	55.0	31.1	43.7	23.3	46.6
	Other	1.7	1.5	1.7	0.0	0.0	5.5	1.8
	Doctorate							
	Social Work	37.1	53.8	32.5	60.0	36.8	52.1	37.2
	Other	14.2	13.6	10.8	8.9	19.5	17.8	13.1
	Medicine or Law	1.7	1.5	0.0	0.0	0.0	1.4	1.0
	Other	0.2	0.8	0.0	0.0	0.0	0.0	0.2
	Total	100.0	100.0	100.0	100.0	100.0	100.0	100.0
	Number	655	132	120	45	87	73	3,660
Baccalaureate	Master's							
	Social Work	64.2	21.4	68.3	53.8	72.5	56.5	58.0
	Other	2.2	0.0	2.4	7.7	0.0	0.0	2.1
	Doctorate							
	Social Work	20.3	60.7	22.0	19.2	11.8	26.1	25.4
	Other	12.5	17.9	7.3	15.4	11.8	13.0	13.2
	Medicine or Law	0.7	0.0	0.0	3.8	2.0	4.3	0.9
	Other	0.0	0.0	0.0	0.0	2.0	0.0	0.4
	Total	100.0	100.0	100.0	100.0	100.0	100.0	100.0
	Number	271	28	41	26	51	23	1,201

* Column totals may not correspond among tables within this report due to variance in response rates.

Almost all social work faculty hold master's degrees in social work (93.8%). Table 13 shows that those faculty members who do not have master's degrees in social work usually hold either a master's or a doctorate in a field other than social work as their highest degree.

TABLE 13

Faculty, by Highest Earned Degree,
with and without a Master's Degree in Social Work, and Level of Program*

Level of Program	Highest Earned Degree	Degree					
		With MSW		Without MSW		Total	
		#	%	#	%	#	%
Graduate and Joint	Master's						
	Social Work	2,177	49.1	0	0.0	2,177	45.9
	Other	29	0.7	52	17.0	81	1.7
	Doctorate						
	Social Work	1,763	39.7	41	13.4	1,804	38.0
	Other	432	9.7	187	61.3	619	13.1
	Medicine or Law	35	0.8	17	5.6	52	1.1
	Other	2	0.0	8	2.6	10	0.2
	Total	4,438	100.0	305	100.0	4,743	100.0
Baccalaureate	Master's						
	Social Work	970	62.9	0	0.0	970	59.5
	Other	6	0.4	24	27.6	30	1.8
	Doctorate						
	Social Work	384	24.9	16	18.4	400	24.5
	Other	170	11.0	38	43.7	208	12.8
	Medicine or Law	11	0.7	5	5.7	16	1.0
	Other	2	0.1	4	4.6	6	0.4
	Total	1,543	100.0	87	100.0	1,630	100.0

* Column totals may not correspond among tables within this report due to variance in response rates.

Rank

Table 14 displays the distribution of rank among social work education faculty in responding programs. At the graduate/joint level, faculty members are fairly evenly distributed between the three highest ranks and the other ranks. As might be expected, there are fewer full professors than associate professors and fewer associate professors than assistant professors at both levels. More faculty are assistant professors than any other rank except men at the graduate/joint level where there are more full professors.

TABLE 14

Faculty, by Rank, Gender, and Level of Program*

Level of Program	Rank	Gender					
		Male		Female		Total	
		#	%	#	%	#	%
Graduate and Joint	Professor	429	23.7	321	10.4	750	15.3
	Associate Professor	321	17.7	516	16.7	837	17.1
	Assistant Professor	297	16.4	607	19.6	904	18.4
	Instructor	233	12.9	557	18.0	790	16.1
	Lecturer	258	14.3	492	15.9	750	15.3
	Clinical Appointment	24	1.3	74	2.4	98	2.0
	Emeritus	18	1.0	9	0.3	27	0.6
	Other	230	12.7	518	16.7	748	15.3
	Total	1,810	100.0	3,094	100.0	4,904	100.0
Baccalaureate	Professor	115	19.9	95	8.9	210	12.8
	Associate Professor	134	23.2	224	21.1	358	21.8
	Assistant Professor	141	24.4	354	33.3	495	30.2
	Instructor	75	13.0	184	17.3	259	15.8
	Lecturer	60	10.4	126	11.9	186	11.3
	Clinical Appointment	0	0.0	77	0.2	2	0.1
	Emeritus	2	0.3	2	0.1	3	0.2
	Other	50	8.7	1	7.2	127	7.7
	Total	577	100.0	1,063	100.0	1,640	100.0

* Column totals may not correspond among tables within this report due to variance in response rates.

The educational attainment of faculty and their rank is displayed in Table 15. Full professors typically have doctorates. At the graduate/joint level, the majority of faculty in all three higher ranks hold doctorates, while the majority of those in the lower three categories hold the master's degree in social work as their highest degree. At the baccalaureate level, most full or associate professors hold doctorates while the majority of those at or below the rank of assistant professor hold master's degrees in social work as their highest degree.

TABLE 15

Faculty, by Rank, Highest Earned Degree, and Level of Program*

Level of Program	Highest Earned Degree	Professor		Associate Professor		Assistant Professor		Instructor		Lecturer		Clinical Appointment		Emeritus		Other		Total	
		#	%	#	%	#	%	#	%	#	%	#	%	#	%	#	%	#	%
Graduate and Joint	Master's																		
	Social Work	38	5.1	95	11.4	233	25.9	671	85.3	553	74.4	74	75.5	9	33.3	497	78.6	2,170	45.5
	Other	3	0.4	5	0.6	13	1.4	15	1.9	19	2.6	2	2.0	0	0.0	27	4.3	84	1.8
	Doctorate																		
	Social Work	491	65.7	566	67.7	525	58.4	59	7.5	99	13.3	6	6.1	10	37.0	56	8.9	1,812	38.0
	Other	210	28.1	164	19.6	111	12.3	32	4.1	57	7.7	15	15.3	8	29.6	44	7.0	641	13.4
	Medicine or Law	4	0.5	4	0.5	15	1.7	9	1.1	13	1.7	0	0.0	0	0.0	7	1.1	52	1.1
	Other	1	0.1	2	0.2	2	0.2	1	0.1	2	0.3	1	1.0	0	0.0	1	0.2	10	0.2
	Total	747	100.0	836	100.0	899	100.0	787	100.0	743	100.0	98	100.0	27	100.0	632	100.0	4,769	100.0
Baccalaureate	Master's																		
	Social Work	65	31.0	149	41.9	258	52.1	216	84.7	165	88.7	2	100.0	9	33.3	107	89.9	963	59.2
	Other	0	0.0	1	0.3	5	1.0	14	5.5	8	4.3	0	0.0	0	0.0	2	1.7	30	1.8
	Doctorate																		
	Social Work	75	35.7	133	37.4	173	34.9	8	3.1	8	4.3	0	0.0	10	37.0	6	5.0	403	24.8
	Other	66	31.4	69	19.4	54	10.9	10	3.9	4	2.2	0	0.0	8	29.6	4	3.4	209	12.9
	Medicine or Law	4	1.9	4	1.1	4	0.8	3	1.2	1	0.5	0	0.0	0	0.0	0	0.0	16	1.0
	Other	0	0.0	0	0.0	1	0.2	4	1.6	0	0.0	0	0.0	0	0.0	0	0.0	5	0.3
	Total	210	100.0	356	100.0	495	100.0	255	100.0	186	100.0	2	100.0	27	100.0	119	100.0	1,626	100.0

*Column totals may not correspond among tables within this report due to variance in response rates.

15

Table 16 displays the distribution of rank by ethnicity. Again, due to the small number of minority faculty members, caution should be taken in interpreting these percentages.

TABLE 16

Faculty, by Rank, Ethnicity and Level of Program*

Level of Program	Rank	Ethnicity						
		African Am.	Asian Am.	Chicano/ Mex. Am.	Am. Indian	Puerto Rican	Other & Foreign	White
Graduate and Joint	Professor	12.1	23.7	8.2	20.0	28.4	13.2	15.5
	Assoc. Prof.	22.0	19.8	19.7	31.1	20.5	23.7	15.7
	Asst. Prof.	25.5	28.2	17.2	15.6	10.2	35.5	16.8
	Instructor	9.6	9.2	9.0	17.8	9.1	7.9	18.0
	Lecturer	11.7	11.5	15.6	8.9	12.5	9.2	16.3
	Clinical Appt.	2.5	0.0	2.5	0.0	0.0	0.0	2.1
	Emeritus	0.1	0.0	0.0	0.0	0.0	0.0	0.7
	Other	16.3	7.6	27.9	6.7	19.3	10.5	15.0
	Total	100.0	100.0	100.0	100.0	100.0	100.0	100.0
	Number	667	131	122	45	88	76	3,768
Baccalaureate	Professor	11.3	21.4	7.7	7.7	12.8	12.5	13.3
	Assoc. Prof.	19.3	25.0	23.1	19.2	4.3	29.2	22.8
	Asst. Prof.	28.5	50.0	10.3	30.8	27.7	25.0	30.9
	Instructor	21.9	0.0	15.4	19.2	19.1	12.5	14.6
	Lecturer	12.0	3.6	10.3	23.1	21.3	20.8	10.7
	Clinical Appt.	0.4	0.0	2.6	0.0	0.0	0.0	0.0
	Emeritus	0.0	0.0	0.0	0.0	0.0	0.0	0.3
	Other	6.6	0.0	30.8	0.0	14.9	0.0	7.6
	Total	100.0	100.0	100.0	100.0	100.0	100.0	100.0
	Number	274	28	39	26	47	24	1,200

* Column totals may not correspond among tables within this report due to variance in response rates.

Primary Responsibility

Tables 17 and 18 show the distribution of the primary responsibility of social work faculty within the social work program. Faculty members with formal administrative titles are included under those specific titles. Programs were asked to report the time faculty spent in classroom teaching, field instruction, field liaison responsibilities, administration, and other social work responsibilities. No definitions were given for these categories. For this report, "primary responsibility" is defined as that responsibility that receives the greatest amount of the faculty member's time. Faculty members who spend equal amounts of time in classroom and field instruction or liaison activities were combined, as were those who spend most of their time in field activities. Individuals who spend most of their time in "other" social work responsibilities are listed as "other."

Table 17 displays the primary responsibilities of social work faculty. The majority of baccalaureate faculty (66.2%) are dedicated to teaching. At the graduate level, almost three out of four faculty members spend their time primarily in teaching. At both levels, most of these faculty are primarily classroom teachers. There is little difference between males and females in this characteristic; however, the percentage of females at the graduate/joint level in field work is clearly higher than that of the males with the same responsibility. More females (50.4% at the graduate/joint level and 62.9% the baccalaureate level) than males serve as dean/director of social work programs. Females outnumber males in all responsibility categories, except one.

TABLE 17

Faculty, by Primary Responsibility, Gender, and Level of Program*

Level of Program	Primary Responsibility	Gender					
		Male		Female		Total	
		#	%	#	%	#	%
Graduate and Joint	Classroom Teaching	1,120	64.9	1,659	56.9	2,779	59.9
	Classroom and Field	18	1.0	45	1.5	63	1.4
	Field Instruction/Liaison	108	6.3	389	13.3	497	10.7
	Total Teaching	1,246	72.2	2,093	71.7	3,339	71.9
	Dean/Director	67	3.9	68	2.3	135	2.9
	Associate Dean/Director	41	2.4	40	1.4	81	1.7
	Assistant Dean/Director	15	0.9	27	0.9	42	0.9
	Director Undergraduate Program	28	1.6	50	1.7	78	1.7
	Director Field Instruction	23	1.3	94	3.2	117	2.5
	Asst. Director Field Instruction	8	0.5	36	1.2	44	0.9
	Dir. Admissions/Minority Recruitment	14	0.8	23	0.8	37	0.8
	Dir. Continuing Education/Work Study	5	0.3	9	0.3	14	0.3
	Dir. Research/Research Administrator	3	0.2	6	0.2	9	0.2
	Alumni/Career Development Coordinator	0	0.0	7	0.2	7	0.2
	Other Administration	84	4.9	117	4.0	201	4.3
	Total Administration	288	16.7	477	16.3	765	16.5
	Other	191	11.1	348	11.9	539	11.6
	Total	1,725	100.0	2,918	100.0	4,643	100.0
Baccalaureate	Classroom Teaching	366	65.0	588	57.6	954	60.2
	Classroom and Field	13	2.3	29	2.8	42	2.7
	Field Instruction/Liaison	10	1.8	42	4.1	52	3.3
	Total Teaching	389	69.1	659	64.5	1,048	66.2
	Dean/Director	91	16.2	154	15.1	245	15.5
	Director Field Instruction	51	9.0	130	12.7	181	11.4
	Other Administration	13	2.3	32	3.1	45	2.8
	Total Administration	155	27.5	316	31.0	471	29.7
	Other	19	3.4	46	4.5	65	4.1
	Total	563	100.0	1,021	100.0	1,584	100.0

* Column totals may not correspond among tables within this report due to variance in response rates.

Table 18 further breaks down the responsibilities of social work faculty. It displays the mean percentage of time spent in classroom teaching, field instruction, field liaison, administration, and other social work responsibilities. The proportion of time spent in the different responsibilities is generally comparable across the two levels. As would be expected, classroom teachers spend most of their time with classroom responsibilities. Baccalaureate administrators spend far more time in the classroom than do their graduate/joint counterparts. Indeed, baccalaureate program directors in graduate/joint programs spend more time in classroom teaching than any other administrator at that level. Considering that baccalaureate programs average less than six faculty members, it is not surprising that baccalaureate faculty members carry multiple responsibilities.

TABLE 18

Mean Percentage of Time Full-time Faculty Members Assigned to Responsibilities in Social Work Programs, by Primary Responsibility and Level of Program

Level of Program	Primary Responsibility	Mean Percentage Assigned				
		Classroom Teaching	Field Instruction	Field Liaison	Admini- stration	Other
Graduate and Joint	Classroom Teaching	78.15	1.04	6.98	1.12	6.68
	Classroom and Field	43.90	22.60	21.31	0.00	0.96
	Field Instruction/Liaison	8.78	24.08	48.70	1.62	1.99
	Dean/Director	18.26	0.42	1.05	74.82	4.43
	Associate Dean/Director	24.94	0.22	3.00	61.30	9.47
	Assistant Dean/Director	18.50	2.38	3.43	67.83	6.64
	Dir. Undergrad Program	46.19	0.96	5.51	41.35	5.87
	Director Field Instruction	16.42	15.21	15.50	48.04	4.16
	Asst. Dir. Field Instruction	12.44	8.14	22.33	47.09	5.00
	Dir. Admissions/ Minority Recruitment	29.16	0.54	2.05	54.19	10.46
	Dir. Continuing Ed./ Work Study	21.54	2.38	6.30	48.54	21.23
	Dir. Research/Res. Admin.	45.67	0.00	0.00	39.29	24.78
	Alumni/Career Dev. Coord.	10.00	0.00	0.00	43.75	20.00
	Other Administration	40.27	2.52	4.25	36.81	13.28
	Other	22.71	0.72	3.26	13.29	57.12
Baccalaureate	Classroom Teaching	81.96	1.81	4.96	2.17	2.69
	Classroom and Field	42.02	20.17	21.86	0.00	0.48
	Field Instruction/Liaison	16.47	39.66	26.03	3.95	3.58
	Dean/Director	55.70	1.79	3.13	34.67	2.97
	Director Field Instruction	47.87	18.87	13.66	15.18	2.50
	Other Administration	50.07	6.80	7.98	21.56	4.90
	Other	29.47	1.67	1.67	25.88	37.81

Years on Full-time Faculty

Table 19 displays the number of years social work faculty were reported to have been on full-time status in the social work program. The survey did not specify the definition of "full-time." It is interesting to note that of the newly hired faculty, half of the baccalaureate and over half of the graduate faculty were hired at the non-professorial ranks. This may indicate a tendency of programs to hire more temporary or adjunct faculty. As would be expected, more graduate/joint full professors have longer service than their colleagues at lower ranks. At the baccalaureate level, associate professors have more seniority. Faculty with 1-5 years of service are most frequently assistant professors.

TABLE 19

Faculty, by Gender, Years on Full-time Faculty, Rank, and Level of Program*

Level of Program	Rank	Gender	Years on Full-time Faculty				
			0	1 – 5	6 – 10	11 & Over	Total
Graduate and Joint	Professor	Male	8	61	54	272	395
		Female	14	32	48	207	301
	Associate Prof.	Male	18	56	100	128	302
		Female	21	89	183	192	485
	Assistant Prof.	Male	39	176	25	15	255
		Female	88	341	67	36	532
	Other	Male	92	83	25	24	224
		Female	233	245	68	62	608
	Total	Male	157	376	204	439	1,176
		Female	356	707	366	497	1,926
Baccalaureate	Professor	Male	5	10	9	76	100
		Female	5	11	10	61	87
	Associate Prof.	Male	8	13	44	63	128
		Female	10	40	63	94	207
	Assistant Prof.	Male	25	74	18	8	125
		Female	55	175	59	39	328
	Other	Male	29	21	2	2	54
		Female	73	69	9	7	158
	Total	Male	67	118	73	149	407
		Female	143	295	141	198	777

* Column totals may not correspond among tables within this report due to variance in response rates.

Tenure

The proportion of full-time social work faculty members with tenure is displayed in Tables 20 and 21. Table 20 shows that tenured faculty with doctorates outnumber those without. Over half of all tenured graduate/joint faculty members hold a doctorate in social work. At the baccalaureate level, four out of ten tenured faculty hold a master's degree in social work as their highest earned degree. Social work faculty with tenure typically hold an advanced degree in social work. Table 21 shows that the percentages of females with tenure in graduate/joint programs and baccalaureate programs have increased for the tenth year in a row. Tenured graduate/joint faculty are more frequently full professors, while tenured baccalaureate faculty are usually associate professors.

TABLE 20

Percentage of Full-time Faculty with Tenure, by Highest Earned Degree and Level of Program*

Highest Earned Degree	Level of Program	
	Graduate and Joint	Baccalaureate
Master's		
Social Work	8.5	42.5
Other	0.5	0.2
Doctorate		
Social Work	67.1	36.6
Other	23.1	19.1
Medicine or Law	0.5	1.4
Other	0.1	0.2
Total: Percent	100.0	100.0
Number	1,357	503

TABLE 21

Percentage of Full-time Faculty with Tenure,
by Rank, Highest Earned Degree, Gender, and Level of Program*

Rank	Highest Earned Degree	Graduate and Joint Programs			Baccalaureate Programs		
		Male	Female	Total	Male	Female	Total
Professor	Doctorate	26.8	20.0	46.8	14.0	8.6	22.6
	Master's	0.9	0.8	1.7	4.6	6.0	10.6
Associate Professor	Doctorate	15.7	26.8	42.5	11.6	17.2	28.8
	Master's	2.2	2.6	4.8	8.4	15.0	23.4
Assistant Professor	Doctorate	0.7	1.5	2.2	1.8	4.2	6.0
	Master's	0.8	1.0	1.8	1.6	6.8	8.4
Total: Percent		47.1	52.7	100.0	42.0	57.8	100.0
Number		628	703	1,331	211	289	500

* Column totals may not correspond among tables within this report due to variance in response rates.

Data were gathered on the salaries of full-time social work faculty. Table 22 displays the median salaries and middle 50% range of salaries of non-administrative faculty (that is, faculty that do not hold an administrative title) by rank and region. Medians are reported here because of the wide range of salaries reported. All salaries reported in Table 22 are adjusted to reflect a nine-month academic year. Raw salary data reported for periods other than nine months were increased or decreased proportionately. Medians and ranges are shown for regions that reported at least five cases at a particular level. This section of the survey was often reported inaccurately or not reported at all; therefore, care should be taken when examining data, especially when comparing salary data from year to year.

One of the factors influencing the data in this table is the definition of "full-time" as those faculty members who spend at least 50% of a full-time equivalent on social work education responsibilities. Therefore, a $15,000 salary likely belongs to a faculty member who only spends half the time of his/her colleague who has a full teaching load. As mentioned above, this section of the survey was most often reported inaccurately. Variables such as time spent in the social work program, months on which the salary is based, and the salary itself are all used to determine the cases and salaries presented in Tables 22-24, and respondents may have reported incorrect data for one or more of the variables. Some of the adjusted salaries in Tables 22-24—23 in Table 22 (10 graduate/joint and 4 baccalaureate), 166 in Table 23 (118 graduate/joint and 74 baccalaureate), and 21 in Table 24 (10 graduate/joint and 4 baccalaureate)—are under $15,000.

As would be expected, full professors receive higher salaries than associate professors do; likewise, associate professors receive higher salaries than assistant professors do. Full professors with appointments in graduate/joint programs make 30.0% more than their baccalaureate-level counterparts do. The difference is smaller at the lower two ranks, with 18.4% and 16.0% between them. The median salaries have increased from last year—4.2%, 4.3%, and 2.9% for graduate/joint full professors, associate professors and assistant professors, respectively. The baccalaureate full, associate and assistant professors also experienced increases of 3.7%, 2.8%, and 2.1%, respectively.

TABLE 22

Median Salary and Middle 50 Percent Salary Range of Full-time Non-administrative Faculty,
by Geographic Region, Level of Program, and Rank[1]

Rank	Region[2]	Graduate and Joint Programs			Baccalaureate Programs		
		Median Salary[3]	Middle 50% Range	# of Faculty	Median Salary[3]	Middle 50% Range	# of Faculty
Professor	1	$72,180	$56,363 - 87,996	52	$54,559	$49,410 - 58,613	7
	2	79,926	54,409 - 86,619	63	37,127	33,858 - 57,431	8
	3	75,682	65,457 - 88,700	55	81,625	54,322 - 82,035	13
	4	70,071	56,904 - 89,306	67	55,077	48,370 - 63,785	15
	5	72,617	63,780 - 86,030	78	56,844	52,011 - 62,903	19
	6	62,928	57,070 - 75,150	41	46,994	43,125 - 51,765	9
	7	64,467	54,555 - 86,788	28	**	**	1
	8	60,556	59,350 - 71,425	9	**	**	3
	9	73,662	56,257 - 85,373	44	53,154	41,022 - 59,428	5
	10	66,717	49,430 - 80,555	18	**	**	1
	Total	71,622	59,525 - 85,530	455	55,077	47,247 – 62,530	81
Associate Professor	1	$58,500	$48,510 - 68,122	51	$50,317	$47,320 - 58,106	8
	2	63,410	51,085 - 68,174	72	50,400	45,750 - 54,578	23
	3	57,765	50,236 - 64,802	82	50,600	45,439 - 57,578	21
	4	50,656	45,386 - 56,525	92	42,921	40,000 - 49,300	27
	5	56,297	50,962 - 65,619	91	49,422	45,133 - 52,075	32
	6	49,914	44,611 - 56,569	47	43,104	41,398 - 44,806	17
	7	55,500	49,054 - 62,644	44	45,814	40,000 - 47,365	11
	8	50,370	47,600 - 52,000	15	44,608	32,891 - 45,754	8
	9	58,508	53,995 - 62,500	24	53,424	40,733 - 56,173	6
	10	49,811	42,468 - 59,452	28	**	**	3
	Total	54,774	48,757 - 63,619	546	46,250	42,506 - 52,341	156
Assistant Professor	1	$45,454	$40,022 - 50,309	48	$39,713	$35,050 - 43,680	13
	2	46,533	42,978 - 50,275	65	42,462	34,088 - 46,021	38
	3	44,423	39,321 - 49,130	78	40,129	37,575 - 47,808	28
	4	43,500	40,000 - 47,601	127	39,694	34,940 - 42,217	56
	5	45,378	42,500 - 51,613	133	39,000	35,855 - 43,458	53
	6	42,685	39,003 - 45,915	72	36,863	35,044 - 40,907	40
	7	47,000	45,050 - 48,076	41	36,818	29,250 - 38,799	17
	8	45,333	43,000 - 47,929	19	36,000	25,500 - 37,710	9
	9	46,400	43,175 - 50,770	32	39,600	30,600 - 42,363	7
	10	47,128	35,219 - 50,744	26	44,055	33,500 - 51,484	5
	Total	45,000	41,246 - 49,113	641	38,795	35,000 - 43,545	266

** Less than five cases reported.

---

[1] Column totals may not correspond among tables within this report due to variance in response rates.

[2] See Table 2 on page 3 for a list of states in each region.

[3] Salary data are adjusted for a nine-month academic year.

Table 23 shows the median salaries reported for full-time faculty members according to their primary responsibility within the social work program. One column displays the actual salaries received by faculty members regardless of the number of months it took them to earn that salary. The other column displays the same salaries adjusted to a nine-month academic year as was done in Table 22. The deans/directors, associate deans/directors, and research directors at the graduate/joint level report the highest median salary. At the baccalaureate level, program directors reported the highest median salary. Of the non-administrative faculty, classroom teachers were highest paid at both levels.

TABLE 23

Median Salary and Range of Full-time Faculty, by Primary Responsibility and Level of Program*

Level of Program	Primary Responsibility	Salary				#
		Adjusted for Months		Unadjusted for Months		
		Median	Range	Median	Range	
Graduate and Joint	Classroom Teaching	$48,700	$3,000-137,383	$49,800	$2,000-137,383	1,465
	Classroom and Field	38,495	4,484-82,356	43,908	4,200-82,356	51
	Field Instruction/Liaison	33,945	4,680- 72,000	38,375	2,600-70,182	212
	Dean/Director	69,849	15,000-175,091	86,141	20,000-214,000	118
	Associate Dean/Director	65,439	831-103,869	73,058	831-123,643	65
	Assistant Dean/Director	46,020	27,709-96,805	55,475	36,050-106,074	40
	Dir. Undergrad Program	53,000	22,471-96,589	55,000	29,961-98,472	72
	Director Field Instruction	42,450	21,211-70,573	50,134	21,211-94,097	107
	Asst./Assoc. Dir. Field Inst.	35,153	16,800-118,597	44,198	18,000-131,774	40
	Dir. Admissions or Minority Recruitment	40,796	18,800-69,841	49,126	18,800-83,992	35
	Dir. Continuing Ed. or Work Study	45,668	32,836-62,792	60,325	35,362-83,722	12
	Dir. Research/Res. Admin.	62,772	30,750-112,500	76,876	41,000-112,500	9
	Alumni/Career Dev. Coord.	36,167	25,778-46,676	47,704	34,370-59,677	6
	Other Administration	51,116	3,457-116,314	56,795	3,841-125,874	157
Baccalaureate	Classroom Teaching	40,000	1,980-83,725	42,000	1,500-83,725	531
	Classroom and Field	35,281	4,484-52,426	38,136	4,484-52,426	37
	Field Instruction/Liaison	36,000	6,000-64,698	39,196	6,000-64,698	35
	Dean/Director	45,243	4,200-85,000	50,270	4,200-102,204	216

* Column totals may not correspond among tables within this report due to variance in response rates.

Table 24 compares the median salaries of full-time non-administrative faculty members, broken down into categories representing ethnicity, gender, highest earned degree, and rank. In general, female faculty members receive lower salaries than do their male counterparts. Over half of the valid cells displaying median salaries for minority faculty members show medians lower than for their white counterparts. Faculty holding master's degrees as their highest earned degree tend to have lower salaries than do their colleagues with doctorates holding the same rank and ethnicity. Comparisons within this table are difficult, given the varying numbers of cases reported among categories.

TABLE 24

Median Salary of Full-time Non-administrative Faculty,
by Ethnicity, Gender, Rank, Highest Earned Degree, and Level of Program*

Level of Program	Rank	Ethnicity	Highest Earned Degree							
			Doctorate				Master's			
			Male		Female		Male		Female	
			Salary†	#	Salary†	#	Salary†	#	Salary†	#
Graduate and Joint	Professor	White	$76,435	195	$68,503	148	$67,950	6	$55,025	10
		Minority	72,000	49	61,516	38	**	2	**	4
	Associate Professor	White	56,964	137	54,778	205	50,717	12	50,357	17
		Minority	54,107	55	55,625	92	55,948	17	51,992	9
	Assistant Professor	White	45,900	125	45,155	236	40,500	27	39,330	57
		Minority	46,000	45	47,000	111	37,766	27	38,700	25
Baccalaureate	Professor	White	57,445	26	57,985	17	54,000	7	50,500	11
		Minority	54,735	8	45,000	5	51,418	5	**	2
	Associate Professor	White	48,770	32	45,900	40	50,470	14	44,091	24
		Minority	47,187	11	43,250	18	49,844	7	43,000	9
	Assistant Professor	White	40,627	34	40,000	55	37,778	21	36,000	72
		Minority	41,300	11	42,363	33	37,897	10	36,306	30

* Column totals may not correspond among tables within this report due to variance in response rates.
** Less than five cases reported.
† Salary data are adjusted for a nine-month academic year.

Table 25 shows that the main source of faculty salaries remains the university itself. Graduate/joint programs use more outside funds than do baccalaureate programs. Classroom teachers generally receive the highest percentage of their salary from inside university sources. As noted before, classroom teachers make up the vast majority of non-administrative faculty, so the means displayed in Table 25 for classroom teachers are a more accurate reflection of this characteristic than the others.

TABLE 25

Mean Percentage of Non-administrative Faculty Salary from Internal University Sources,
by Primary Responsibility, Type of Appointment, and Level of Program

Level of Program	Primary Responsibility	Type of Appointment		Total
		Full-time	Part-time	
Graduate and Joint	Classroom Teaching Classroom and Field Field Instruction/Liaison Other	96.6 94.9 72.6 70.1	96.6 100.0 97.1 82.2	91.1
Baccalaureate	Classroom Teaching Classroom and Field Field Instruction/Liaison Other	98.4 97.0 84.7 82.6	97.0 0.0 100.0 97.5	96.7

Number of Publications

Programs were asked to report on the number of faculty publications that actually appeared in print during the preceding academic or calendar year, whichever year conforms to their record-keeping system. The five categories of publications were defined as refereed articles, books published by formal publishing companies, published book chapters and conference proceedings, monographs, and book reviews. To adjust for multiple authorship, respondents were asked to enter the fraction of authorship undertaken by the faculty member. For example, a faculty member who wrote an article with another colleague would be reported as having written 0.5 of an article. Blank spaces in this section of the form were interpreted as being equal to zero, although many of these cases simply may be missing data. In addition, the reliability of the data from this section of the report depends on the ability of the programs to report accurately the number of publications for all faculty, which is questionable.

Taken as a whole, on average, faculty members published .26 articles, .04 books, .11 book chapters, .10 monographs, and .05 book reviews. Incomplete data were received on many faculty, so these numbers may be somewhat misleading. Among faculty members who published a total of at least one item (*n*=1,358), an average of 1.24 articles, .19 books, .54 book chapters, .50 monographs, and .26 book reviews were published. It is clear that refereed articles are the publishing medium of choice among social work faculty. Females and baccalaureate faculty members appear to publish less frequently than do their male and graduate/joint counterparts. All of these figures are very similar from year to year.

BACCALAUREATE STUDENTS

Baccalaureate social work education programs reported on various aspects of their student body on Schedule II. As noted in Table 1, 372 of 420 programs (88.6%) returned data on Schedule II. The tables in this section report data only on juniors and seniors because some programs do not allow students to declare majors until their junior year. Also, due to the deadline for statistics, many programs do not have access to data showing the major declaration of incoming freshmen. Program data are listed individually in Appendix A in Tables 100 and 101. Again, the schedules requested different data on the same population. Responses varied within the schedules, so comparison between tables may be unreliable. For instance, one table reporting the number of juniors and seniors enrolled (one section of Schedule II) may not agree with another table reporting that same population's ethnicity (another section of the form).

Table 26 reports junior and senior enrollment in baccalaureate programs. Baccalaureate programs typically have small student bodies. Over half of the baccalaureate programs have fewer than 75 juniors and seniors enrolled. Distribution across the categories is similar to previous years' statistics. The median junior and senior enrollment size this year was 51, down from the previous five years.

TABLE 26

Accredited Baccalaureate Programs, by Size of Full-time Junior and Senior Year Enrollment*

Junior and Senior Enrollment	#	%
Under 25	75	20.2
25 - 49	102	27.4
50 - 74	73	19.6
75 - 99	58	15.6
100 - 149	51	13.7
150 and over	13	3.5
Total	372	100.0

* Column totals may not correspond among tables within this report due to variance in response rates.

The total reported enrollment of full-time baccalaureate social work degree students is 36,283. This reflects an decrease from last year. However, this year's response rate was lower than last year's. Freshmen and sophomores accounted for 13,092 of full-time students. Baccalaureate programs reported that 6,763 students are enrolled part-time in their program and 18,499 students are enrolled in one or more social work courses, but not working toward a social work degree.

The gender breakdown of juniors and seniors and 1999-2000 graduates is displayed in Table 27. Females continue to represent the majority of baccalaureate students (87.5%) and graduates (87.8%). Both percentages are the highest they have been in years.

TABLE 27

Juniors and Seniors Enrolled Full-time in Baccalaureate Programs on 11/1/00
and Students Awarded Baccalaureate Degrees in 1999-2000 by Gender*

Gender	Juniors and Seniors Enrolled		Students Awarded Degrees	
	#	%	#	%
Female	19,403	87.5	10,332	87.8
Male	2,585	11.7	1,430	12.1
Unknown	175	0.8	11	1.0
Total	22,163	100.0	11,773	100.0

* Column totals may not correspond among tables within this report due to variance in response rates.

The ethnic distribution of juniors and seniors and 1999-2000 baccalaureate degree recipients is shown in Table 28. The proportions of ethnic minorities receiving baccalaureate degrees decreased this year. The proportion of minority juniors and seniors decreased also. Changes from year to year may be due to the variation of response rates. "African American" continues to be the most frequent ethnic minority identification among juniors and seniors enrolled in baccalaureate programs, outnumbering the other ethnic minorities by a large margin. Chicano/Mexican Americans, Puerto Ricans, and "Other Minority" are the next most frequent. Although the survey did not allow the specification of minorities in the Other Minority category, some respondents chose to write in various Hispanic ethnic groups.

TABLE 28

Juniors and Seniors Enrolled Full-time in Baccalaureate Programs on 11/1/00
and Students Awarded Baccalaureate Degrees in 1999-2000 by Ethnicity*

Ethnicity	Juniors and Seniors Enrolled		Students Awarded Degrees	
	#	%	#	%
African American	3,999	18.0	2,090	17.8
Asian American	339	1.5	229	1.9
Chicano/Mexican American	983	4.4	522	4.4
American Indian	258	1.2	111	0.9
Puerto Rican	851	3.8	307	2.6
Other Minority	427	1.9	229	1.9
Total Minorities	6,857	30.9	3,488	29.6
Foreign	158	0.7	71	0.6
White	14,851	67.0	8,050	68.4
Unknown	297	1.3	164	1.4
Total	22,163	100.0	11,773	100.0

* Column totals may not correspond among tables within this report due to variance in response rates.

MASTER'S STUDENTS

Data on master's and doctoral students were gathered with Schedules III and IV, respectively. In previous years' reports the data from these schedules were reported in this section in many of the same tables. Because the doctoral schedule was changed, those data are now reported after this section. As is true throughout this report, the data in some tables may not be comparable to those in others due to varying responses to different parts of the survey instrument. Program data are listed individually in Appendix A.

Enrollment

Full-time enrollments in master's programs increased steadily from the mid-1950s to 1978. Table 29 shows that in 1979 full-time enrollments began to fall, bottoming out in 1986 at a 15-year low. After 1986 programs reported an increasing number of full-time students in every year except 1989, 1995 and 1998. To compensate for the missing programs' data, a statistically projected total full-time enrollment for 1999 is 22,189. This projection assumes that the mean of the responding programs' enrollments, minus the five highest values, is the value of the missing programs' enrollments. Part-time students make up 39.8% of the responding master's programs' enrollments. Furthermore, part-time students outnumber full-time students in 33 of the 126 programs responding to the survey and 57 programs reported that at least 40% of their students are enrolled part-time.

TABLE 29

Students Enrolled in Master's Programs 1975-2000**

Year	Full-time	Part-time	Year	Full-time	Part-time
1975	16,676	3,203	1988	16,239*	9,024*
1976	16,869	3,239	1989	15,777*	9,420*
1977	17,533	3,912	1990	17,475*	9,945*
1978	17,672	4,333	1991	19,468*	10,232*
1979	17,397	4,942*	1992	20,671*	10,795*
1980	17,122	5,274	1993	21,063*	11,132*
1981	16,552	5,761	1994	21,622*	11,590*
1982	15,131	6,174	1995	21,088*	11,016*
1983	14,265	7,225	1996	22,832*	12,636*
1984	14,275	7,294	1997	23,247*	12,318*
1985	14,055*	7,944*	1998	20,409*	11,350*
1986	13,981*	8,733*	1999	22,315*	13,219*
1987	15,241*	8,044*	2000	20,369*	13,446*

** Column totals may not correspond among tables within this report due to variance in response rates. Only 126 of 139 master's programs responded to this part of the 2000 survey.
* Response rate of less than 100 percent.

Applications and Admissions

Table 30 shows that the number of applications received is down from last year. Interestingly, the percentage of applications accepted and registered continues to rise. Although some of a continued decrease in the number of applications received may be attributed to the poor response rate, there continues to be a downward trend in the number of applications received.

TABLE 30

Applications for Admission to First-year Status in Master's Degree Programs
in 1999 and 2000 by Action Taken

Year	Program	Action							
		Total Received		Considered for Admission		Accepted		Registered	
		#	%	#	%	#	%	#	%
2000	Full-time (n=122)	20,644	100.0	18,740	90.8	14,093	68.3	7,819	37.9
	Part-time (n=117)	9,666	100.0	8,822	91.3	6,715	69.5	5,026	52.0
	Total	30,262	100.0	27,514	90.9	20,808	68.8	12,845	42.4
1999	Full-time (n=124)	24,472	100.0	22,231	90.8	15,735	64.3	8,698	35.5
	Part-time (n=122)	9,767	100.0	9,043	92.6	6,622	67.8	4,875	49.9
	Total	34,239	100.0	31,274	91.3	22,357	65.3	13,573	39.6

Table 31 displays data concerning action taken on applications for advanced standing status in master's degree programs. The majority of applications (72.1%) for advanced standing came from individuals who held a baccalaureate degree in social work from an institution other than the one to which the application was made. An additional 23.8% of applications were received from graduates of baccalaureate programs under the same auspices as the prospective master's programs. The applicants who choose to stay in the same university from which they received their baccalaureate degree are much more likely to be accepted and enroll than are their colleagues who apply to a master's program in a university different from the one which awarded their baccalaureate degree.

TABLE 31

Applications for Advanced Standing Status in Master's Degree Programs in 2000
by Source/Basis and Action

Action	Source or Basis							
	Baccalaureate Social Work Program				Other Education		Total	
	Own School		Other School					
	#	%	#	%	#	%	#	%
Received	1,362	100.0	4,133	100.0	235	100.0	5,730	100.0
Accepted	1,162	85.3	3,232	78.2	170	72.3	4,564	79.7
Enrolled	892	65.5	2,013	48.7	100	42.6	3,005	52.4

Degrees Awarded

As would be expected, the number of degrees awarded to students completing master's and doctoral degrees is proportionate to the number of students enrolled at the same time. Therefore, as Table 32 shows, the number of master's degrees awarded increased from year to year until the 1978-79 academic year. In the 1980s, the number of master's degrees awarded fluctuated, with a general downward trend until the 1986-87 year. This year responding programs reported 15,016 master's degrees awarded. Applying the same projection methodology used to compensate for missing data to estimate total full-time enrollment (described on page 29), the total number of master's degree graduates for 2000 is estimated to be 17,156.

TABLE 32

Graduate Students Awarded Master's Degrees,
Academic Year 1974-75 through 1999-2000**

Academic Year	Master's Degree	Academic Year	Master's Degree
1974-75	8,824	1987-88	9,891*
1975-76	9,080	1988-89	9,509*
1976-77	9,254	1989-90	10,063*
1977-78	9,476	1990-91	10,969*
1978-79	10,080*	1991-92	11,582*
1979-80	9,820	1992-93	12,583*
1980-81	9,750	1993-94	12,856*
1981-82	9,556	1994-95	12,918*
1982-83	9,034*	1995-96	14,484*
1983-84	8,053*	1996-97	15,058*
1984-85	8,798*	1997-98	13,660*
1985-86	8,134*	1998-99	15,061*
1986-87	8,811*	1999-2000	15,016*

* Response rate of less than 100 percent.
** Column totals may not correspond among tables within this report due to variance in response rates. Only 124 of 139 programs responded to this part of the survey.

Demographic Characteristics

Table 33 displays the gender breakdown of graduate students. Females continue to make up the vast majority of master's degree students (84.1%).

TABLE 33

Percentage of Full- and Part-time Master's Students
Enrolled on 11/1/00 and Master's Students Awarded Degrees 1999-2000, by Gender*

Gender	Enrolled			Awarded Degrees
	Full-time	Part-time	Total	
Male	14.0	17.3	15.3	15.3
Female	85.5	82.0	84.1	84.6
Unknown	0.6	0.7	0.6	0.1
Total	100.0	100.0	100.0	100.0
Number	20,117	13,306	33,423	15,016

* Column totals may not correspond among tables within this report due to variance in response rates.

Table 34 displays the age of graduate students enrolled full-time and part-time in graduate social work education. Females aged 25 and under are the largest group among full-time master's students. Part-time master's students are most frequently females aged 31-40. Part-time males are more likely to be in the over-40 age group while full-time males are more likely to be aged 26-30 or 31-40. In general, the proportions displayed here are comparable to those of previous years.

TABLE 34

Percentage of Full- and Part-time Master's Students Enrolled on 11/1/00, by Gender and Age*

Age	Gender	Full-time	Part-time
25 & under	Male	3.4	1.7
	Female	36.6	15.6
26 - 30	Male	3.8	4.6
	Female	21.4	22.0
31 - 40	Male	3.8	5.4
	Female	14.6	22.9
41 & over	Male	3.0	5.5
	Female	12.8	21.5
Total	Male	14.0	17.3
	Female	85.5	82.0
Unknown		0.6	0.7
Total	Percent	100.0	100.0
	Number	20,117	13,306

* Column totals may not correspond among tables within this report due to variance in response rates.

32

The percentage of ethnic minorities enrolled in master's programs continues to increase, as does the percentage of minorities graduating. African Americans continue to be the largest ethnic minority group.

TABLE 35

Percentage of Full- and Part-time Master's Students Enrolled on 11/1/00
and Master's Students Awarded Degrees 1999-2000, by Ethnicity*

Ethnicity	Enrolled		Awarded Degrees
	Full-time	Part-time	
African American	15.2	17.6	13.8
Asian American	3.7	2.4	3.0
Chicano/Mexican American	3.6	4.3	3.7
American Indian	0.9	1.0	0.8
Puerto Rican	2.3	2.4	2.2
Other Minority	2.8	2.9	2.5
Total Minorities	28.5	30.7	26.0
Foreign	1.5	0.8	1.1
White	67.7	65.3	69.8
Unknown	2.3	3.2	3.1
Total	100.0	100.0	100.0
Number	20,117	13,306	15,016

* Column totals may not correspond among tables within this report due to variance in response rates.

Concentration of Study

Data were gathered on the primary methods concentration of master's degree students enrolled in schools of social work. Schedule III did not define any of the "methods of practice categories" or "fields of practice or social problem categories." Programs were asked to place student information in cells that represented "methods" and "social problems." Tables 36 and 37 display that information in two different ways.

Table 36 shows that most master's degree students have or will have declared a methods concentration. Most students study a method of practice in conjunction with a primary field of practice or social problem concentration. "Direct practice" is the most popular method and "generic" practice runs a distant second.

TABLE 36

Master's Degree Students Enrolled on 11/1/00, by Primary Methods Concentration*

Methods	Concentration Framework							
	Methods Only		Methods Combined with Field of Practice or Social Prob.		Field of Practice or Social Problem Only (No Methods)		Total	
	#	%	#	%	#	%	#	%
Direct Practice	5,616	49.3	9,838	53.5	---	---	15,454	48.0
Community Organization and Planning	111	1.0	633	3.4	---	---	744	2.3
Administration or Management	426	3.7	602	3.3	---	---	1,028	3.2
Combination of Direct Practice with C.O. and Planning or Administration or Management	300	2.6	1,129	6.1	---	---	1,429	4.4
Combination of C.O. and Planning with Administration or Management	414	3.6	375	2.0	---	---	789	2.4
Generic	1,820	16.0	2,128	11.6	---	---	3,948	12.3
Other	452	4.0	1,184	6.4	---	---	1,636	5.1
Not Yet Determined	1,451	12.7	2,505	13.6	---	---	3,956	12.3
None (Field of Practice or Social Problem Only)†	792	7.0	---	---	2,438	100.0	3,230	10.0
Total	11,382	100.0	18,394	100.0	2,438	100.0	32,214	100.0

* Column totals may not correspond among tables within this report due to variance in response rates.

† Due to data entry errors, values were placed in the Methods Only column for this row. In previous years' reports, the fact that the definition of this row made a value in the Methods Only column impossible was recognized.

Table 37 displays the distribution of students who have declared a particular field of practice or social problem concentration. Mental health continues to be the concentration taken by the most master's degree students (9.7%). Child welfare, "other," and family services (in that order) are runners-up. Relatively few students study other concentrations.

TABLE 37

Master's Degree Students Enrolled on 11/1/00, by Primary Field of Practice or Social Problem Concentration*

Type of Concentration	#	%
Aging/Gerontological Social Work	556	1.7
Alcohol, Drug or Substance Abuse	240	0.7
Child Welfare	2,388	7.4
Community Planning	491	1.5
Corrections/Criminal Justice	189	0.6
Family Services	2,201	6.8
Group Services	133	0.4
Health	1,377	4.3
Occupational/Industrial Social Work	147	0.5
Mental Health or Community Mental Health	3,129	9.7
Mental Retardation	58	0.2
Public Assistance/Public Welfare	41	0.1
Rehabilitation	59	0.2
School Social Work	1,011	3.1
Other	2,274	7.1
Combinations	758	2.4
Not Yet Determined	5,780	17.9
None (Methods Concentration Only)	11,382	35.3
Total	32,214	100.0

* Column totals may not correspond among tables within this report due to variance in response rates.

Concentration of Field Instruction

Although students may choose to study a particular field of practice or social problem, the location of their field instruction may not correspond with their study concentration. Table 38 shows the primary field of practice in which master's students were placed on November 1, 2000. The most frequent concentrations in this table are the same as in Table 37, but many students who study in one social problem area may work in another field of practice in their practicum. Mental health claims 14.7% of field placements. Following mental health, family service, child welfare, and health lead all the other fields of practice. Many master's students (35.5%) either were not yet assigned field instruction on November 1, 2000 or were not to be in field instruction this year.

TABLE 38

Master's Degree Students Enrolled on 11/1/00, by Primary Field of Practice in Field Instruction*

Type of Concentration	#	%
Aging/Gerontological Social Work	1,006	3.1
Alcohol, Drug or Substance Abuse	784	2.4
Child Welfare	2,683	8.3
Community Planning	752	2.3
Corrections/Criminal Justice	810	2.5
Family Service	3,006	9.3
Group Services	376	1.2
Health	2,503	7.8
Occupational/Industrial Social Work	225	0.7
Mental Health or Community Mental Health	4,727	14.7
Mental Retardation	225	0.7
Public Assistance/Public Welfare	225	0.7
Rehabilitation	182	0.6
School Social Work	2,318	7.2
Other	979	3.0
Not Yet Assigned Field Instruction	4,817	14.9
Not To Be In Field Instruction This Academic Year	6,637	20.6
Total	32,255	100.0

* Column totals may not correspond among tables within this report due to variance in response rates.

Financial Aid

Table 39 shows that a higher percentage of full-time students who are ethnic minorities receive financial aid than are enrolled.

TABLE 39

Full-time Master's Students Receiving Financial Grants on 11/1/00, by Ethnicity*

Ethnicity	#	%
African American	2,015	18.2
American Indian	131	3.6
Asian American	375	6.1
Chicano/Mexican American	680	1.2
Puerto Rican	162	1.5
Other Minority	293	2.8
Total Minorities	3,656	33.1
Foreign	111	1.0
White	6,999	63.4
Unknown	274	2.5
Total	11,040	100.0

* Column totals may not correspond among tables within this report due to variance in response rates.

Table 40 shows the different sources of the financial aid received by full-time master's and doctoral students as of November 1, 2000. This represents all awards made, regardless of number of sources. For example, if one student represented in Table 39 received an award from three different sources, that student would be counted three times in Table 40.

Master's degree students who received financial aid from sources other than their field placement received it most often from formal loan programs, followed by their school or university. Other sources were infrequent in comparison. Among those awards given by field instruction agencies, social welfare agencies and state or local government were the most frequent. The main sources of financial aid for graduate social work education have not greatly varied from year to year.

TABLE 40

Financial Grants Awarded to Full-time Master's Students on 11/1/00, by Source of Funds

Source of Funds	Funds Not Tied to Current Field Instruction		Funds Paid by Field Instruction Agency		Total	
	#	%	#	%	#	%
Public Funds						
Federal Government						
Child Welfare	596	2.8	220	8.1	816	3.4
Office of Aging	1	0.0	3	0.1	4	0.0
NIAAA	3	0.0	0	0.0	3	0.0
NIDA	2	0.0	0	0.0	2	0.0
NIMH	0	0.0	7	0.3	7	0.0
VA	15	0.1	149	5.5	164	0.7
FCWSP (Work Study)	1,166	5.4	358	13.2	1,524	6.3
State or Local Government	812	3.8	535	19.7	1,347	5.6
Veterans Benefits	74	0.3	14	0.5	88	0.4
Other	408	1.9	151	5.6	559	2.3
Voluntary Funds						
Social Welfare Agencies	187	0.9	523	19.3	710	2.9
Foundations/Other Sources	664	3.1	351	12.9	1,015	4.2
School or University	5,542	25.8	90	3.3	5,632	23.3
Foreign Governments	612	2.8	48	1.8	660	2.7
Formal Loan Programs	9,660	45.0	1	0.0	9,661	39.9
Work Study (not federal)	416	1.9	180	6.6	596	2.5
Research or Graduate Assistantships	964	4.5	32	1.2	996	4.1
Other	366	1.7	49	1.8	415	1.7
Total	21,488	100.0	2,711	100.0	24,199	100.0

Student-Faculty Ratio

Table 41 displays student-faculty ratios for master's and doctoral programs. For the purpose of calculating ratios, full-time students were counted as one and part-time students were counted as one-half. Faculty were counted according to the amount of time they spent at the master's level. For instance, faculty members who spend 100% of their time in social work, but split their time between the master's program and the doctoral program would be counted as 50% to the master's ratio and 50% to the doctoral ratio. Likewise, part-time faculty members who spend 30% of their time in social work and split it between the two programs would be counted as 15% to master's and 15% to doctoral. Programs in which the time allotted to doctoral and master's programs was missing in over 25% of their faculty entries were not included in Table 41.

The median ratio is virtually unchanged from last year. There was only a slight variation in the distribution of the ratios from last year. The methodology could be responsible for the variation in this table from year to year. There appears to be an increase in part-time students. If a program has many part-time students and a normal faculty size, it could drive the ratios reported in this table down. There is no simple explanation for the variation from year to year.

TABLE 41

Student-Faculty Ratio in Master's Programs on 11/1/00

Student-Faculty Ratio	#	%
Less than 6.0:1	17	16.0
6.0:1 - 8.9:1	43	40.6
9.0:1 - 11.9:1	21	19.8
12.0 1 - 14.9:1	18	17.0
15.0:1 and over	7	6.6
Total	106	100.0
Median	8.3:1	

* Column totals may not correspond among tables within this report due to variance in response rates.

DOCTORAL STUDENTS

As noted earlier, data on master's and doctoral students were gathered with Schedules III and IV, respectively. With the advice of doctoral program directors, this year the Commission on Information Management and Research revised Schedule IV to more accurately reflect the current structure of doctoral programs. In previous years' reports master's and doctoral program data were reported in many of the same tables. Because the doctoral schedule was changed, those data are now reported in a separate section. As is true throughout this report, the data in some tables may not be comparable to those in others due to varying responses to different parts of the survey instrument. Program data are listed individually in Appendix A.

Applications and Admissions

This is the first year that this report contains application and admissions action data for doctoral programs. Table 42 shows that less than two-thirds of applications received by doctoral programs are considered for admission. Less than half of those are accepted, but most of the applications accepted eventually register.

TABLE 42

Applications for Admission to Doctoral Programs
in 2000, by Action Taken

Year	Action							
	Total Received		Considered for Admission		Accepted		Registered	
	#	%	#	%	#	%	#	%
2000	1,846	100.0	1,152	62.4	565	30.6	402	21.8

Enrollment

Table 43 displays doctoral program enrollments over 25 years. It is reported here to maintain continuity between annual reports and to give historical perspective. The 2000 figures are not included in this table because the survey asked the enrollment questions in a different way. This year programs were asked to report data on students who are taking coursework and those who have completed coursework, in addition to their full-time and part-time status. Numbers from this year may be used to continue Table 43 by adding the two full-time and two part-time columns in Table 45 together. There is no way to know, however, if programs reported students in the same way in 1975-1999.

Furthermore, if those numbers are used, one finds that, in spite of a 79.1% response rate, full-time enrollment increased to the second-highest level in 26 years. Part-time enrollment fell, however, to one of the lowest levels in recent years. The change in the survey could be responsible for these facts, so the 2000 figures have been withheld from Table 43. Future reports will include a table that compares like data for historical perspective.

41

TABLE 43

Students Enrolled in Doctoral Programs 1975-1999

Year	Full-time	Part-time	Year	Full-time	Part-time
1975	712	**	1988	1,003	911
1976	769	**	1989	857*	989*
1977	866	**	1990	838*	956*
1978	821	**	1991	1,133	978
1979	954	174*	1992	1,000*	1,005*
1980	825	213*	1993	1,085*	949*
1981	868	226	1994	1,102*	995*
1982	922	284	1995	1,003*	946*
1983	855	227	1996	1,134*	953*
1984	798*	1,024	1997	1,356*	1,080*
1985	702*	728*	1998	1,127*	975*
1986	601*	841*	1999	1,126*	827*
1987	703*	820*			

** No data collected
* Response rate of less than 100 percent.

Degrees Awarded

The number of doctoral degrees awarded has fluctuated over the years. Because of the small number of doctoral programs, any missing data will have an impact on the total number of degrees awarded. So while the number of doctoral degrees reported is down significantly this year, it is likely due to the poor response rate.

TABLE 44

Doctoral Degrees Awarded
Academic Year 1974-75 through 1999-2000**

Academic Year	#	Academic Year	#
1974-75	155	1987-88	332
1975-76	179	1988-89	189*
1976-77	179	1989-90	247*
1977-78	178	1990-91	245
1978-79	174*	1991-92	243*
1979-80	213	1992-93	229*
1980-81	226	1993-94	294*
1981-82	284	1994-95	279*
1982-83	227*	1995-96	258*
1983-84	245*	1996-97	286*
1984-85	181*	1997-98	266*
1985-86	297*	1998-99	267*
1986-87	195*	1999-2000	229*

* Response rate of less than 100 percent.
** Column totals may not correspond among tables within this report due to variance in response rates. Only 53 of 67 doctoral programs responded to this part of the survey.

Demographic Characteristics

Table 45 displays the gender breakdown of doctoral students and graduates. The proportions of males and females is consistent across the different columns, with females making up almost two-thirds of all doctoral students and graduates. This is a characteristic that does not change much from year to year.

TABLE 45

Percentage of Full- and Part-time Doctoral Students
Enrolled on 11/1/00 and Awarded Degrees 1999-2000, by Gender*

Gender	Taking Coursework			Completed Coursework			Degrees Awarded
	Full-time	Part-time	Total	Full-time	Part-time	Total	
Male	26.0	27.1	26.4	28.5	25.4	27.1	27.5
Female	74.0	72.9	73.6	71.5	74.6	72.9	72.5
Total	100.0	100.0	100.0	100.0	100.0	100.0	100.0
Number	749	417	1,166	530	456	986	229

* Column totals may not correspond among tables within this report due to variance in response rates.

The revised survey also affected the way that the age of doctoral students is reported. Programs were asked to report the mean age of male and female students according to their enrollment status in the program. Table 46 shows that full-time students are younger than part-time students and students taking coursework are generally younger than those who have completed coursework.

TABLE 46

Mean Age of Doctoral Students Enrolled on 11/1/00, by Gender

Gender	Taking Coursework		Completed Coursework	
	Full-time	Part-time	Full-time	Part-time
Male	39.1	42.2	40.9	42.1
Female	37.8	42.1	40.3	42.8

The ethnic distribution of doctoral students enrolled and graduated is displayed in Table 47. African Americans make up over half of all doctoral students who are ethnic minorities. Foreign students make up a relatively large proportion of full-time students.

TABLE 47

Percentage of Full- and Part-time Doctoral Students
Enrolled on 11/1/00 and Awarded Degrees 1999-2000, by Ethnicity*

Ethnicity	Taking Coursework		Completed Coursework		Degrees Awarded
	Full-time	Part-time	Full-time	Part-time	
African American	15.9	14.6	13.0	14.5	10.5
American Indian	1.7	1.4	0.6	1.1	0.4
Asian American	4.1	4.1	3.0	2.2	3.1
Chicano/Mexican American	1.6	3.1	2.5	1.5	1.3
Puerto Rican	0.8	0.7	1.1	0.9	3.1
Other Minority	2.3	2.9	1.3	1.8	0.9
Total Minorities	26.4	26.9	21.5	21.9	19.2
Foreign	13.1	2.2	10.6	5.7	9.2
White	59.3	68.1	65.8	69.5	71.6
Unknown	1.2	2.9	2.1	2.9	0.0
Total	100.0	100.0	100.0	100.0	100.0
Number	749	417	530	456	229

* Column totals may not correspond among tables within this report due to variance in response rates.

Financial Aid

Table 48 displays the ethnicity of students who received financial grants. Previous years' surveys asked for the ethnicity of full-time students who received financial grants. The revised doctoral survey made no distinction between full-time and part-time students for this question, but did separate students according to whether they had completed coursework. The distribution across ethnic categories is similar to the enrollment figures.

TABLE 48

Doctoral Students Receiving Financial Grants in 2000, by Ethnicity*

Ethnicity	Taking Coursework		Completed Coursework	
	#	%	#	%
African American	118	17.3	47	16.2
American Indian	9	1.3	1	0.3
Asian American	23	3.4	9	3.1
Chicano/Mexican American	14	2.1	4	1.4
Puerto Rican	3	0.4	2	0.7
Other Minority	8	1.2	3	1.0
Total Minorities	175	25.7	66	22.7
Foreign	89	13.0	38	13.1
White	409	60.0	186	63.9
Unknown	9	1.3	1	0.3
Total	682	100.0	291	100.0

* Column totals may not correspond among tables within this report due to variance in response rates.

The sources of financial aid are noted in Table 49. The survey was dramatically revised in this area to more accurately reflect how financial aid is tracked in institutions. The institutions and schools of social work are the most common sources of financial aid to all students. Among students taking coursework, the schools provide more awards than their institutions, but among students who have completed coursework the institutions grant more awards.

TABLE 49

Financial Grants Awarded to Doctoral Students in 2000, by Source of Funds

Source of Funds	Students Taking Coursework			Students Completed Coursework		
	Tuition Assistance Only	Stipend Support Only	Both Tuition and Stipend	Tuition Assistance Only	Stipend Support Only	Both Tuition and Stipend
University Funds	135	50	147	88	19	31
School of Social Work Funds	92	33	294	33	12	55
Funded Faculty Grants	8	36	75	12	15	30
Grants Received Directly by Student	1	4	14	0	6	5
Other	5	6	35	1	0	2
Total	241	129	565	134	52	123
Formal Student Loans			94			38

PROGRAMS IN CANDIDACY FOR ACCREDITATION

The characteristics of programs in candidacy status for accreditation varied somewhat since last year. Fifty-one programs were polled to determine the ethnic and gender identification of their graduates. Of those 51 programs, there were 30 stand-alone baccalaureate programs, 6 stand-alone master's programs, 13 graduate programs jointly administered with baccalaureate programs, and 2 baccalaureate programs jointly administered with graduate programs. As noted in Table 1, 45 programs responded to Schedule V. Table 42 shows that baccalaureate programs reported 355 graduates and master's programs reported 274 graduates.

It is clear that African Americans greatly outnumber members of other ethnic minority categories graduating from baccalaureate programs in candidacy. The proportion of male to female students is similar to accredited programs. The proportion of minorities graduating from baccalaureate candidacy programs (36.3%) is higher than that of fully accredited programs (see Table 28). Master's programs in candidacy status graduated 20.8% minorities, which is less than accredited programs.

TABLE 50

Students Awarded Degrees in Programs in Candidacy 1999-2000, by Ethnicity and Gender

Ethnicity	Baccalaureate Programs				Master's Programs			
	Male	Female	Unknown	Total	Male	Female	Unknown	Total
African American	11	64	1	76	3	22	0	25
Asian American	0	10	0	10	1	1	0	2
Chicano/Mexican American	1	11	0	12	3	14	0	17
American Indian	0	3	0	3	1	4	0	5
Puerto Rican	5	6	0	11	0	6	0	6
Other Minority	2	15	0	17	0	2	0	2
Total Minorities	19	109	1	129	8	49	0	57
Foreign	0	2	0	2	0	2	0	2
White	17	204	3	224	17	188	0	205
Unknown	0	0	0	0	0	10	0	10
Total	36	315	4	355	25	249	0	274

RECENT TRENDS IN SOCIAL WORK EDUCATION

Tables 51 and 52 display selected characteristics of social work education over the last five years. General trends may be seen in these displays, but they must be interpreted with caution. During the last fifteen years, the response rate has not been 100% on any schedule except for the doctoral surveys, which were 100% in 1991. As noted earlier, response rates to specific items also vary within schedules.

TABLE 51

Highlights of Recent Trends in Baccalaureate Social Work Education

	1996	1997	1998	1999	2000
Accredited Baccalaureate Programs*					
Baccalaureate Only	301	309	310	313	313
Joint	87	91	100	104	107
Percent Response to Survey	92.5	92.3	83.2	90.6	88.6
Institutional Auspices (Baccalaureate Only)					
Percent Public	49.7	49.0	49.1	48.0	46.3
Percent Private	50.3	51.0	50.9	52.0	53.7
Faculty (Baccalaureate Only)					
Total Number	1,818	1,774	1,638	1,761	1,615
Percent Women	64.2	63.6	64.0	64.8	64.7
Percent Ethnic Minority	25.4	24.2	24.7	25.4	26.5
Percent Doctorates	36.6	38.1	38.4	38.1	37.5
Students					
Full-time Degree Students	41,214	40,696	35,816	37,557	36,283
Percent Juniors or Seniors	65.5	65.7	65.5	66.0	63.9
Percent Women	85.4	86.5	86.9	85.3	87.5
Percent Ethnic Minority	31.0	31.3	33.6	32.7	30.9
Part-time Degree Students	7,824	7,354	6,627	7,334	6,763
Others Taking Social Work Courses	17,415	17,959	16,856	18,002	18,499
Degrees Awarded					
Total Number	12,356	12,949	11,435	12,798	11,773
Percent Women	85.9	86.1	87.5	86.9	87.8
Percent Ethnic Minority	26.9	27.5	29.2	30.3	29.6

None of the statistics in this table represent a 100 percent response rate.
* Represents all accredited programs, not the number of programs responding to this survey.

TABLE 52

Highlights of Recent Trends in Graduate Social Work Education

	1996	1997	1998	1999	2000
Programs*					
Accredited Master's Programs	117	119	126	131	139
Doctoral Programs	56	58	62	62	67
Percent Response Rate to Survey					
Accredited Master's Programs	95.7	96.6	88.1	95.4	90.6
Doctoral Programs	96.4	98.3	88.7	87.1	79.1
Faculty (Graduate and Joint)					
Total Number	4,429	4,695	4,432	4,267	5,048
Percent Women	61.0	61.8	62.0	63.0	63.1
Percent Ethnic Minority	22.7	22.3	22.4	22.8	23.0
Percent Doctorates	51.1	51.7	51.3	51.7	51.4
Full-time Professors	688	684	644	613	589
Percent Women	37.1	36.3	37.8	41.6	45.3
Percent Ethnic Minority	24.3	22.6	20.8	21.5	22.8
Full-time Associate Professors	754	783	722	707	675
Percent Women	59.9	57.9	58.1	60.5	62.1
Percent Ethnic Minority	26.6	28.3	28.4	28.7	29.8
Full-time Assistant Professors	710	760	735	697	659
Percent Women	65.6	68.2	68.4	69.2	68.0
Percent Ethnic Minority	29.9	30.4	30.5	28.4	29.6
Median Salary for Full-time Faculty					
Professor	$62,700	$66,444	$66,808	$68,754	$71,622
Associate Professor	49,130	50,570	51,403	52,523	54,774
Assistant Professor	39,000	40,241	42,000	43,720	45,000
Students: Master's Programs					
Full-time Students	22,832	23,247	20,409	22,315	20,369
Percent Women	83.5	83.8	84.0	83.8	85.5
Percent Ethnic Minority	23.7	25.0	25.5	26.0	28.5
Part-time Students	12,636	12,318	11,350	13,219	13,446
Applications for First Year Status	44,968	40,075	34,533	34,239	30,262
Percent Accepted	50.1	57.4	59.6	65.3	68.8
Applications for Advanced Standing	6,283	6,179	5,974	6,440	5,730
Master's Degrees Awarded	14,484	15,058	13,660	15,061	15,016
Percent Women	83.3	83.8	83.8	84.6	84.6
Percent Ethnic Minority	21.7	23.6	21.9	24.2	26.0
Students: Doctoral Programs					
Full-time Students	1,134	1,356	1,127	1,126	1,279†
Percent Women	70.1	71.5	71.1	73.1	72.9†
Percent Ethnic Minority	23.6	27.7	27.3	29.2	29.6†
Part-time Students	953	1,080	975	827	873†
Doctoral Degrees Awarded	258	286	266	267	229
Percent Women	69.9	65.7	69.9	74.2	72.5
Percent Ethnic Minority	16.3	17.8	13.5	20.6	19.2

None of the statistics in this table represent a 100 percent response rate.

* Represents all accredited programs, not the number of programs responding to this survey.

† See text on page 41 for notes on interpreting doctoral figures from this year.

APPENDIX A

Reference Tables

List of Reference Tables

TABLE 100

Number of Juniors and Seniors, by Gender and Ethnicity, and Number of Freshman and Sophomore Full-time Degree Students Enrolled in Baccalaureate Programs on 11/1/00

Program	Men									Women									Unk	Total	Frosh and Soph	Total
	African Amer	Amer Indian	Asian Amer	Chicano	Puerto Rican	White	Other	Foreign	Total	African Amer	Amer Indian	Asian Amer	Chicano	Puerto Rican	White	Other	Foreign	Total				
TOTAL: Number	597	53	59	147	91	1,478	78	33	2,585	3,368	205	279	836	759	13,261	346	125	19,403	175	22,163	13,092	35,255
Percent	2.7%	0.2%	0.3%	0.7%	0.4%	6.7%	0.4%	0.1%	11.7%	15.2%	0.9%	1.3%	3.8%	3.4%	59.8%	1.6%	0.6%	87.5%	0.8%	100.0%		
ABILENE CHRISTIAN	3	0	0	0	0	5	0	0	8	0	0	1	0	0	28	0	1	30	0	38	21	59
ADELPHI UNIV	2	0	0	0	1	5	0	0	8	26	0	3	0	5	47	3	0	84	0	92	19	111
ALABAMA A&M UNIV	5	0	0	0	0	0	0	0	5	40	0	0	0	0	2	0	0	42	0	47	50	97
ALABAMA STATE UNIV	7	0	0	0	0	0	0	0	7	39	0	0	2	0	3	0	0	44	0	51	74	125
ALVERNIA COLL	0	0	0	0	0	1	0	0	1	0	0	1	0	1	11	1	0	14	0	15	17	32
ANDERSON UNIV	0	0	0	0	0	3	0	0	3	0	0	0	0	0	36	0	1	37	0	40	33	73
ANDREWS UNIV	1	0	1	1	0	2	0	0	5	10	0	4	5	0	10	0	4	33	0	38	16	54
ANNA MARIA COLL	0	0	1	0	0	1	0	0	2	0	0	0	0	0	15	0	0	15	0	17	11	28
APPALACHIAN STATE	1	0	0	0	0	4	0	0	5	3	0	0	0	0	85	0	0	88	0	93	45	138
ARIZONA STATE UNIV	3	3	0	6	0	7	0	0	19	9	16	1	25	0	104	0	1	156	0	175	34	209
ARKANSAS STATE UNIV	5	0	0	0	0	10	0	0	15	16	0	0	1	0	64	0	0	81	0	96	75	171
ASHLAND UNIV	0	0	0	0	0	0	0	0	0	1	0	0	0	0	18	1	0	20	0	20	16	36
ATLANTIC UNION COLL	4	0	0	0	0	0	0	1	9	6	0	0	0	0	1	1	5	15	0	24	24	48
AUBURN UNIV	1	0	0	0	0	4	0	0	5	11	0	0	0	0	40	1	0	52	0	57	17	74
AUGSBURG COLL	2	0	0	0	0	4	0	0	6	2	0	1	0	0	36	0	0	39	0	45	24	69
AUGUSTANA/U SIOUX FA	0	0	0	0	0	1	0	0	1	0	0	0	0	0	23	0	0	23	0	24	18	42
AUSTIN PEAY STATE	1	0	0	0	0	2	0	0	3	20	0	2	3	0	50	4	0	79	0	82	47	129
AZUSA PACIFIC UNIV	0	0	1	0	0	4	0	0	5	2	0	2	9	0	23	0	0	36	0	41	36	77
BALL STATE UNIV	2	0	0	1	0	6	0	0	10	15	1	0	2	0	75	0	0	94	0	104	560	664
BARTON COLL	0	0	0	0	0	1	0	0	1	11	1	0	0	0	17	0	1	30	0	31	17	48
BAYLOR UNIV	1	0	0	0	0	2	0	0	3	2	0	0	8	0	38	2	2	52	0	55	53	108
BELMONT UNIV	0	0	0	0	0	1	0	0	1	0	0	0	0	0	16	0	0	16	0	17	25	42
BEMIDJI STATE UNIV	0	0	0	0	0	3	0	0	3	0	3	0	0	0	56	0	0	59	0	62	35	97
BETHANY COLL/WV	0	0	0	0	0	2	0	0	2	0	0	0	0	0	10	0	0	10	0	12	1	13
BETHEL COLL/KS	0	0	0	0	0	3	0	0	3	0	0	0	0	0	12	0	0	12	0	15	12	27
BETHEL COLL/MN	1	0	0	0	0	1	0	0	2	1	0	0	0	0	38	0	0	40	0	42	45	87
BLOOMSBURG UNIV	3	0	0	0	0	8	0	0	11	3	0	0	0	4	33	0	0	40	0	51	24	75
BLUFFTON COLL	0	0	0	0	0	2	0	0	2	0	0	0	0	0	13	0	0	13	0	15	18	33
BOISE STATE UNIV	1	0	1	0	0	11	0	0	13	0	1	2	4	0	53	0	0	64	0	77	92	169
BOWIE STATE UNIV	*	*	*	*	*	*	*	*	*	*	*	*	*	*	*	*	*	*	*	*	28	28
BOWLING GREEN STATE	0	0	0	0	0	3	0	0	3	2	0	0	1	0	90	0	0	93	0	96	64	160
BRESCIA UNIV	0	0	0	0	0	5	0	0	5	2	0	0	0	0	34	0	0	36	0	41	17	58
BRIAR CLIFF COLL	0	0	0	0	0	1	0	0	1	3	1	2	2	0	22	0	0	30	0	31	9	40
BRIDGEWATER STATE	0	1	0	0	0	5	0	0	6	6	0	1	2	0	62	0	2	76	0	82	44	126
BRIGHAM YOUNG/HI	0	1	1	0	0	6	11	4	24	0	0	5	1	0	16	16	4	43	0	67	36	103
BRIGHAM YOUNG/UT	0	0	0	0	0	19	1	0	20	1	1	3	2	0	94	6	0	107	0	127	4	131
BUENA VISTA UNIV	0	1	0	0	0	2	0	0	3	0	0	0	1	0	26	0	1	28	0	31	11	42
BUFFALO STATE COLL	4	0	0	0	0	19	0	0	23	13	0	0	0	10	93	2	0	118	0	141	115	256

TABLE 100

Number of Juniors and Seniors, by Gender and Ethnicity, and Number of Freshman and Sophomore Full-time Degree Students Enrolled in Baccalaureate Programs on 11/1/00

Program	Men									Women									Unk	Total	Frosh and Soph	Total
	African Amer	Amer Indian	Asian Amer	Chicano	Puerto Rican	White	Other	Foreign	Total	African Amer	Amer Indian	Asian Amer	Chicano	Puerto Rican	White	Other	Foreign	Total				
CABRINI COLL	0	0	0	0	0	0	0	0	0	2	0	0	0	2	46	0	0	50	0	50	0	50
CAL STATE UNIV/CHI	1	0	0	4	0	6	0	0	15	3	0	3	13	0	46	0	1	73	0	88	34	122
CAL STATE UNIV/FRES	4	1	1	40	0	12	15	0	77	26	3	3	110	0	38	21	0	223	0	300	49	349
CAL STATE UNIV/LB	3	0	3	2	0	3	1	0	12	8	0	6	42	0	27	3	0	86	0	98	64	162
CALVIN COLL	2	0	0	0	0	7	0	0	9	2	0	0	1	0	64	0	0	67	0	76	58	134
CAMPBELL UNIV	0	0	0	0	0	1	0	0	1	0	0	0	1	0	14	0	1	16	0	17	16	33
CAPITAL UNIV	1	1	1	0	0	3	0	0	5	30	0	0	2	0	40	2	0	74	0	79	22	101
CARLOW COLL	0	0	0	0	0	1	0	0	1	8	0	0	0	0	9	0	0	17	0	18	0	18
CARROLL COLL/MT	0	0	0	0	0	0	0	0	0	0	0	0	0	0	3	0	0	3	0	3	0	3
CARROLL COLL/WI	1	0	0	0	0	2	0	0	3	6	0	0	1	0	30	0	0	37	0	40	22	62
CARTHAGE COLL	1	0	0	0	0	0	0	0	1	1	0	0	0	1	15	0	0	17	0	18	20	38
CASTLETON STATE COLL	0	0	0	0	0	3	0	0	3	0	0	0	0	0	23	0	0	23	0	26	26	52
CATHOLIC UNIV/DC	2	0	0	0	0	3	1	0	6	2	0	0	0	0	14	1	0	17	0	23	30	53
CATHOLIC UNIV/PR	0	0	0	0	16	0	0	0	16	0	0	0	0	107	0	0	0	107	0	123	133	256
CEDAR CREST COLL	0	0	0	0	0	0	0	0	0	1	0	0	0	0	21	0	0	22	0	22	10	32
CEDARVILLE COLL	0	0	0	0	0	2	0	0	2	0	0	0	0	0	28	0	0	28	0	30	18	48
CENTRAL CONNECTICUT	2	0	0	0	2	3	1	0	8	3	1	0	0	5	40	2	0	51	0	59	0	59
CENTRAL MISSOURI	0	0	0	0	0	7	0	0	7	6	1	0	1	0	56	1	1	66	0	73	50	123
CHRISTOPHER NEWPORT	6	0	0	0	0	6	0	0	12	30	0	0	0	0	58	0	0	94	0	106	17	123
CLARK ATLANTA UNIV	4	0	0	0	0	0	0	0	4	40	0	0	0	1	0	0	0	41	0	45	32	77
CLEVELAND STATE UNIV	*	*	*	*	*	*	*	*	*	*	*	*	*	*	*	*	*	*	*	*	75	75
COLL MISERICORDIA	0	0	0	0	0	1	0	0	1	0	0	0	0	0	25	0	0	25	0	26	16	42
COLL MOUNT ST JOSEPH	1	0	0	0	0	0	0	0	1	8	0	0	0	0	10	0	0	18	0	19	29	48
COLL NEW ROCHELLE	0	0	0	0	0	0	0	0	0	5	0	0	0	2	8	3	1	19	0	19	12	31
COLL ST BEN/ST JOHNS	0	0	0	0	0	3	0	0	3	0	0	1	1	0	30	0	0	32	0	35	24	59
COLL ST CAT/U ST THO	1	0	0	0	0	2	0	0	3	4	0	4	1	0	92	1	1	103	0	106	0	106
COLL ST SCHOLASTICA	0	0	0	0	0	2	0	0	2	0	1	0	0	0	21	0	0	22	0	24	17	41
COLORADO STATE UNIV	0	0	1	0	0	11	0	0	12	2	0	1	5	0	90	6	0	104	0	116	42	158
COLUMBIA COLL/MO	1	0	0	0	0	4	*	*	5	8	1	0	0	*	32	*	*	42	0	47	23	70
COLUMBIA COLL/SC	*	*	*	*	*	*	0	0	*	*	*	*	*	1	*	0	0	*	*	*	37	37
CONCORD COLL	1	0	0	0	0	6	0	0	7	5	0	2	0	0	41	0	1	49	0	56	50	106
CONCORDIA COLL/MN	0	0	0	0	0	1	0	0	1	0	0	0	0	0	19	0	1	20	0	21	6	27
CONCORDIA COLL/NY	0	0	0	1	1	0	0	0	1	3	0	1	0	0	12	0	1	17	0	18	19	37
CONCORDIA UNIV WISC	0	0	0	0	0	1	0	0	2	2	0	0	0	0	12	0	0	14	0	16	8	24
COPPIN STATE COLL	*	*	*	*	*	*	*	*	*	*	*	*	*	*	*	*	*	*	*	*	41	41
CREIGHTON UNIV	0	0	0	0	0	1	0	0	1	1	0	0	1	0	12	0	0	14	0	15	5	20
DANA COLL	1	0	0	0	0	2	0	0	3	2	1	0	1	0	17	0	0	21	0	24	18	42
DAVID LIPSCOMB UNIV	1	0	0	0	0	1	0	1	3	1	0	1	0	0	20	0	1	23	0	26	21	47
DEFIANCE COLL	0	0	0	0	0	1	0	0	1	1	0	0	0	0	15	0	0	16	0	17	10	27
DELAWARE STATE UNIV	5	0	0	0	0	1	0	0	6	35	0	0	0	1	1	0	0	38	0	44	80	124
DELTA STATE UNIV	1	0	0	0	0	1	0	0	2	32	0	0	0	0	18	0	0	50	0	52	40	92

54

TABLE 100

Number of Juniors and Seniors, by Gender and Ethnicity, and Number of Freshman and Sophomore Full-time Degree Students Enrolled in Baccalaureate Programs on 11/1/00

Program	Men: African Amer	Men: Amer Indian	Men: Asian Amer	Men: Chicano	Men: Puerto Rican	Men: White	Men: Other	Men: Foreign	Men: Total	Women: African Amer	Women: Amer Indian	Women: Asian Amer	Women: Chicano	Women: Puerto Rican	Women: White	Women: Other	Women: Foreign	Women: Total	Unk	Juniors and Seniors: Total	Frosh and Soph	Total
DOMINICAN COLL	1	0	0	0	4	0	0	0	5	6	0	0	0	1	14	0	0	21	0	26	14	40
DORDT COLL	0	0	0	0	0	2	0	0	2	1	0	0	0	0	28	0	0	29	0	31	36	67
EAST CAROLINA UNIV	4	0	0	0	0	6	0	0	10	34	0	0	0	0	64	1	0	99	0	109	6	115
EAST CENTRAL UNIV	1	1	0	0	0	3	0	0	5	0	7	0	0	0	44	1	0	52	0	57	17	74
EAST TENNESSEE STATE	2	0	0	0	0	10	0	0	12	2	1	0	0	0	64	0	0	67	0	79	36	115
EASTERN COLL	0	0	1	0	1	5	0	0	7	2	0	1	0	1	37	0	0	41	0	48	43	91
EASTERN KENTUCKY	0	0	0	0	0	4	0	0	4	5	0	0	0	0	95	0	0	100	0	104	80	184
EASTERN MENNONITE	0	0	1	0	0	6	0	0	7	0	0	0	0	1	22	2	0	25	0	32	22	54
EASTERN MICHIGAN	3	0	0	0	0	8	0	0	11	20	0	3	1	0	70	0	0	100	0	111	66	177
EASTERN NAZARENE	0	0	0	0	0	1	0	0	1	1	0	1	0	0	16	2	0	20	0	21	10	31
EDINBORO UNIV	1	0	0	0	0	9	0	0	10	2	0	0	0	0	55	0	0	57	0	67	70	137
ELIZABETHTOWN COLL	0	0	0	0	0	3	0	0	3	0	0	0	0	2	25	0	0	27	0	30	18	48
ELMS COLL	1	0	0	0	1	1	0	0	3	3	0	1	0	2	24	0	0	30	0	33	14	47
EVANGEL UNIV	1	0	0	0	0	4	0	0	5	0	0	0	1	0	24	0	0	25	0	30	25	55
FERRIS STATE UNIV	4	0	1	0	0	5	0	0	11	1	0	0	0	0	94	0	0	95	0	106	61	167
FERRUM COLL	2	0	0	0	0	1	0	0	3	2	0	0	0	0	19	0	0	21	0	24	10	34
FLORIDA ATLANTIC	3	0	0	1	0	6	0	0	10	26	0	1	8	0	56	0	5	96	0	106	23	129
FLORIDA INTERNATL	7	0	0	0	0	2	9	0	18	42	0	4	0	0	15	45	3	109	0	127	0	127
FLORIDA STATE UNIV	4	0	0	0	0	23	2	0	29	52	2	2	0	0	140	16	0	212	0	241	10	251
FORT HAYS STATE UNIV	0	0	0	1	0	9	0	0	10	0	0	0	4	0	44	0	1	49	1	60	38	98
FROSTBURG STATE UNIV	1	0	0	0	0	1	0	0	2	1	0	1	0	0	39	0	1	42	0	44	24	68
GALLAUDET UNIV	3	0	0	0	0	3	0	1	7	5	0	0	1	1	14	0	0	21	0	28	0	28
GANNON UNIV	0	0	0	0	0	1	0	1	2	2	0	0	0	0	17	0	0	19	0	21	16	37
GEORGE MASON UNIV	3	0	0	0	0	4	0	0	7	22	0	5	13	4	95	0	0	139	0	146	67	213
GEORGIA STATE UNIV	0	0	0	0	0	0	0	0	0	0	0	0	0	0	0	0	0	0	61	61	31	92
GEORGIAN COURT COLL	0	0	0	0	0	0	0	0	0	3	0	1	0	6	38	1	0	49	0	49	21	70
GORDON COLL	0	0	0	0	0	10	0	0	10	0	0	0	0	1	43	1	1	46	0	56	31	87
GOSHEN COLL	0	0	0	0	0	4	0	0	4	1	0	1	0	0	15	0	4	21	0	25	13	38
GOVERNORS STATE UNIV	2	0	0	1	0	0	0	0	3	4	0	1	0	0	10	0	0	15	0	18	0	18
GRAMBLING STATE UNIV	1	0	0	0	0	5	0	0	6	*	*	*	*	*	*	*	*	*	0	*	63	63
GRAND VALLEY STATE	1	0	0	0	0	5	0	0	6	3	0	0	1	0	64	2	0	70	0	76	84	160
HARDIN-SIMMONS UNIV	1	0	0	0	0	0	0	0	2	2	0	2	3	0	24	0	0	31	0	33	23	56
HARDING UNIV	0	0	0	0	0	6	0	0	6	0	0	0	0	1	39	0	0	40	0	46	17	63
HERITAGE COLL	0	0	0	5	0	1	0	0	6	0	1	0	18	0	7	0	0	26	0	32	0	32
HOOD COLL	0	0	0	0	0	0	0	0	0	0	0	0	0	0	17	2	0	21	0	21	3	24
HOPE COLL	0	0	0	0	0	4	0	0	4	0	0	0	1	0	43	0	0	44	0	48	0	48
HOWARD PAYNE UNIV	2	0	0	0	0	1	0	0	3	2	0	0	1	0	13	0	0	16	0	19	10	29
HUMBOLDT STATE UNIV	0	0	1	1	0	9	0	1	12	4	5	0	8	0	26	3	0	46	0	58	40	98
IDAHO STATE UNIV	0	0	0	1	0	27	0	0	28	1	0	1	6	0	113	0	0	121	3	152	71	223
ILLINOIS STATE UNIV	1	0	0	0	0	8	0	0	9	14	1	1	0	0	96	1	0	113	0	122	81	203
INDIANA STATE UNIV	0	0	0	0	0	1	0	0	1	3	0	0	0	0	25	0	0	28	0	29	52	81

TABLE 100

Number of Juniors and Seniors, by Gender and Ethnicity, and Number of Freshman and Sophomore Full-time Degree Students Enrolled in Baccalaureate Programs on 11/1/00

Program	Men: African Amer	Amer Indian	Asian Amer	Chicano	Puerto Rican	White	Other	Foreign	Men Total	Women: African Amer	Amer Indian	Asian Amer	Chicano	Puerto Rican	White	Other	Foreign	Women Total	Unk	J&S Total	Frosh and Soph	Total
INDIANA UNIV	0	0	0	1	0	16	1	0	18	22	3	1	2	1	130	2	0	164	0	182	35	217
INDIANA WESLEYAN	2	0	0	0	0	2	0	0	4	1	0	0	1	0	17	0	1	20	0	24	40	64
INTERAMERICAN/ARE	0	0	0	0	12	0	0	0	12	0	0	0	0	111	0	0	0	111	0	123	113	236
INTERAMERICAN/MET	0	0	0	0	10	0	0	0	10	0	0	0	0	114	0	0	0	114	0	124	92	216
IONA COLL	2	0	0	0	1	4	1	0	8	1	0	0	0	4	14	2	0	21	0	29	12	41
JACKSON STATE UNIV	20	0	0	0	0	0	0	0	20	119	0	0	0	0	0	0	0	119	0	139	85	224
JACKSONVILLE STATE	5	0	0	0	0	10	0	0	15	34	0	1	0	0	67	1	0	101	0	116	84	200
JAMES MADISON UNIV	0	0	0	0	0	6	0	0	6	4	0	1	0	0	65	1	0	72	0	78	51	129
JUNIATA COLL	0	0	0	0	0	0	0	0	0	1	0	0	0	0	16	0	0	17	0	17	13	30
KANSAS STATE UNIV	2	2	0	2	0	1	0	0	7	2	2	1	0	0	0	0	0	5	82	94	47	141
KEAN UNIV	*	*	*	*	*	*	*	*	*	*	*	*	*	*	*	*	*	*	*	*	49	49
KENTUCKY CHRISTIAN	0	0	0	0	0	1	0	0	1	2	0	0	0	0	12	0	0	14	0	15	22	37
KENTUCKY STATE UNIV	3	0	0	0	0	1	0	0	4	7	0	0	0	0	9	0	0	16	0	20	25	45
KEUKA COLL	0	0	0	0	0	3	0	0	3	0	0	1	0	0	16	0	0	17	0	20	17	37
KUTZTOWN UNIV	2	0	0	0	1	3	0	0	6	4	1	2	0	4	27	0	0	38	0	44	57	101
LA SALLE UNIV	1	0	0	0	0	0	0	0	1	7	0	0	0	2	9	0	0	18	0	19	15	34
LA SIERRA UNIV	5	0	0	1	0	2	0	0	8	3	0	3	7	0	13	0	0	26	0	34	16	50
LEHMAN COLL	15	0	1	0	5	1	0	0	22	88	0	4	0	122	11	0	0	225	0	247	0	247
LEWIS-CLARK STATE	1	0	0	0	0	15	0	0	16	0	0	1	0	0	58	0	3	62	0	78	331	409
LOCK HAVEN UNIV	2	0	0	0	1	2	0	0	5	2	0	0	0	0	58	0	0	60	0	65	54	119
LONG ISLAND UNIV/CWP	0	0	1	0	0	2	0	0	3	4	0	0	0	0	11	2	0	17	0	20	0	20
LONGWOOD COLL	1	0	0	0	0	3	0	0	4	3	0	3	0	0	33	0	0	39	0	43	29	72
LORAS/CLARK COLLS	0	0	0	0	0	2	0	0	2	0	0	0	0	1	26	0	0	27	0	29	16	45
LOUISIANA COLL	0	0	0	0	0	3	0	0	3	0	0	0	0	0	14	0	0	14	0	17	24	41
LOURDES COLL	0	1	0	0	0	0	0	0	1	3	0	0	0	0	13	0	0	16	0	17	9	26
LOYOLA UNIV CHICAGO	1	0	0	0	0	2	0	0	3	4	0	2	0	3	12	0	0	22	1	26	22	48
LUBBOCK CHRISTIAN	0	0	0	0	0	8	0	0	8	1	0	0	3	0	28	0	1	33	0	41	24	65
LUTHER COLL	0	0	0	0	0	3	0	0	3	0	0	0	0	0	23	0	0	25	0	28	24	52
MACMURRAY COLL	0	0	0	0	0	1	0	0	1	0	0	0	0	0	14	0	1	15	0	16	9	25
MADONNA UNIV	*	*	*	*	*	*	*	*	*	*	*	*	*	*	*	*	*	*	*	*	20	20
MALONE COLL	0	0	0	0	0	1	0	0	1	0	0	0	0	0	21	0	0	22	0	23	33	56
MANCHESTER COLL	1	0	0	0	0	1	0	0	2	0	0	0	0	0	16	0	1	18	0	18	28	46
MANSFIELD UNIV	0	0	0	0	0	9	0	0	9	0	0	0	0	0	36	0	1	37	0	46	38	84
MARIAN COLL	0	0	0	0	0	0	0	0	0	0	0	1	0	0	16	1	0	18	0	18	23	41
MARQUETTE UNIV	0	0	0	0	0	2	0	0	2	2	0	0	0	0	25	0	0	27	0	29	15	44
MARS HILL COLL	1	0	0	0	0	2	0	0	3	1	0	0	0	0	39	0	0	40	0	43	14	57
MARSHALL UNIV	2	0	0	0	0	6	0	0	9	2	0	0	0	0	36	0	0	41	0	50	22	72
MARYCREST INTERNATL	0	0	0	0	0	1	0	0	1	0	0	0	0	0	12	0	0	13	0	14	3	17
MARYGROVE COLL	3	0	0	0	0	2	0	0	6	16	0	0	0	0	3	1	0	22	0	28	16	44
MARYWOOD UNIV	0	0	0	0	0	1	0	0	1	0	0	0	0	0	15	0	0	15	0	16	21	37

TABLE 100

Number of Juniors and Seniors, by Gender and Ethnicity, and Number of Freshman and Sophomore Full-time Degree Students Enrolled in Baccalaureate Programs on 11/1/00

Program	Men									Women									Unk	Total	Frosh and Soph	Total
	African Amer	Amer Indian	Asian Amer	Chicano	Puerto Rican	White	Other	Foreign	Total	African Amer	Amer Indian	Asian Amer	Chicano	Puerto Rican	White	Other	Foreign	Total				
MERCY COLL	4	0	0	0	3	1	0	0	8	14	0	1	0	13	8	1	0	37	0	45	0	45
MERCYHURST COLL	0	0	0	0	0	2	0	0	2	0	0	0	0	0	18	2	0	20	0	22	14	36
MEREDITH COLL	0	0	0	0	0	0	0	0	0	4	0	1	0	0	24	0	0	29	0	29	5	34
METHODIST COLL	1	0	0	0	2	0	0	0	3	11	0	0	2	1	14	0	0	28	0	31	22	53
METRO STATE COLL DEN	1	0	0	2	0	11	0	0	14	5	0	1	11	0	58	0	2	77	4	95	100	195
METRO STATE UNIV	1	0	1	0	0	4	0	0	6	3	0	4	1	1	24	0	1	34	0	40	0	40
MIAMI UNIV	0	0	0	0	0	5	0	0	5	5	0	0	2	0	54	0	1	62	0	67	54	121
MICHIGAN STATE UNIV	1	0	0	0	0	7	0	0	8	10	0	0	1	2	55	0	1	69	0	77	50	127
MIDDLE TENNESSEE ST	6	0	0	0	0	24	2	0	32	16	0	0	0	0	107	0	0	123	0	155	60	215
MIDWESTERN STATE	0	0	0	0	0	5	0	1	6	5	2	0	4	0	35	0	2	48	0	54	32	86
MILLERSVILLE UNIV	1	0	0	0	0	6	0	0	7	8	0	0	0	2	55	0	0	65	0	72	48	120
MINNESOTA STATE/MANK	1	0	1	0	0	5	0	0	7	0	0	4	0	0	89	0	0	93	6	106	84	190
MINNESOTA STATE/MOOR	0	1	2	0	0	11	0	0	14	0	1	2	0	0	100	0	0	103	0	117	76	193
MINOT STATE UNIV	0	4	0	0	0	5	0	1	10	0	4	0	0	0	27	0	1	32	0	42	25	67
MISSISSIPPI STATE/ST	2	0	0	0	0	2	0	0	4	36	0	0	0	0	22	0	0	58	0	62	25	87
MISSISSIPPI VALLEY	5	0	0	0	0	1	0	0	6	83	0	0	0	0	0	0	0	83	0	89	77	166
MISSOURI WESTERN	0	0	0	0	0	1	0	0	1	2	0	0	0	0	37	0	0	39	0	40	43	83
MOLLOY COLL	0	0	0	0	0	4	0	0	4	9	0	0	0	3	43	2	0	57	0	61	10	71
MONMOUTH UNIV	0	0	0	0	0	4	0	0	4	3	0	0	0	6	45	0	0	54	0	58	30	88
MOREHEAD STATE UNIV	2	0	0	0	0	9	6	0	17	3	0	0	0	0	54	50	0	107	0	124	44	168
MORGAN STATE UNIV	12	0	0	0	0	0	0	0	12	87	0	0	0	0	3	0	0	90	0	102	53	155
MOUNT MARY COLL	0	0	0	0	0	0	0	0	0	2	0	2	0	0	18	0	0	22	0	22	7	29
MOUNT MERCY COLL	0	0	0	0	0	0	0	0	0	0	1	0	0	0	18	0	0	19	0	19	25	44
MOUNT SENARIO COLL	0	0	0	0	0	1	0	0	1	1	0	0	0	0	11	0	0	12	0	13	20	33
MURRAY STATE UNIV	0	0	0	0	0	5	0	0	5	10	0	1	1	2	84	0	1	99	0	104	39	143
NAZARETH COLL ROCH	0	0	0	0	0	2	0	0	2	9	0	0	0	0	42	2	0	53	0	55	16	71
NEB WESLEYAN/UNION	0	0	0	0	0	1	0	0	1	1	0	1	0	0	13	0	0	15	0	16	4	20
NEW MEXICO HIGHLANDS	1	0	0	6	0	5	0	0	12	2	4	0	31	0	2	0	0	39	0	51	6	57
NEW MEXICO STATE	2	2	0	8	0	1	0	0	13	4	2	1	50	0	33	0	0	90	0	103	111	214
NEW YORK UNIV	3	0	0	0	0	7	0	0	10	7	0	6	0	8	40	1	1	63	0	73	34	107
NIAGARA UNIV	0	0	0	0	0	2	0	0	2	2	1	0	1	0	26	1	0	31	0	33	17	50
NORTH CAROLINA CENT	2	0	0	0	0	1	0	0	3	22	0	0	0	0	2	0	0	24	0	27	28	55
NORTHEASTERN ILL	3	0	0	3	3	11	0	0	20	30	0	1	15	7	29	13	1	96	0	116	16	132
NORTHEASTERN STATE	0	2	1	0	0	9	0	0	12	5	17	0	1	0	43	0	0	66	0	78	0	78
NORTHERN ARIZONA	0	4	0	0	0	4	0	0	8	0	16	1	3	0	39	0	0	59	0	67	48	115
NORTHERN KENTUCKY	2	0	0	0	0	3	0	0	5	8	0	0	0	0	52	0	0	60	0	65	54	119
NORTHERN MICHIGAN	1	1	0	0	0	8	0	0	10	1	3	2	0	0	55	0	0	61	0	71	42	113
NORTHWEST NAZARENE	0	0	0	0	0	10	0	0	10	0	0	1	1	0	22	0	0	24	0	34	30	64
NORTHWESTERN COLL	0	0	0	0	0	1	0	0	1	0	0	0	0	0	23	0	0	23	0	24	19	43
NORTHWESTERN STATE	8	1	0	0	0	6	0	0	15	43	2	1	0	0	59	3	0	108	0	123	100	223
OAKWOOD COLL	15	0	0	0	0	0	0	2	17	24	0	0	0	0	0	0	1	25	0	42	32	74

TABLE 100

Number of Juniors and Seniors, by Gender and Ethnicity, and Number of Freshman and Sophomore Full-time Degree Students Enrolled in Baccalaureate Programs on 11/1/00

Program	Men									Women									Unk	Total	Frosh and Soph	Total
	African Amer	Amer Indian	Asian Amer	Chicano	Puerto Rican	White	Other	Foreign	Total	African Amer	Amer Indian	Asian Amer	Chicano	Puerto Rican	White	Other	Foreign	Total		Total		
SOUTHWEST TEXAS	2	0	0	3	0	3	0	0	8	6	1	1	29	0	65	0	0	104	0	112	39	151
SPALDING UNIV	2	2	0	0	0	5	0	1	10	4	0	0	0	0	20	0	2	26	0	36	11	47
SPRING ARBOR COLL	0	0	0	0	0	1	0	0	1	1	0	1	0	0	18	0	1	21	0	22	16	38
ST CLOUD STATE UNIV	1	0	0	1	0	6	0	1	10	1	0	1	2	0	102	0	1	120	0	130	115	245
ST FRANCIS COLL	0	0	0	0	0	3	0	0	3	0	1	0	0	0	12	0	0	13	3	19	14	33
ST JOSEPH COLL	0	0	0	1	0	0	0	0	0	2	0	1	0	0	19	0	0	29	0	29	11	40
ST LOUIS UNIV	2	0	1	1	0	1	0	0	5	3	0	0	0	0	33	0	0	38	0	43	25	68
ST MARYS COLL	0	0	0	0	0	0	0	0	0	1	0	0	2	0	18	0	0	21	0	21	22	43
ST OLAF COLL	1	0	0	1	0	3	0	1	6	0	0	0	2	0	19	1	0	22	0	28	26	54
STEPHEN F AUSTIN	4	1	0	0	0	7	0	0	11	26	0	0	1	3	57	0	0	84	0	95	63	158
SUNY/ALBANY	0	1	0	0	2	4	0	0	8	9	0	2	1	3	44	0	0	59	0	67	0	67
SUNY/BROCKPORT	3	0	0	0	0	14	1	0	18	11	1	0	0	0	102	9	0	123	0	141	17	158
SUNY/STONY BROOK	2	0	1	0	0	5	0	0	8	12	0	4	0	5	27	4	0	52	0	60	0	60
SYRACUSE UNIV	9	0	1	1	1	8	0	0	20	14	0	0	1	2	47	0	0	64	1	85	93	178
TALLADEGA COLL	8	0	0	0	0	0	0	0	8	25	0	0	0	0	0	0	0	25	0	33	28	61
TAYLOR UNIV	0	0	0	0	0	2	0	0	2	0	0	0	1	0	27	0	0	28	0	30	37	67
TEMPLE UNIV	9	0	0	0	1	7	0	1	19	55	1	1	0	12	50	0	1	129	0	148	80	228
TENNESSEE STATE UNIV	3	0	0	0	0	3	1	0	7	31	0	0	0	0	3	1	0	35	0	42	39	81
TEXAS A&M UNIV/COM	2	0	0	0	0	4	0	0	6	22	0	0	3	0	37	0	0	62	0	68	22	90
TEXAS CHRISTIAN UNIV	2	0	1	0	0	8	0	1	14	5	1	0	4	0	52	0	2	65	0	79	44	123
TEXAS LUTHERAN UNIV	2	0	0	1	0	1	0	0	4	1	0	0	0	0	9	0	0	14	0	18	5	23
TEXAS TECH UNIV	2	0	0	8	0	4	0	0	14	2	0	0	18	0	43	0	0	63	0	77	19	96
TEXAS WOMAN'S UNIV	0	0	0	0	0	0	0	0	0	13	0	0	5	0	23	0	0	41	0	41	18	59
TROY STATE UNIV	0	0	0	0	0	4	0	0	4	15	0	0	0	0	26	0	0	42	0	46	35	81
TUSKEGEE UNIV	15	0	0	0	0	0	0	0	15	33	0	0	0	0	0	1	2	35	0	50	10	60
U OF AKRON	2	1	0	0	0	2	0	0	5	13	0	0	0	0	40	0	0	55	0	60	0	60
U OF ALABAMA	2	0	0	0	0	5	0	0	7	16	0	0	0	0	49	1	1	66	0	73	54	127
U OF ALABAMA/BIR	1	0	0	0	0	1	0	0	2	12	0	0	0	0	19	0	0	32	0	34	0	34
U OF ALASKA/ANK	0	2	0	0	0	3	0	0	5	4	0	0	1	0	21	2	0	28	0	33	17	50
U OF ALASKA/FAIR	0	1	1	0	0	3	0	0	5	5	5	1	1	1	25	5	1	43	13	61	15	76
U OF ARKANSAS/FAY	3	1	0	0	0	13	0	0	17	4	1	0	1	0	55	0	1	62	0	79	36	115
U OF ARKANSAS/PB	7	0	0	0	0	0	0	0	7	26	0	0	0	0	0	0	0	26	0	33	30	63
U OF CENTRAL FLORIDA	4	0	1	0	0	5	3	0	13	18	0	2	2	13	55	2	0	92	0	105	0	105
U OF CINCINNATI	2	0	0	0	0	3	0	0	5	11	0	0	0	0	49	0	0	62	0	67	0	67
U OF DETROIT MERCY	0	0	0	0	0	0	0	0	0	12	0	1	1	0	4	0	0	17	0	17	3	20
U OF FINDLAY	0	0	0	0	0	2	0	0	2	0	0	0	0	0	14	0	0	16	0	18	17	35
U OF GEORGIA	2	0	0	0	0	3	0	0	5	13	0	0	5	0	74	0	0	92	0	97	51	148
U OF HAWAII	0	0	3	0	0	0	4	0	7	0	0	15	0	0	6	8	2	31	0	38	0	38
U OF ILLINOIS/CHI	1	0	1	2	1	4	0	0	10	8	1	4	5	1	42	8	1	75	0	85	0	85
U OF ILLINOIS/SPR	0	0	0	0	0	8	0	0	8	10	0	0	0	0	48	0	0	58	0	58	0	66
U OF INDIANAPOLIS	1	0	0	0	0	2	0	0	3	4	0	0	0	0	10	0	2	16	0	19	25	44

TABLE 100

Number of Juniors and Seniors, by Gender and Ethnicity, and Number of Freshman and Sophomore Full-time Degree Students Enrolled in Baccalaureate Programs on 11/1/00

Program	Men									Women									Unk	Total	Frosh and Soph	Total
	African Amer	Amer Indian	Asian Amer	Chicano	Puerto Rican	White	Other	Foreign	Total	African Amer	Amer Indian	Asian Amer	Chicano	Puerto Rican	White	Other	Foreign	Total				
OHIO STATE UNIV	2	0	0	0	0	6	0	0	8	13	1	1	0	0	114	3	1	133	0	141	177	318
OHIO UNIV	0	0	0	0	0	9	0	1	10	3	0	0	2	0	57	0	1	64	0	74	31	105
OLIVET NAZARENE UNIV	0	0	0	0	0	3	0	0	3	5	0	0	1	0	37	0	0	43	0	46	48	94
ORAL ROBERTS UNIV	2	0	0	0	0	3	0	0	5	10	0	0	1	0	16	0	2	29	0	34	14	48
OUR LADY OF LAKE	0	0	0	5	0	0	0	0	5	8	0	0	33	0	6	1	0	50	0	55	33	88
PACIFIC LUTHERAN	1	0	3	0	0	4	0	0	8	3	1	1	1	0	32	0	1	39	0	47	0	47
PACIFIC UNION COLL	0	0	1	1	0	0	1	0	3	1	0	0	2	0	6	0	0	9	0	12	14	26
PHILLY COLL BIBLE	2	0	0	0	0	6	0	1	9	2	0	0	0	0	50	0	1	53	0	62	35	97
PITTSBURG STATE UNIV	1	2	0	1	0	7	0	0	14	3	3	0	4	0	34	0	0	44	0	58	27	85
PLYMOUTH STATE COLL	0	0	0	0	0	2	0	0	2	1	0	0	0	0	17	0	0	19	0	21	20	41
PRAIRIE VIEW A&M	20	0	0	0	0	2	0	6	28	75	0	0	1	0	6	0	10	92	0	120	51	171
PRESENTATION COLL	2	1	0	0	0	1	1	0	5	0	0	0	0	0	8	0	0	8	0	13	18	31
PROVIDENCE COLL	0	0	0	0	0	1	0	0	1	0	0	0	0	0	29	0	0	30	0	31	17	48
RADFORD UNIV	0	0	0	0	0	5	0	0	5	5	0	1	0	0	49	0	0	55	0	60	31	91
RAMAPO COLL	0	0	0	0	0	2	1	1	4	5	0	0	0	0	42	4	2	54	0	58	60	118
REGIS COLL	0	0	0	0	0	0	0	0	0	3	1	0	0	0	19	3	0	26	0	26	12	38
RHODE ISLAND COLL	2	0	0	0	0	6	2	0	10	8	0	0	0	0	73	0	0	83	0	93	41	134
ROCHESTER INST TECH	4	0	2	0	0	7	0	0	13	2	0	0	0	0	26	0	1	29	0	42	24	66
RUTGERS UNIV/NB	1	0	0	0	1	3	1	0	5	13	0	3	0	4	51	1	0	72	0	77	8	85
RUTGERS UNIV/NRK	4	0	1	0	1	0	5	0	11	12	0	1	0	12	16	11	0	52	0	63	8	71
SACRED HEART UNIV	0	0	0	0	0	1	0	0	1	1	0	0	0	1	21	0	0	23	0	24	10	34
SAGINAW VALLEY STATE	2	0	0	0	0	5	0	0	7	10	0	0	1	0	54	0	0	65	0	72	3	75
SALEM STATE COLL	1	0	0	0	0	6	2	0	9	6	0	1	0	4	41	5	0	57	0	66	45	111
SALVE REGINA UNIV	0	0	0	0	0	4	0	0	4	1	0	0	0	0	28	0	0	29	0	33	27	60
SAN DIEGO STATE UNIV	*	*	*	*	*	*	*	*	*	*	*	*	*	*	*	*	*	*	*	*	43	43
SAN FRANCISCO STATE	6	0	4	11	0	7	0	0	28	17	0	39	26	0	48	5	2	137	0	165	0	165
SAVANNAH STATE UNIV	3	0	0	0	0	0	0	0	3	56	0	0	0	0	1	1	0	58	0	61	15	76
SHEPHERD COLL	1	0	0	0	0	3	0	0	4	5	0	0	1	0	14	2	0	22	0	26	30	56
SHIPPENSBURG UNIV	0	0	0	0	0	6	0	0	6	4	0	0	0	0	89	0	0	93	0	99	66	165
SIENA COLL	0	0	0	0	0	2	0	0	2	1	1	0	0	0	16	3	0	21	0	23	26	49
SKIDMORE COLL	*	*	*	*	*	*	*	*	*	*	*	*	*	*	*	*	*	*	*	*	30	30
SLIPPERY ROCK UNIV	3	0	0	2	0	10	0	0	15	2	0	0	0	0	43	0	1	48	0	63	54	117
SOUTH CAROLINA STATE	9	0	0	0	0	1	0	0	10	67	0	0	0	0	1	0	0	68	0	78	77	155
SOUTHEAST MISSOURI	0	0	0	0	0	7	0	0	7	7	0	0	0	0	76	0	0	86	0	93	49	142
SOUTHEASTERN LOU	1	0	0	0	0	24	0	0	25	18	0	0	0	0	131	0	0	149	0	174	92	266
SOUTHERN CONNECTICUT	3	0	0	0	0	3	0	0	9	10	0	1	0	0	46	1	0	66	0	75	0	75
SOUTHERN ILL/CAR	8	0	0	2	0	23	0	0	33	40	1	1	0	0	134	0	0	178	0	211	52	263
SOUTHERN ILL/EDW	2	0	0	0	0	10	0	0	12	8	0	0	0	0	55	0	0	63	0	75	11	86
SOUTHERN UNIV	16	0	0	0	0	2	0	0	18	108	0	0	0	0	0	0	0	108	0	126	27	153
SOUTHERN UNIV A&M	10	0	0	0	0	0	0	0	10	100	0	0	0	0	1	0	0	101	0	111	111	222
SOUTHWEST MISSOURI	0	0	0	0	0	15	0	0	15	7	1	0	0	0	118	0	0	131	0	146	78	224

59

TABLE 100

Number of Juniors and Seniors, by Gender and Ethnicity, and Number of Freshman and Sophomore Full-time Degree Students Enrolled in Baccalaureate Programs on 11/1/00

Program	Men									Women									Unk	Total	Frosh and Soph	Total
	African Amer	Amer Indian	Asian Amer	Chicano	Puerto Rican	White	Other	Foreign	Total	African Amer	Amer Indian	Asian Amer	Chicano	Puerto Rican	White	Other	Foreign	Total				
U OF IOWA	0	0	0	1	0	1	0	0	9	0	0	0	0	0	44	0	0	73	0	82	41	123
U OF KANSAS	0	3	0	0	0	9	0	0	12	5	3	3	2	0	101	0	0	117	0	129	0	129
U OF KENTUCKY	10	0	0	0	0	16	0	0	26	25	0	1	2	0	100	0	0	128	0	154	37	191
U OF LOUISIANA/MON	1	0	0	0	0	2	0	0	3	39	0	0	1	0	40	0	0	80	0	83	59	142
U OF MAINE/PI	0	0	0	0	0	4	0	0	4	0	1	0	0	0	16	2	4	23	0	27	72	99
U OF MARY	1	2	0	0	0	4	0	0	7	0	2	0	0	0	28	0	0	30	0	37	20	57
U OF MARY HARD-BAY	1	1	0	0	0	2	0	0	4	6	0	0	9	0	14	1	0	30	0	34	25	59
U OF MARYLAND	5	0	2	0	1	12	0	0	21	24	2	8	0	6	76	0	1	118	0	139	53	192
U OF MICHIGAN/FL	4	0	0	0	0	10	0	0	14	14	0	0	1	1	87	0	0	102	0	116	27	143
U OF MISSISSIPPI	4	0	0	0	0	6	0	0	10	27	1	0	0	0	56	0	0	85	0	95	22	117
U OF MISSOURI/COL	0	0	1	0	0	3	0	0	4	1	0	0	3	0	57	0	0	62	0	66	63	129
U OF MISSOURI/STL	2	0	1	1	0	3	0	0	6	12	0	1	1	0	49	0	6	69	0	75	22	97
U OF MONTANA	0	1	0	0	0	8	0	0	10	0	6	1	0	0	74	0	0	82	0	92	59	151
U OF MONTEVALLO	2	0	0	0	0	2	0	0	4	4	0	0	0	0	28	0	0	32	0	36	25	61
U OF NEBRASKA/KEA	0	0	0	0	0	0	0	0	0	0	1	0	1	0	74	0	0	76	0	76	23	99
U OF NEBRASKA/OMA	0	0	1	0	0	1	0	0	2	0	0	1	3	0	31	0	0	35	0	37	0	37
U OF NEVADA/LV	3	0	1	1	0	7	0	0	13	4	1	2	11	0	46	0	6	68	0	81	20	101
U OF NEVADA/REN	*	*	*	*	*	*	*	*	*	*	*	*	*	*	*	*	*	*	*	*	40	40
U OF NEW HAMPSHIRE	0	0	0	0	0	4	0	0	4	0	0	0	2	0	56	0	0	62	0	66	38	104
U OF NORTH ALABAMA	2	0	1	1	0	7	0	1	11	14	2	0	0	0	58	0	0	77	0	88	54	142
U OF NORTH CAR/CHT	5	1	1	0	0	3	0	0	9	17	0	1	0	0	32	0	0	50	0	59	34	93
U OF NORTH CAR/GRB	1	0	0	0	0	3	0	0	4	32	0	2	0	0	52	0	0	86	0	90	90	180
U OF NORTH CAR/PEM	5	2	0	1	0	7	0	0	15	18	17	0	2	0	22	0	0	59	0	74	27	101
U OF NORTH DAKOTA	0	0	0	0	0	5	0	0	7	0	7	0	3	0	62	0	0	72	0	79	44	123
U OF NORTH TEXAS	2	0	0	3	0	6	1	0	13	8	0	0	3	0	50	1	0	62	0	75	45	120
U OF NORTHERN IOWA	1	0	0	0	0	10	0	0	12	4	1	1	0	0	119	1	0	129	0	141	48	189
U OF OKLAHOMA	1	1	0	1	0	3	0	0	6	8	4	1	0	0	45	3	0	61	0	67	52	119
U OF PITTSBURGH	5	0	0	0	0	6	0	0	11	19	1	1	0	0	92	0	2	115	0	126	0	126
U OF PUERTO RICO/HU	0	0	0	0	16	0	0	0	16	0	0	0	0	104	0	0	0	104	0	120	92	212
U OF PUERTO RICO/RP	*	*	*	*	*	*	*	*	*	*	*	*	*	*	*	*	*	*	*	*	0	0
U OF RIO GRANDE	0	0	0	0	0	0	0	0	0	0	0	0	0	0	16	0	0	16	0	16	24	40
U OF SACRED HEART	*	*	*	*	*	*	*	*	*	*	*	*	*	*	*	*	*	*	*	*	30	30
U OF SOUTH DAKOTA	0	0	0	0	0	1	0	1	2	0	1	0	0	0	40	0	1	41	0	43	31	74
U OF SOUTH FLORIDA	4	0	0	0	0	5	0	0	9	32	0	0	0	9	68	4	1	114	0	123	0	123
U OF SOUTHERN COLO	1	0	0	1	0	3	0	0	6	3	0	2	18	0	31	0	2	57	0	63	32	95
U OF SOUTHERN IND	0	0	0	0	0	0	0	0	7	0	0	0	0	0	54	0	0	54	0	61	75	136
U OF SOUTHERN MAINE	1	0	0	0	0	5	0	0	6	0	2	0	0	0	59	0	0	61	0	67	4	71
U OF SOUTHERN MISS	2	2	0	0	0	2	0	0	6	24	0	0	0	0	26	0	0	50	0	56	0	56
U OF ST FRANCIS/IL	*	*	*	*	*	*	*	*	*	*	*	*	*	*	*	*	*	*	*	*	10	10
U OF ST FRANCIS/IN	3	0	0	0	1	6	0	0	10	4	0	0	2	0	9	0	0	15	0	25	30	55
U OF TENNESSEE/CHAT	2	1	0	0	0	4	0	0	7	14	0	0	0	0	37	0	0	51	0	58	27	85

TABLE 100

Number of Juniors and Seniors, by Gender and Ethnicity, and Number of Freshman and Sophomore Full-time Degree Students Enrolled in Baccalaureate Programs on 11/1/00

Program	Men									Women									Unk	Total	Frosh and Soph	Total
	African Amer	Amer Indian	Asian Amer	Chicano	Puerto Rican	White	Other	Foreign	Total	African Amer	Amer Indian	Asian Amer	Chicano	Puerto Rican	White	Other	Foreign	Total				
U OF TENNESSEE/KNX	0	0	0	0	0	2	0	0	2	4	0	0	0	0	45	0	0	49	0	51	71	122
U OF TENNESSEE/MAR	0	0	0	0	0	5	0	0	5	11	0	0	0	0	45	0	1	57	0	62	24	86
U OF TEXAS/ARL	2	0	0	0	0	6	0	0	8	22	1	4	14	0	42	0	0	83	0	91	34	125
U OF TEXAS/AUS	4	0	0	1	0	9	0	0	14	2	0	4	32	0	71	0	0	109	0	123	51	174
U OF TEXAS/PAN	0	0	0	3	0	0	0	0	3	2	0	0	34	0	1	0	0	37	0	40	0	40
U OF TOLEDO	3	1	0	0	0	3	0	0	7	21	1	0	0	0	48	0	0	73	0	80	54	134
U OF VERMONT	0	0	0	0	0	4	0	0	4	0	0	0	0	0	41	2	0	43	0	47	28	75
U OF WASHINGTON	0	0	1	1	0	2	0	0	4	6	2	15	4	0	46	3	0	77	0	81	8	89
U OF WEST VIRGINIA	3	0	0	0	0	8	0	0	13	19	1	2	3	0	56	0	0	87	0	100	14	114
U OF WISCONSIN/EAU	0	0	0	1	0	3	0	1	5	0	0	0	5	0	104	0	0	109	0	114	85	199
U OF WISCONSIN/GBY	0	0	0	0	0	7	0	0	7	0	3	1	0	0	41	0	0	45	0	52	18	70
U OF WISCONSIN/MAD	0	0	0	0	0	2	0	0	2	0	0	1	0	0	35	0	0	36	0	38	0	38
U OF WISCONSIN/MIL	3	1	0	1	0	10	0	0	15	9	1	1	1	0	72	0	0	84	0	99	77	176
U OF WISCONSIN/OSH	0	0	1	0	0	9	0	0	10	1	2	2	0	1	60	0	0	66	0	76	90	166
U OF WISCONSIN/RIV	0	0	0	0	0	2	0	0	2	0	0	1	0	0	46	0	0	47	0	49	44	93
U OF WISCONSIN/SUP	0	2	0	0	0	9	0	2	13	0	2	0	0	0	35	0	1	38	0	51	26	77
U OF WISCONSIN/WHI	4	0	3	0	0	23	0	0	30	4	0	0	0	0	164	0	0	168	0	198	104	302
URSULINE COLL	0	0	0	0	0	0	0	0	0	7	0	0	1	0	2	0	0	9	0	9	5	14
UTAH STATE UNIV	0	0	0	0	0	8	0	0	8	1	0	0	1	0	67	0	0	69	0	77	90	167
VALPARAISO UNIV	0	0	0	0	0	1	0	0	1	1	0	1	0	0	26	0	0	28	0	29	16	45
VIRGINIA COMMONWEAL	2	0	0	0	0	6	0	0	8	16	0	2	0	0	36	0	0	54	0	62	85	147
VIRGINIA INTERMONT	*	*	*	*	*	*	*	*	*	*	*	*	*	*	*	*	*	*	*	*	6	6
VIRGINIA STATE UNIV	1	0	0	0	0	0	0	0	1	9	0	0	0	0	0	0	0	9	0	10	38	48
WALLA WALLA COLL	0	0	0	0	0	4	0	0	4	1	0	0	2	0	20	0	1	24	0	28	19	47
WARREN WILSON COLL	0	0	0	0	0	0	0	0	0	0	0	0	0	0	8	0	0	8	0	8	12	20
WASHBURN UNIV	1	1	0	1	0	10	0	0	13	4	0	0	4	0	39	0	0	49	0	62	16	78
WAYNE STATE UNIV	8	0	0	1	0	4	0	0	13	40	2	3	7	0	72	4	1	129	0	142	0	142
WEBER STATE UNIV	1	0	0	1	0	10	0	0	12	0	0	0	2	0	58	0	0	60	0	72	64	136
WEST TEXAS A&M UNIV	0	0	0	0	0	1	1	0	2	6	0	0	8	0	44	0	0	58	0	60	31	91
WEST VIRGINIA UNIV	0	0	2	0	0	13	1	0	16	5	0	1	0	0	85	2	0	93	0	109	155	264
WESTERN CAROLINA	0	0	0	0	0	6	0	0	6	2	2	0	0	0	37	0	0	41	0	47	16	63
WESTERN CONNECTICUT	0	0	0	1	0	3	0	0	4	0	2	1	6	0	31	1	1	42	0	46	72	118
WESTERN ILLINOIS	0	0	0	1	0	5	0	0	6	6	0	1	1	0	64	0	1	73	0	79	41	120
WESTERN KENTUCKY	2	0	0	0	0	6	0	0	8	15	0	1	2	0	53	0	0	71	0	79	65	144
WESTERN MARYLAND	0	0	0	0	0	5	0	0	5	0	0	2	0	0	26	0	0	28	0	33	25	58
WESTERN NEW ENGLAND	0	0	0	0	0	5	0	0	5	0	0	0	0	1	32	0	0	33	0	38	18	56
WESTERN NEW MEXICO	1	0	0	0	0	1	0	0	2	0	0	0	9	0	4	0	0	13	0	15	26	41
WHEELOCK COLL	1	0	0	0	0	2	0	0	3	7	1	0	0	4	23	0	0	36	0	39	11	50
WHITTIER COLL	*	*	*	*	*	*	*	*	*	*	*	*	*	*	*	*	*	*	*	*	8	8
WICHITA STATE UNIV	0	0	0	0	0	3	0	0	3	4	1	0	0	0	43	0	0	48	0	51	31	82
WIDENER UNIV	2	0	0	0	0	0	0	0	2	3	0	0	0	0	19	0	0	22	0	24	11	35

61

TABLE 100

Number of Juniors and Seniors, by Gender and Ethnicity, and Number of Freshman and Sophomore Full-time Degree Students Enrolled in Baccalaureate Programs on 11/1/00

Program	Juniors and Seniors																				Frosh and Soph	Total
	Men									Women									Unk	Total		
	African Amer	Amer Indian	Asian Amer	Chicano	Puerto Rican	White	Other	Foreign	Total	African Amer	Amer Indian	Asian Amer	Chicano	Puerto Rican	White	Other	Foreign	Total				
WILLIAM WOODS UNIV	0	0	0	0	0	0	0	0	0	0	0	0	0	0	10	1	0	11	0	11	10	21
WINONA STATE UNIV	*	*	*	*	*	*	*	*	*	*	*	*	*	*	*	*	*	*	*	*	60	60
WINTHROP UNIV	5	0	0	0	0	3	0	0	8	27	0	1	1	0	43	0	0	72	0	80	45	125
WRIGHT STATE UNIV	1	0	0	0	0	5	0	0	6	12	0	0	1	0	62	1	0	82	0	88	2	90
XAVIER UNIV	0	0	0	0	0	6	0	0	6	2	0	1	0	0	31	0	0	34	0	40	19	59
YORK COLL	5	0	2	1	0	0	0	0	12	43	0	3	9	0	2	3	0	69	0	81	78	159
YOUNGSTOWN STATE	2	0	0	0	0	3	1	0	6	11	0	0	0	0	52	1	0	64	0	70	87	157

* Missing data

62

TABLE 101

Students Awarded Baccalaureate Degrees Academic Year 1999-2000, by Gender and Ethnicity

Program	Men									Women									Unknown	Total
	African Amer	Amer Indian	Asian Amer	Chicano	Puerto Rican	White	Other	Foreign	Total	African Amer	Amer Indian	Asian Amer	Chicano	Puerto Rican	White	Other	Foreign	Total		
TOTAL: Number	344	13	38	82	34	834	48	14	1,430	1,746	97	191	437	272	7,215	181	57	10,332	11	11,773
Percent	2.9%	0.1%	0.3%	0.7%	0.3%	7.1%	0.4%	0.1%	12.1%	14.8%	0.8%	1.6%	3.7%	2.3%	61.3%	1.5%	0.5%	87.8%	0.1%	100.0%
ABILENE CHRISTIAN	0	0	0	0	0	1	0	0	1	0	0	0	2	0	12	1	0	15	0	16
ADELPHI UNIV	5	0	0	0	0	3	1	0	9	21	0	1	0	2	24	1	0	49	0	58
ALABAMA A&M UNIV	1	0	0	0	0	1	0	0	2	16	0	0	0	0	4	0	0	20	0	22
ALABAMA STATE UNIV	5	0	0	0	0	0	0	0	5	16	0	0	0	0	3	0	0	19	0	24
ALVERNIA COLL	0	0	0	0	0	0	0	0	0	0	0	1	0	0	7	0	0	8	0	8
ANDERSON UNIV	0	0	0	0	0	3	0	0	3	1	0	0	0	0	16	0	1	18	0	21
ANDREWS UNIV	0	0	0	0	0	0	0	0	0	5	0	0	3	0	5	0	0	13	0	13
ANNA MARIA COLL	1	0	0	0	0	2	0	0	3	0	0	0	0	0	5	0	0	5	0	8
APPALACHIAN STATE	0	0	0	0	0	1	0	0	1	1	0	0	0	0	37	0	1	39	0	40
ARIZONA STATE UNIV	0	1	0	3	0	8	0	0	12	5	9	1	12	0	55	0	0	82	0	94
ARKANSAS STATE UNIV	0	0	0	0	0	3	0	0	3	9	0	0	0	0	44	0	0	53	0	56
ASHLAND UNIV	0	0	0	0	0	1	0	0	1	0	0	0	0	0	13	0	0	13	0	14
ATLANTIC UNION COLL	0	0	0	0	0	0	0	0	0	1	0	0	0	0	1	0	2	4	0	4
AUBURN UNIV	1	0	0	0	0	0	0	0	1	4	0	0	1	0	21	0	0	26	0	27
AUGSBURG COLL	0	0	0	0	0	2	0	0	2	1	0	1	0	0	20	0	0	22	0	24
AUGUSTANA/U SIOUX FA	0	0	0	0	0	1	1	0	2	0	0	0	0	0	18	0	0	18	0	20
AUSTIN PEAY STATE	3	0	0	0	0	5	0	0	8	2	0	0	0	0	25	1	0	28	0	36
AZUSA PACIFIC UNIV	0	0	0	0	0	0	0	0	0	1	0	2	0	0	7	1	1	12	0	12
BALL STATE UNIV	0	0	0	0	0	3	0	0	3	0	0	0	1	0	59	1	1	62	0	65
BARTON COLL	1	0	0	0	0	0	0	0	1	6	0	0	0	0	6	0	0	12	0	13
BAYLOR UNIV	0	0	0	0	0	5	0	0	5	4	0	0	1	0	13	1	1	19	0	24
BELMONT UNIV	0	0	0	0	0	1	0	0	1	2	0	0	1	0	30	0	0	33	0	34
BEMIDJI STATE UNIV	0	0	0	0	0	0	0	0	0	0	1	0	0	0	13	0	0	14	0	14
BETHANY COLL/WV	0	0	0	0	0	1	0	0	1	0	0	0	0	0	3	0	0	3	0	4
BETHEL COLL/KS	0	0	0	0	0	0	0	0	0	1	0	0	0	0	7	0	0	8	0	8
BETHEL COLL/MN	0	0	0	0	0	1	0	0	1	0	0	0	0	0	19	0	0	19	0	20
BLOOMSBURG UNIV	0	0	0	0	0	3	0	0	3	0	0	0	0	0	48	0	0	48	0	51
BLUFFTON COLL	0	0	0	0	0	4	0	0	4	0	0	0	0	0	7	0	0	7	0	11
BOISE STATE UNIV	0	0	0	0	0	3	0	0	3	0	0	1	0	0	24	0	0	28	0	31
BOWIE STATE UNIV	6	0	0	0	0	1	0	0	7	17	0	1	0	0	3	2	0	23	0	30
BOWLING GREEN STATE	0	0	0	0	0	2	0	0	2	0	0	0	1	0	37	0	0	38	0	40
BRESCIA UNIV	0	0	0	0	0	3	0	0	3	1	0	0	0	0	20	0	0	21	0	24
BRIAR CLIFF COLL	0	0	0	0	0	0	0	0	0	0	0	0	1	0	4	0	0	5	0	5
BRIDGEWATER STATE	0	0	0	0	0	5	0	0	5	2	0	0	0	0	26	0	0	29	0	34
BRIGHAM YOUNG/HI	0	1	5	0	0	3	3	1	13	0	0	2	0	0	13	6	5	26	0	39
BRIGHAM YOUNG/UT	0	0	1	0	0	7	0	0	8	0	0	2	1	0	57	2	0	62	0	70
BUENA VISTA UNIV	0	0	0	0	0	1	0	0	1	1	0	0	0	0	11	0	0	11	0	12
BUFFALO STATE COLL	4	0	0	0	0	11	1	0	16	8	0	0	0	5	59	0	0	73	0	89
CABRINI COLL	0	0	0	0	0	0	0	0	0	1	0	0	0	0	4	0	1	6	0	6
CAL STATE UNIV/CHI	2	1	1	0	0	3	0	0	7	1	0	0	5	0	21	0	0	36	0	43
CAL STATE UNIV/FRES	1	0	1	14	0	2	9	0	27	10	0	2	30	0	20	12	0	76	0	103
CAL STATE UNIV/LB	1	0	2	2	0	4	1	1	11	15	0	14	18	0	23	6	0	86	0	97

TABLE 101

Students Awarded Baccalaureate Degrees Academic Year 1999-2000, by Gender and Ethnicity

Program	Men									Women									Unknown	Total
	African Amer	Amer Indian	Asian Amer	Chicano	Puerto Rican	White	Other	Foreign	Total	African Amer	Amer Indian	Asian Amer	Chicano	Puerto Rican	White	Other	Foreign	Total		
CALVIN COLL	0	0	0	0	0	2	0	0	2	0	0	1	0	0	35	0	0	36	0	38
CAMPBELL UNIV	0	0	0	0	0	0	0	0	0	0	0	0	0	0	0	0	0	0	0	0
CAPITAL UNIV	6	0	0	0	0	6	0	0	12	21	0	0	1	0	28	0	0	50	0	62
CARLOW COLL	0	0	0	0	0	1	0	0	1	4	0	0	0	0	4	0	0	8	0	9
CARROLL COLL/MT	0	0	0	0	0	1	0	0	1	0	0	0	0	0	8	0	0	8	0	9
CARROLL COLL/WI	0	0	0	0	0	1	0	0	1	0	0	0	0	0	2	0	0	2	0	3
CARTHAGE COLL	2	0	0	0	0	0	0	0	2	2	0	0	0	0	9	0	0	11	0	13
CASTLETON STATE COLL	0	0	0	0	0	2	0	0	2	0	0	0	0	0	14	0	0	14	0	16
CATHOLIC UNIV/DC	0	0	0	0	0	0	0	0	0	0	0	0	0	0	9	1	0	10	0	10
CATHOLIC UNIV/PR	0	0	0	0	5	0	0	0	5	0	0	0	0	58	0	0	0	58	0	63
CEDAR CREST COLL	0	0	0	0	0	1	0	0	1	0	0	0	0	0	21	0	0	21	0	22
CEDARVILLE COLL	0	0	0	0	0	0	0	0	0	0	0	0	0	0	5	0	0	5	0	5
CENTRAL CONNECTICUT	1	0	0	0	0	1	0	0	2	6	0	2	0	0	15	0	0	23	0	25
CENTRAL MISSOURI	1	0	0	0	0	1	0	0	2	11	1	1	2	0	37	0	0	52	0	54
CHRISTOPHER NEWPORT	1	0	0	0	0	1	0	0	2	4	0	0	0	0	14	0	0	18	0	20
CLARK ATLANTA UNIV	0	0	0	0	0	0	0	0	0	9	0	0	0	0	0	0	0	9	0	9
CLEVELAND STATE UNIV	*	*	*	*	*	*	*	*	*	*	*	*	*	*	*	*	*	*	*	*
COLL MISERICORDIA	0	0	0	0	0	5	0	0	5	0	0	0	0	0	14	0	0	14	0	19
COLL MOUNT ST JOSEPH	0	0	0	0	0	1	0	0	1	3	0	0	0	0	6	0	0	9	0	10
COLL NEW ROCHELLE	0	0	0	0	0	0	0	0	0	3	0	0	0	2	2	1	0	8	0	8
COLL ST BEN/ST JOHNS	0	0	0	1	0	0	0	0	1	0	0	1	0	0	18	0	0	19	0	20
COLL ST CAT/U ST THO	1	0	0	1	0	2	0	0	4	4	0	1	0	0	47	0	0	52	0	56
COLL ST SCHOLASTICA	0	0	0	0	0	2	0	0	2	0	0	0	0	0	7	0	0	7	0	9
COLORADO STATE UNIV	0	0	0	1	0	5	0	0	6	0	0	1	2	0	35	1	0	39	0	45
COLUMBIA COLL/MO	0	0	0	0	0	2	0	0	2	4	1	0	0	0	11	0	0	16	0	18
COLUMBIA COLL/SC	0	0	0	0	0	0	0	0	0	18	0	0	0	0	7	0	0	25	0	25
CONCORD COLL	0	0	0	0	0	3	0	0	3	2	0	0	0	0	27	0	0	29	0	32
CONCORDIA COLL/MN	0	0	0	0	0	1	0	0	1	0	0	1	0	0	19	0	0	20	0	21
CONCORDIA COLL/NY	1	0	0	0	0	0	0	0	1	1	0	0	0	0	1	0	2	4	0	5
CONCORDIA UNIV WISC	1	0	0	0	0	1	0	0	2	0	0	0	0	0	6	0	0	6	0	8
COPPIN STATE COLL	5	0	0	0	0	0	0	0	5	19	0	0	0	0	0	0	0	19	0	24
CREIGHTON UNIV	0	0	0	0	0	0	0	0	0	1	0	0	0	0	5	0	0	6	0	6
DANA COLL	0	0	0	0	0	0	0	0	0	0	0	0	0	0	9	0	0	9	0	9
DAVID LIPSCOMB UNIV	0	0	0	0	0	3	0	0	3	0	0	0	0	0	11	0	0	11	0	14
DEFIANCE COLL	0	0	0	0	0	0	0	0	0	0	0	0	0	0	6	0	0	6	0	6
DELAWARE STATE UNIV	6	0	0	0	0	2	0	0	8	16	0	0	0	3	8	0	0	27	0	35
DELTA STATE UNIV	1	0	0	0	0	2	0	0	3	22	0	0	0	0	10	0	0	32	0	35
DOMINICAN COLL	0	0	0	0	0	0	0	0	0	1	0	0	0	3	7	0	0	11	0	11
DORDT COLL	0	0	0	0	0	1	0	0	1	0	0	0	0	0	11	0	0	11	0	12
EAST CAROLINA UNIV	2	1	0	0	0	6	0	0	9	20	0	0	0	0	34	0	0	54	0	63
EAST CENTRAL UNIV	0	0	0	0	0	3	0	0	3	2	1	0	0	0	18	0	0	21	0	24
EAST TENNESSEE STATE	1	0	0	0	0	2	0	0	3	1	0	0	0	0	27	0	0	28	0	31
EASTERN COLL	0	0	0	0	0	3	0	0	3	4	0	0	0	0	13	1	0	18	0	21
EASTERN KENTUCKY	1	0	0	0	0	2	0	0	3	2	0	0	0	0	41	0	0	43	0	46
EASTERN MENNONITE	0	0	1	0	0	4	0	0	5	0	0	0	0	0	15	0	2	17	0	22

TABLE 101

Students Awarded Baccalaureate Degrees Academic Year 1999-2000, by Gender and Ethnicity

Program	Men									Women									Unknown	Total
	African Amer	Amer Indian	Asian Amer	Chicano	Puerto Rican	White	Other	Foreign	Total	African Amer	Amer Indian	Asian Amer	Chicano	Puerto Rican	White	Other	Foreign	Total		
EASTERN MICHIGAN	2	0	0	0	0	10	0	0	12	17	1	1	3	0	58	0	0	82	0	94
EASTERN NAZARENE	0	0	0	0	0	0	0	0	0	0	0	1	0	0	3	0	0	4	0	4
EDINBORO UNIV	1	0	0	0	0	2	0	0	3	1	0	0	0	0	29	0	0	30	0	33
ELIZABETHTOWN COLL	0	0	0	0	0	1	0	0	1	0	0	0	0	0	11	0	0	11	0	12
ELMS COLL	1	0	0	0	0	1	0	0	2	1	0	0	0	2	12	0	0	15	0	17
EVANGEL UNIV	0	0	0	0	0	1	0	0	1	0	0	0	0	0	9	0	0	9	0	10
FERRIS STATE UNIV	1	0	0	0	0	3	0	0	4	1	0	0	0	0	33	0	0	34	0	38
FERRUM COLL	1	0	0	0	0	1	1	0	3	1	0	0	0	0	8	0	0	9	0	12
FLORIDA ATLANTIC	6	0	0	2	0	9	0	0	17	22	0	1	9	0	51	0	0	83	0	100
FLORIDA INTERNATL	5	0	0	0	0	8	1	1	15	28	0	1	0	0	19	41	0	89	0	104
FLORIDA STATE UNIV	0	0	1	0	0	13	4	0	18	27	0	0	0	0	90	7	0	124	0	142
FORT HAYS STATE UNIV	0	0	0	0	0	2	0	0	2	0	1	0	1	0	20	0	0	22	0	24
FROSTBURG STATE UNIV	0	0	0	0	0	3	0	0	3	5	0	0	0	0	21	0	0	26	0	29
GALLAUDET UNIV	1	0	0	0	0	2	0	0	3	1	0	0	1	0	8	0	0	10	0	13
GANNON UNIV	0	0	0	0	0	5	0	0	5	0	0	0	0	0	9	0	0	9	0	14
GEORGE MASON UNIV	0	0	0	0	0	2	0	0	2	0	0	0	0	0	37	0	0	37	0	39
GEORGIA STATE UNIV	2	0	0	0	0	2	0	0	4	11	0	0	0	0	14	4	0	29	0	33
GEORGIAN COURT COLL	0	0	0	0	0	0	0	0	0	2	0	0	0	6	16	0	0	24	0	24
GORDON COLL	0	0	0	0	0	1	0	0	1	0	0	0	0	0	21	1	0	22	0	23
GOSHEN COLL	0	0	0	0	0	1	0	0	1	0	0	0	0	0	7	0	0	7	0	8
GOVERNORS STATE UNIV	0	0	0	0	0	0	0	0	0	5	0	0	0	0	2	0	0	7	0	7
GRAMBLING STATE UNIV	10	0	0	0	0	1	0	0	11	31	0	0	0	0	0	0	0	31	0	42
GRAND VALLEY STATE	2	0	0	0	0	3	0	0	5	2	0	0	0	0	17	0	0	19	0	24
HARDIN-SIMMONS UNIV	0	0	0	1	0	1	0	0	2	0	0	0	0	0	9	0	0	9	0	11
HARDING UNIV	0	0	0	0	0	0	0	0	0	2	0	0	0	0	22	0	0	24	0	24
HERITAGE COLL	0	0	0	1	0	0	0	0	1	0	2	4	0	0	3	0	0	9	0	10
HOOD COLL	0	0	0	0	0	0	0	0	0	2	0	0	0	0	12	1	0	15	0	15
HOPE COLL	0	0	0	0	0	1	0	0	1	2	0	0	0	0	13	0	0	15	0	16
HOWARD PAYNE UNIV	0	0	0	0	0	1	0	0	1	1	0	0	1	0	4	0	0	6	0	7
HUMBOLDT STATE UNIV	0	0	1	0	0	1	1	0	3	0	2	8	0	1	18	1	0	29	0	32
IDAHO STATE UNIV	1	0	0	1	0	15	0	1	18	0	0	1	0	0	37	2	0	42	0	60
ILLINOIS STATE UNIV	2	0	0	1	0	5	0	0	8	9	0	4	0	0	79	2	0	94	0	102
INDIANA STATE UNIV	0	0	0	0	0	0	0	0	0	2	0	0	0	0	13	0	0	15	0	15
INDIANA UNIV	3	0	0	1	0	7	0	0	11	9	0	3	0	0	58	0	0	70	0	81
INDIANA WESLEYAN	0	0	0	0	0	0	0	0	0	0	0	0	0	0	13	0	0	13	0	13
INTERAMERICAN/ARE	0	0	0	0	8	0	0	0	8	0	0	0	0	38	0	0	0	38	0	46
INTERAMERICAN/MET	*	*	*	*	*	*	*	*	*	*	*	*	*	*	*	*	*	*	*	*
IONA COLL	1	0	0	0	0	1	0	0	2	3	0	0	0	1	7	5	1	17	0	19
JACKSON STATE UNIV	21	0	0	0	0	2	0	0	24	32	0	0	0	0	1	0	0	33	0	57
JACKSONVILLE STATE	5	0	0	0	0	3	0	0	8	21	0	2	1	0	39	0	0	63	0	71
JAMES MADISON UNIV	1	0	1	0	0	8	1	0	11	2	0	1	0	0	42	1	0	46	0	57
JUNIATA COLL	0	0	0	0	0	1	0	0	1	0	0	0	0	0	5	0	0	5	0	6
KANSAS STATE UNIV	1	0	0	0	0	4	0	0	5	5	0	1	0	0	18	0	0	24	0	29
KEAN UNIV	*	*	*	*	*	*	*	*	*	*	*	*	*	*	*	*	*	*	*	*
KENTUCKY CHRISTIAN	0	0	0	0	0	0	0	0	0	0	0	0	0	0	6	0	0	6	0	6

TABLE 101

Students Awarded Baccalaureate Degrees Academic Year 1999-2000, by Gender and Ethnicity

Program	Men									Women									Unknown	Total
	African Amer	Amer Indian	Asian Amer	Chicano	Puerto Rican	White	Other	Foreign	Total	African Amer	Amer Indian	Asian Amer	Chicano	Puerto Rican	White	Other	Foreign	Total		
KENTUCKY STATE UNIV	0	0	0	0	0	1	0	0	1	1	0	0	0	0	8	0	0	9	0	10
KEUKA COLL	0	0	0	0	0	2	0	0	4	0	0	0	0	0	6	0	0	12	0	16
KUTZTOWN UNIV	0	0	0	0	0	2	0	0	2	0	0	0	0	0	9	0	0	9	4	15
LA SALLE UNIV	0	0	0	1	0	0	0	0	1	7	0	0	2	0	3	0	0	12	0	13
LA SIERRA UNIV	1	0	0	0	0	0	0	0	1	1	0	1	6	0	2	0	0	10	0	11
LEHMAN COLL	12	0	2	0	4	1	0	0	19	32	0	1	0	36	8	0	0	77	0	96
LEWIS-CLARK STATE	1	0	0	0	0	4	0	2	7	1	1	0	2	0	20	0	2	26	0	33
LOCK HAVEN UNIV	0	0	0	0	0	1	0	0	1	0	1	0	0	0	30	0	0	31	0	32
LONG ISLAND UNIV/CWP	0	0	0	0	0	1	0	0	1	0	0	0	0	0	0	1	0	1	0	2
LONGWOOD COLL	1	0	0	0	0	1	0	0	2	3	0	0	0	0	13	0	0	16	0	18
LORAS/CLARK COLLS	0	0	0	0	0	4	0	0	4	0	0	0	0	0	20	0	0	20	0	24
LOUISIANA COLL	0	0	0	0	0	1	0	0	1	1	0	0	0	0	7	0	0	8	0	9
LOURDES COLL	0	0	0	0	0	0	0	0	0	1	1	0	1	0	10	1	0	14	0	14
LOYOLA UNIV CHICAGO	0	0	3	0	0	0	0	0	3	0	0	1	0	2	18	0	0	23	5	31
LUBBOCK CHRISTIAN	0	0	0	0	0	2	0	0	2	0	0	0	1	0	15	0	1	17	0	19
LUTHER COLL	0	0	0	0	0	2	0	0	2	0	0	0	0	0	12	0	0	12	0	14
MACMURRAY COLL	2	0	0	0	0	4	0	0	6	0	0	0	0	0	8	0	1	9	0	15
MADONNA UNIV	0	0	0	0	0	5	0	0	5	4	0	1	0	0	17	1	0	23	0	28
MALONE COLL	0	0	0	0	0	3	0	0	3	1	0	0	0	0	19	0	0	20	0	23
MANCHESTER COLL	0	0	0	0	0	3	0	0	3	0	0	0	0	0	3	1	0	4	0	7
MANSFIELD UNIV	0	0	0	0	0	2	0	0	2	1	0	0	0	0	20	0	0	21	0	23
MARIAN COLL	0	0	0	0	0	1	0	0	1	0	1	0	1	0	7	0	0	9	0	10
MARQUETTE UNIV	0	0	0	0	0	0	0	0	0	0	0	0	0	0	14	0	0	14	0	14
MARS HILL COLL	0	0	0	0	0	2	0	0	2	1	0	0	0	0	11	0	0	12	0	14
MARSHALL UNIV	0	0	0	0	0	0	0	0	0	0	0	0	0	0	13	0	0	15	0	15
MARYCREST INTERNATL	0	0	0	0	0	0	0	0	0	3	1	0	0	0	6	0	0	10	0	10
MARYGROVE COLL	1	0	0	0	0	0	0	0	1	12	0	0	0	0	2	0	0	14	0	15
MARYWOOD UNIV	0	0	0	0	0	2	0	0	2	0	0	0	0	0	17	0	0	17	0	19
MERCY COLL	4	0	0	0	0	0	0	0	4	5	0	0	0	3	3	2	0	13	0	17
MERCYHURST COLL	0	0	0	0	0	4	0	0	4	1	0	0	0	0	8	0	0	9	0	13
MEREDITH COLL	0	0	0	0	0	0	0	0	0	4	0	0	0	0	25	0	0	29	0	29
METHODIST COLL	0	0	0	0	0	1	0	0	1	5	0	0	0	0	8	0	0	13	0	14
METRO STATE COLL DEN	1	0	0	1	0	3	0	0	5	7	1	1	4	0	18	1	0	32	0	37
METRO STATE UNIV	0	1	0	0	0	1	0	0	2	4	0	2	1	0	8	0	2	17	0	19
MIAMI UNIV	0	1	0	0	0	0	0	0	1	0	0	0	0	0	26	0	0	26	0	27
MICHIGAN STATE UNIV	0	0	0	0	0	2	0	0	2	2	0	1	0	0	26	0	0	29	0	31
MIDDLE TENNESSEE ST	1	0	0	0	0	3	0	0	4	6	0	0	0	0	36	0	0	42	0	46
MIDWESTERN STATE	0	0	0	1	0	9	0	0	10	1	1	0	3	0	29	0	0	34	0	44
MILLERSVILLE UNIV	1	0	0	0	0	6	0	0	7	1	0	0	0	1	36	0	0	38	0	45
MINNESOTA STATE/MANK	1	0	0	0	0	3	0	0	4	0	0	1	0	0	41	0	0	42	0	46
MINNESOTA STATE/MOOR	0	0	0	0	0	1	0	0	1	1	0	1	0	0	51	0	1	58	0	59
MINOT STATE UNIV	1	0	0	0	0	1	0	0	2	1	0	0	0	0	16	0	4	22	0	24
MISSISSIPPI STATE/ST	2	0	0	0	0	1	0	0	3	6	0	0	0	0	12	0	0	18	0	21
MISSISSIPPI VALLEY	4	0	0	0	0	1	0	0	5	26	0	0	0	0	0	0	0	26	0	31
MISSOURI WESTERN	0	0	0	0	0	0	0	0	0	0	1	0	0	0	17	0	0	18	0	18

TABLE 101

Students Awarded Baccalaureate Degrees Academic Year 1999-2000, by Gender and Ethnicity

Program	Men									Women									Unknown	Total
	African Amer	Amer Indian	Asian Amer	Chicano	Puerto Rican	White	Other	Foreign	Total	African Amer	Amer Indian	Asian Amer	Chicano	Puerto Rican	White	Other	Foreign	Total		
MOLLOY COLL	0	0	0	0	0	2	0	0	2	4	0	0	0	1	18	0	0	23	0	25
MONMOUTH UNIV	3	0	0	0	0	0	0	0	3	2	0	0	0	1	20	0	0	27	0	30
MOREHEAD STATE UNIV	0	0	0	0	0	3	1	0	4	0	0	0	0	0	21	16	0	37	0	41
MORGAN STATE UNIV	7	0	0	0	0	0	0	0	7	43	0	0	0	0	2	0	0	45	0	52
MOUNT MARY COLL	0	0	0	0	0	0	0	0	0	5	0	0	0	0	2	0	0	7	0	7
MOUNT MERCY COLL	0	0	0	0	0	1	0	0	1	1	0	0	0	0	16	0	0	17	0	18
MOUNT SENARIO COLL	0	0	0	0	0	2	0	0	2	0	1	0	0	0	5	0	0	6	0	8
MURRAY STATE UNIV	0	0	0	0	0	0	0	0	0	2	0	0	0	0	27	0	0	29	0	29
NAZARETH COLL ROCH	1	0	0	0	1	1	0	0	3	0	1	0	0	1	16	0	0	18	0	21
NEB WESLEYAN/UNION	0	0	0	0	0	0	0	0	0	0	0	0	0	0	7	0	0	7	0	7
NEW MEXICO HIGHLANDS	0	2	0	0	0	0	0	0	2	0	9	0	7	0	8	0	0	24	0	26
NEW MEXICO STATE	3	0	0	4	0	10	0	0	17	1	3	0	15	0	16	0	0	35	0	52
NEW YORK UNIV	0	0	0	0	0	3	0	0	3	3	0	5	0	1	12	2	0	23	0	26
NIAGARA UNIV	0	0	0	0	0	1	0	0	1	0	0	0	0	0	10	0	1	11	0	12
NORTH CAROLINA CENT	1	0	0	0	0	0	0	0	1	8	0	0	0	0	1	0	0	9	0	10
NORTHEASTERN ILL	0	0	0	1	0	1	0	0	2	6	0	0	10	2	14	2	0	34	0	36
NORTHEASTERN STATE	0	2	0	0	0	2	0	0	4	1	9	1	2	0	30	0	0	43	0	47
NORTHERN ARIZONA	1	0	0	0	0	6	0	0	7	1	1	1	0	0	20	0	0	23	0	30
NORTHERN KENTUCKY	0	0	0	0	0	1	0	0	1	0	0	0	0	0	26	0	0	26	0	27
NORTHERN MICHIGAN	0	0	0	0	0	3	0	0	3	0	1	0	0	0	22	0	0	23	0	26
NORTHWEST NAZARENE	0	0	0	0	0	2	0	0	3	1	0	0	1	0	17	0	0	19	0	22
NORTHWESTERN COLL	0	0	0	0	0	0	0	0	0	0	0	0	0	0	8	0	0	8	0	8
NORTHWESTERN STATE	1	0	0	0	0	2	0	0	3	14	1	0	2	0	21	1	0	41	0	44
OAKWOOD COLL	5	0	0	0	0	0	0	0	5	10	0	0	0	0	0	0	0	11	0	16
OHIO STATE UNIV	0	0	0	0	0	3	0	0	3	4	1	0	0	0	63	3	1	72	0	75
OHIO UNIV	0	0	0	0	0	2	0	0	2	1	0	0	1	0	29	0	0	31	0	33
OLIVET NAZARENE UNIV	0	0	0	0	0	3	0	0	3	3	0	0	0	0	12	0	0	16	0	19
ORAL ROBERTS UNIV	0	0	0	0	0	2	0	0	2	1	1	0	0	0	10	0	1	13	0	15
OUR LADY OF LAKE	0	0	0	4	0	1	0	0	5	5	0	0	26	0	10	1	0	43	0	48
PACIFIC LUTHERAN	2	0	0	0	0	4	0	0	6	1	0	0	0	0	6	0	0	7	0	13
PACIFIC UNION COLL	0	0	0	0	0	0	0	0	0	0	0	1	1	1	1	4	0	7	0	7
PHILLY COLL BIBLE	0	0	0	0	0	0	0	0	0	1	0	1	0	0	9	0	0	11	0	11
PITTSBURG STATE UNIV	0	0	0	0	0	3	0	0	3	3	0	0	0	0	17	0	0	22	0	25
PLYMOUTH STATE COLL	0	0	0	0	0	4	1	0	5	0	0	0	0	0	10	0	0	12	0	17
PRAIRIE VIEW A&M	11	0	0	1	0	0	0	0	12	28	1	1	0	0	3	0	1	34	0	46
PRESENTATION COLL	0	0	0	0	0	0	0	0	0	0	0	0	0	0	3	0	0	3	0	3
PROVIDENCE COLL	1	0	0	0	0	2	0	0	3	0	0	0	0	0	16	0	0	16	0	19
RADFORD UNIV	0	0	0	0	0	8	0	0	8	1	0	0	0	0	46	0	0	47	0	55
RAMAPO COLL	0	0	0	0	0	2	1	0	4	1	0	0	0	0	27	2	1	31	0	35
REGIS COLL	0	0	0	0	0	0	0	0	0	2	0	2	0	1	9	1	0	15	0	15
RHODE ISLAND COLL	1	0	0	0	0	2	1	0	4	6	0	0	0	0	32	2	0	40	0	44
ROCHESTER INST TECH	0	0	0	0	0	1	0	0	1	1	0	0	0	0	16	0	1	18	0	19
RUTGERS UNIV/NB	1	0	0	0	0	2	0	0	3	8	0	2	0	2	30	0	0	42	0	45
RUTGERS UNIV/NRK	4	0	0	0	2	0	1	0	7	6	0	3	0	6	1	7	0	23	0	30
SACRED HEART UNIV	0	0	1	0	0	3	0	0	4	1	0	0	0	1	17	0	0	19	0	23

TABLE 101

Students Awarded Baccalaureate Degrees Academic Year 1999-2000, by Gender and Ethnicity

Program	Men African Amer	Amer Indian	Asian Amer	Chicano	Puerto Rican	White	Other	Foreign	Total	Women African Amer	Amer Indian	Asian Amer	Chicano	Puerto Rican	White	Other	Foreign	Total	Unknown	Total
SAGINAW VALLEY STATE	1	0	0	2	0	13	0	0	16	7	0	0	1	0	49	0	0	60	0	76
SALEM STATE COLL	0	0	0	0	0	3	0	0	3	3	0	0	0	2	16	1	0	22	0	25
SALVE REGINA UNIV	0	0	0	0	0	1	0	0	1	0	0	0	0	0	8	0	0	8	0	9
SAN DIEGO STATE UNIV	1	1	3	3	0	2	0	0	12	3	2	9	26	0	22	0	0	69	0	81
SAN FRANCISCO STATE	1	0	7	5	0	5	0	0	18	10	0	36	19	0	24	2	0	94	1	113
SAVANNAH STATE UNIV	1	0	0	0	0	0	0	0	1	13	0	0	0	0	0	1	0	14	0	15
SHEPHERD COLL	0	0	0	0	0	2	0	0	2	1	0	0	0	0	11	1	0	13	0	15
SHIPPENSBURG UNIV	1	0	0	0	0	8	0	0	9	2	0	0	0	0	50	0	0	52	0	61
SIENA COLL	0	0	0	0	0	0	0	0	0	0	0	1	0	0	19	0	0	20	0	20
SKIDMORE COLL	*	*	*	*	*	*	*	*	*	*	*	*	*	*	*	*	*	*	*	*
SLIPPERY ROCK UNIV	0	0	0	0	0	5	0	0	5	5	0	0	0	0	31	0	0	37	0	42
SOUTH CAROLINA STATE	4	0	0	0	0	0	0	0	4	37	0	0	0	0	0	0	0	37	0	41
SOUTHEAST MISSOURI	0	0	0	0	0	3	0	0	3	1	0	0	0	0	48	0	0	49	0	52
SOUTHEASTERN LOU	0	0	0	0	0	3	0	0	3	7	0	0	0	0	64	0	0	71	0	74
SOUTHERN CONNECTICUT	1	0	0	0	1	4	0	0	6	4	0	1	0	3	23	1	0	32	0	38
SOUTHERN ILL/CAR	4	0	0	0	0	8	0	3	15	20	0	0	1	0	89	0	2	112	0	127
SOUTHERN ILL/EDW	2	0	0	0	0	7	0	0	9	9	0	0	0	0	30	0	0	39	0	48
SOUTHERN UNIV	5	0	0	0	0	0	0	0	5	42	0	0	0	0	1	0	0	43	0	48
SOUTHERN UNIV A&M	6	0	0	0	0	0	0	0	6	47	2	0	0	0	1	0	0	48	0	54
SOUTHWEST MISSOURI	0	0	0	0	0	11	0	0	11	1	2	1	0	0	52	0	1	58	0	69
SOUTHWEST TEXAS	2	0	0	4	0	6	0	0	12	10	0	2	24	0	58	0	1	95	0	107
SPALDING UNIV	1	0	0	0	0	3	0	2	6	3	0	0	0	0	7	0	0	10	0	16
SPRING ARBOR COLL	0	0	0	0	0	1	0	0	1	0	0	0	0	0	7	0	0	7	0	8
ST CLOUD STATE UNIV	0	0	0	0	0	2	0	0	2	0	0	1	1	0	49	0	1	60	0	62
ST FRANCIS COLL	0	0	0	0	0	0	0	0	0	0	1	0	0	0	9	0	0	10	0	10
ST JOSEPH COLL	0	0	0	0	0	0	0	0	0	6	1	0	0	5	15	0	0	28	0	28
ST LOUIS UNIV	0	0	0	0	0	2	0	0	2	1	0	2	3	0	20	0	0	26	0	28
ST MARY'S COLL	0	0	0	0	0	0	0	0	0	0	0	0	0	0	7	0	0	7	0	7
ST OLAF COLL	0	0	0	0	0	0	0	0	0	0	0	0	0	1	6	0	0	7	0	7
STEPHEN F AUSTIN	3	1	0	0	0	4	0	0	8	8	0	0	2	0	36	0	0	46	0	54
SUNY/ALBANY	1	0	0	0	0	4	0	0	6	3	0	0	0	0	16	2	0	23	0	29
SUNY/BROCKPORT	0	0	0	0	0	6	0	0	6	4	0	1	0	0	64	3	0	73	0	79
SUNY/STONY BROOK	0	0	0	0	1	2	0	0	3	1	0	2	0	1	14	0	0	18	0	21
SYRACUSE UNIV	0	0	0	0	0	5	0	0	8	2	0	0	0	1	20	0	0	30	0	38
TALLADEGA COLL	3	0	0	0	0	0	0	0	3	6	0	0	0	0	0	0	0	6	0	9
TAYLOR UNIV	0	0	0	0	0	3	0	0	3	0	0	0	0	1	10	0	0	11	0	14
TEMPLE UNIV	7	0	0	0	1	6	0	0	15	32	0	2	0	4	30	0	0	80	0	95
TENNESSEE STATE UNIV	2	0	0	0	0	1	0	0	3	23	0	0	0	0	1	0	0	24	0	27
TEXAS A&M UNIV/COM	1	0	0	1	0	5	0	0	7	6	0	0	0	0	23	0	0	29	0	36
TEXAS CHRISTIAN UNIV	0	0	0	0	0	1	0	0	1	5	1	0	0	0	20	1	1	27	0	28
TEXAS LUTHERAN UNIV	1	0	0	0	0	0	0	0	1	0	0	0	2	0	5	0	0	7	0	8
TEXAS TECH UNIV	0	0	0	1	0	2	0	0	3	1	0	0	8	0	16	0	0	25	0	28
TEXAS WOMAN'S UNIV	0	0	0	0	0	0	0	0	0	8	0	2	5	0	32	0	0	47	0	47
TROY STATE UNIV	1	0	0	0	0	4	0	0	5	9	0	0	0	0	31	0	0	40	0	45
TUSKEGEE UNIV	7	0	0	0	0	0	0	0	7	15	0	0	0	0	0	0	0	15	0	22

TABLE 101

Students Awarded Baccalaureate Degrees Academic Year 1999-2000, by Gender and Ethnicity

Program	Men									Women									Unknown	Total
	African Amer	Amer Indian	Asian Amer	Chicano	Puerto Rican	White	Other	Foreign	Total	African Amer	Amer Indian	Asian Amer	Chicano	Puerto Rican	White	Other	Foreign	Total		
U OF AKRON	3	0	0	0	0	3	0	0	6	18	0	0	0	0	59	0	0	77	1	84
U OF ALABAMA	1	0	0	0	0	0	0	0	1	4	0	0	1	0	40	0	0	45	0	46
U OF ALABAMA/BIR	2	0	0	0	0	2	0	0	4	6	0	0	0	0	16	0	1	23	0	27
U OF ALASKA/ANK	0	0	1	0	0	2	1	0	4	0	0	0	0	0	20	4	0	24	0	28
U OF ALASKA/FAIR	2	0	0	0	0	3	1	0	6	0	0	1	0	1	12	3	0	17	0	23
U OF ARKANSAS/FAY	1	0	0	0	0	4	0	0	5	2	0	0	0	0	22	0	0	24	0	29
U OF ARKANSAS/PB	2	0	0	0	0	0	0	0	2	6	0	0	0	1	0	0	0	7	0	9
U OF CENTRAL FLORIDA	2	0	0	0	2	7	0	0	11	7	0	2	1	6	30	4	0	50	0	61
U OF CINCINNATI	2	0	0	0	0	2	0	0	4	4	0	0	0	0	23	2	0	29	0	33
U OF DETROIT MERCY	4	0	0	0	0	2	0	0	6	3	1	0	0	0	3	0	1	8	0	14
U OF FINDLAY	1	0	0	0	0	0	0	0	1	0	0	0	0	0	10	0	0	10	0	11
U OF GEORGIA	1	0	0	0	0	1	0	0	2	6	0	0	1	0	47	0	1	55	0	57
U OF HAWAII	0	0	1	1	1	1	0	0	4	2	0	12	0	0	3	0	0	17	0	21
U OF ILLINOIS/CHI	1	0	0	1	1	1	0	0	4	3	0	1	4	1	19	1	0	29	0	33
U OF ILLINOIS/SPR	0	0	0	0	0	4	0	0	4	4	0	0	0	0	13	0	0	17	0	21
U OF INDIANAPOLIS	0	0	0	0	0	1	0	0	1	0	0	0	0	0	5	0	0	5	0	6
U OF IOWA	1	0	1	0	0	3	0	0	5	0	1	1	1	0	24	0	0	27	0	32
U OF KANSAS	0	0	0	0	0	4	0	0	4	2	0	0	1	0	51	0	0	54	0	58
U OF KENTUCKY	10	0	0	0	0	12	0	0	22	9	0	0	1	0	61	0	1	72	0	94
U OF LOUISIANA/MON	3	0	0	0	0	2	0	0	5	17	0	0	1	0	20	0	0	38	0	43
U OF MAINE/PI	0	0	0	0	0	1	1	1	3	0	0	1	0	0	10	2	4	17	0	20
U OF MARY	0	0	0	0	0	1	0	0	1	0	0	0	0	0	14	2	0	16	0	17
U OF MARY HARD-BAY	0	0	0	0	0	1	0	0	1	1	0	1	0	1	15	0	0	18	0	19
U OF MARYLAND	1	0	0	0	0	6	1	0	8	14	0	1	0	1	49	0	3	68	0	76
U OF MICHIGAN/FL	2	0	0	0	0	16	0	0	18	17	0	0	0	0	61	0	0	78	0	96
U OF MISSISSIPPI	2	0	0	0	0	0	0	0	2	18	0	0	0	0	32	0	0	50	0	52
U OF MISSOURI/COL	1	0	0	0	0	3	0	0	4	4	0	1	1	0	24	0	0	30	0	34
U OF MISSOURI/STL	2	0	0	0	0	1	0	0	3	11	0	0	0	0	37	0	0	48	0	51
U OF MONTANA	0	0	0	0	0	4	2	0	6	0	0	3	0	0	37	0	2	42	0	48
U OF MONTEVALLO	0	0	0	0	0	2	0	0	2	5	0	0	0	0	18	0	0	23	0	25
U OF NEBRASKA/KEA	0	0	0	0	0	3	0	0	3	0	0	0	0	0	27	0	0	27	0	30
U OF NEBRASKA/OMA	0	0	0	0	0	1	0	0	1	1	0	0	0	0	14	0	0	15	0	16
U OF NEVADA/LV	4	0	0	3	0	7	0	0	14	14	0	0	2	0	21	2	1	40	0	54
U OF NEVADA/REN	0	0	0	0	0	1	1	0	2	1	0	0	0	1	22	0	0	24	0	26
U OF NEW HAMPSHIRE	0	0	0	0	0	4	2	0	6	1	0	1	0	0	23	0	0	25	0	31
U OF NORTH ALABAMA	1	0	0	0	0	2	0	0	3	4	0	1	0	0	22	2	0	29	0	32
U OF NORTH CAR/CHT	0	0	0	0	0	1	0	0	1	15	0	1	2	0	30	0	0	48	0	49
U OF NORTH CAR/GRB	1	0	0	0	0	2	0	0	3	17	0	0	1	0	25	0	0	43	0	46
U OF NORTH CAR/PEM	4	0	0	1	0	2	0	0	7	10	6	0	0	1	14	0	0	31	0	38
U OF NORTH DAKOTA	0	0	0	0	0	3	0	0	3	0	2	0	0	0	28	0	2	32	0	35
U OF NORTH TEXAS	1	0	0	0	0	2	0	0	3	5	0	0	8	0	28	0	0	41	0	44
U OF NORTHERN IOWA	0	1	0	0	0	6	0	0	7	2	0	0	3	0	64	1	0	70	0	77
U OF OKLAHOMA	1	1	0	0	0	3	0	0	5	2	5	2	3	0	27	1	0	40	0	45
U OF PITTSBURGH	1	0	0	0	0	11	1	0	13	10	0	0	0	0	39	0	0	49	0	62
U OF PUERTO RICO/HU	0	0	0	0	6	0	0	0	6	0	0	0	0	55	0	0	0	55	0	61

TABLE 101

Students Awarded Baccalaureate Degrees Academic Year 1999-2000, by Gender and Ethnicity

Program	Men									Women									Unknown	Total
	African Amer	Amer Indian	Asian Amer	Chicano	Puerto Rican	White	Other	Foreign	Total	African Amer	Amer Indian	Asian Amer	Chicano	Puerto Rican	White	Other	Foreign	Total		
U OF PUERTO RICO/RP	*	*	*	*	*	*	*	*	*	*	*	*	*	*	9	*	*	9	*	*
U OF RIO GRANDE	0	0	0	0	0	1	0	0	1	0	0	0	0	0	9	0	0	9	0	10
U OF SACRED HEART	*	*	*	*	*	*	*	*	*	*	*	*	*	*	*	*	*	*	*	*
U OF SOUTH DAKOTA	0	0	0	0	0	1	0	0	1	0	0	0	1	0	17	0	0	18	0	19
U OF SOUTH FLORIDA	0	0	0	1	0	3	0	0	4	15	1	0	6	1	46	0	0	69	0	73
U OF SOUTHERN COLO	0	0	0	2	0	6	0	0	8	2	0	0	1	0	14	0	0	17	0	25
U OF SOUTHERN IND	1	0	0	0	0	1	0	0	2	1	0	0	0	0	28	0	0	29	0	31
U OF SOUTHERN MAINE	0	0	0	0	0	5	0	0	5	0	0	1	0	0	44	0	0	45	0	50
U OF SOUTHERN MISS	0	0	1	0	0	0	0	0	1	11	0	0	0	0	21	0	0	32	0	33
U OF ST FRANCIS/IL	1	0	0	0	0	1	0	0	2	3	0	0	0	0	5	0	0	8	0	10
U OF ST FRANCIS/IN	0	0	0	0	0	0	0	0	0	0	0	0	0	0	0	0	0	0	0	0
U OF TENNESSEE/CHAT	0	0	0	0	0	1	0	0	1	6	0	0	0	0	8	0	0	14	0	15
U OF TENNESSEE/KNX	0	0	0	0	0	1	0	0	1	7	0	0	0	0	32	0	0	39	0	40
U OF TENNESSEE/MAR	6	0	0	0	0	1	0	0	7	0	0	0	0	0	17	0	0	17	0	24
U OF TEXAS/ARL	1	1	0	1	0	4	0	0	7	16	1	4	5	0	27	0	0	53	0	60
U OF TEXAS/AUS	1	0	0	2	0	6	0	1	10	0	0	7	8	0	53	0	1	69	0	79
U OF TEXAS/PAN	0	0	0	6	0	0	0	0	6	0	0	0	37	0	0	0	0	37	0	43
U OF TOLEDO	0	0	0	0	0	1	0	0	1	9	0	0	0	0	22	0	0	33	0	34
U OF VERMONT	0	0	0	0	0	2	0	0	2	0	0	0	0	0	16	0	0	16	0	18
U OF WASHINGTON	1	0	6	2	0	3	0	0	12	0	3	13	1	1	37	0	0	55	0	67
U OF WEST VIRGINIA	0	0	1	0	0	8	0	0	9	5	0	1	2	0	40	0	0	48	0	57
U OF WISCONSIN/EAU	0	0	0	0	0	4	0	0	4	0	0	1	0	0	46	0	1	47	0	51
U OF WISCONSIN/GBY	0	0	0	0	0	0	0	0	0	0	0	0	0	0	20	0	1	21	0	21
U OF WISCONSIN/MAD	0	0	0	0	0	2	0	0	2	0	0	1	1	0	25	0	0	26	0	28
U OF WISCONSIN/MIL	0	0	0	0	0	6	1	0	7	10	1	2	6	0	47	0	2	68	0	75
U OF WISCONSIN/OSH	0	0	0	0	0	9	0	0	9	2	0	0	1	0	51	0	0	54	0	63
U OF WISCONSIN/RIV	0	0	0	0	0	0	0	0	0	0	0	0	0	1	24	0	0	25	0	25
U OF WISCONSIN/SUP	0	0	0	1	0	4	0	0	5	0	0	0	0	0	11	0	0	11	0	16
U OF WISCONSIN/WHI	0	0	0	0	0	1	0	0	2	0	0	0	0	0	53	0	0	61	0	63
URSULINE COLL	0	0	0	0	0	0	0	0	0	4	0	0	0	0	4	0	0	8	0	8
UTAH STATE UNIV	0	0	0	0	0	7	0	0	7	0	0	0	1	0	37	0	0	38	0	45
VALPARAISO UNIV	0	0	0	1	0	0	0	0	1	0	0	0	0	0	4	0	0	4	0	5
VIRGINIA COMMONWEAL	0	0	0	0	0	4	0	0	4	11	0	0	0	0	19	0	0	30	0	34
VIRGINIA INTERMONT	*	*	*	*	*	*	*	*	*	*	*	*	*	*	*	*	*	*	*	*
VIRGINIA STATE UNIV	1	0	0	0	0	0	0	0	1	11	0	0	0	0	0	1	0	11	0	12
WALLA WALLA COLL	0	0	0	1	0	4	0	0	5	0	0	0	2	0	11	0	0	14	0	19
WARREN WILSON COLL	0	0	0	0	0	0	0	0	0	1	0	0	0	0	6	0	0	7	0	7
WASHBURN UNIV	1	0	0	0	0	2	0	0	3	3	1	0	0	0	29	0	0	33	0	36
WAYNE STATE UNIV	0	0	0	0	0	2	0	0	2	23	0	0	0	0	46	2	0	71	0	73
WEBER STATE UNIV	1	0	0	0	0	9	0	0	10	1	0	0	5	0	42	0	0	48	0	58
WEST TEXAS A&M UNIV	0	0	0	0	0	1	0	0	1	2	0	0	2	0	25	0	0	29	0	30
WEST VIRGINIA UNIV	1	0	0	0	0	3	0	0	4	2	0	0	0	0	48	0	0	50	0	54
WESTERN CAROLINA	0	0	0	0	0	3	0	0	3	0	2	0	0	0	15	0	0	17	0	20
WESTERN CONNECTICUT	1	0	1	0	0	1	0	0	3	0	0	0	0	0	23	0	1	24	0	27
WESTERN ILLINOIS	2	0	0	0	0	1	0	0	3	10	0	0	1	0	26	0	0	37	0	40

TABLE 101

Students Awarded Baccalaureate Degrees Academic Year 1999-2000, by Gender and Ethnicity

Program	Men									Women									Unknown	Total
	African Amer	Amer Indian	Asian Amer	Chicano	Puerto Rican	White	Other	Foreign	Total	African Amer	Amer Indian	Asian Amer	Chicano	Puerto Rican	White	Other	Foreign	Total		
WESTERN KENTUCKY	1	0	0	0	0	0	0	0	1	3	0	0	1	0	21	0	0	25	0	26
WESTERN MARYLAND	0	0	0	0	0	0	0	0	0	1	0	0	0	1	15	0	0	17	0	17
WESTERN NEW ENGLAND	0	0	0	0	0	0	0	0	0	0	0	1	0	1	8	0	0	10	0	10
WESTERN NEW MEXICO	0	0	0	0	0	0	0	0	0	0	0	0	5	0	3	0	0	8	0	8
WHEELOCK COLL	0	0	0	0	0	1	0	0	1	5	0	0	2	0	21	0	0	28	0	29
WHITTIER COLL	0	0	0	0	0	1	0	0	1	0	0	3	11	0	0	0	0	14	0	15
WICHITA STATE UNIV	1	0	0	0	0	2	0	0	3	3	0	1	2	0	25	0	0	31	0	34
WIDENER UNIV	0	0	0	0	0	3	0	0	3	4	0	1	0	0	9	0	0	14	0	17
WILLIAM WOODS UNIV	0	0	0	0	0	0	0	0	0	0	0	0	0	0	5	1	0	6	0	6
WINONA STATE UNIV	1	0	0	0	0	7	0	1	10	0	0	0	1	0	36	0	0	37	0	47
WINTHROP UNIV	2	0	0	0	0	0	0	0	2	17	0	0	1	0	25	0	0	43	0	45
WRIGHT STATE UNIV	2	0	0	0	0	3	0	0	6	5	0	0	1	0	31	0	0	37	0	43
XAVIER UNIV	0	0	0	0	0	0	0	0	0	3	0	0	0	0	14	0	0	17	0	17
YORK COLL	1	0	0	2	0	1	0	0	5	43	0	1	5	0	1	0	0	57	0	62
YOUNGSTOWN STATE	1	0	0	1	0	4	0	0	6	12	0	0	1	0	33	0	1	50	0	56

* Missing data

71

TABLE 200

Applications for Admission to First-year Status in Full-time Master's Degree Programs During 2000, by Action Taken

Program	Applications			Registered			Total Newly Enrolled in 2000	Withdrawals	Enrollment by 11/1/00			
	Total Received	Considered for Admission	Accepted	Accepted But Not Registered	Accepted and Registered	Accepted in Prior Years			Advanced Standing in First Year	Others Still in First Year	In Second Year	Enrollment First Year/ Full-time
TOTAL:	20,644	18,740	14,093	6,274	7,819	176	7,938	362	305	778	225	8,491
ADELPHI UNIV	240	165	140	25	115	2	110	7	0	0	16	94
ALABAMA A&M UNIV	30	30	23	0	23	0	23	0	0	0	0	23
ANDREWS UNIV	19	19	14	3	11	0	11	0	0	1	0	12
ARIZONA STATE UNIV	230	224	205	75	130	0	126	4	0	1	0	127
AUGSBURG COLL	31	31	30	17	13	1	14	0	0	0	0	14
BARRY UNIV	109	109	97	57	40	0	36	4	0	0	0	36
BOISE STATE UNIV	33	22	14	5	9	0	8	1	0	0	0	8
BOSTON COLL	402	386	249	157	92	4	96	0	0	40	0	136
BOSTON UNIV	383	354	288	179	109	0	83	26	0	24	0	107
BRIGHAM YOUNG/UT	147	147	47	8	39	0	39	0	0	0	0	39
BRYN MAWR COLL	117	103	81	37	44	0	43	1	0	12	0	55
CAL STATE UNIV/FRES	90	90	53	0	53	0	53	0	0	0	0	53
CAL STATE UNIV/LB	*	*	*	*	*	*	*	*	*	*	*	*
CAL STATE UNIV/SB	136	99	53	16	37	0	37	0	0	0	0	37
CAL STATE UNIV/STAN	81	62	58	19	39	0	39	0	0	0	0	39
CASE WESTERN RESERVE	254	224	215	92	123	0	119	4	0	0	0	119
CATHOLIC UNIV/DC	115	75	69	30	39	2	39	2	0	0	0	39
CLARK ATLANTA UNIV	110	110	69	36	33	0	31	2	0	0	0	31
CLEVE ST U/U AKRON	54	46	22	0	22	0	22	0	0	0	0	22
COLL ST CAT/U ST THO	54	53	42	17	25	1	26	0	0	0	0	26
COLORADO STATE UNIV	56	54	26	8	18	0	18	0	0	0	0	18
COLUMBIA UNIV	755	741	590	284	306	12	284	34	0	18	0	302
DELAWARE STATE UNIV	379	79	75	21	54	0	46	8	0	0	0	46
EAST CAROLINA UNIV	85	85	51	29	22	0	22	0	0	0	0	22
EASTERN MICHIGAN	5	5	3	0	3	0	3	0	0	0	0	3
FLORIDA INTERNATL	*	*	*	*	*	*	*	*	*	*	*	*
FLORIDA STATE UNIV	104	84	74	49	25	0	25	0	0	0	0	25
FORDHAM UNIV	444	311	263	184	79	0	79	0	0	254	0	333
GALLAUDET UNIV	26	26	24	11	13	1	17	0	3	5	3	19
GRAMBLING STATE UNIV	56	56	25	5	20	0	20	0	0	0	0	20
GRAND VALLEY STATE	75	60	50	10	40	4	51	3	10	20	45	26
HOWARD UNIV	218	200	172	83	89	15	118	1	15	20	1	137
HUNTER COLL	556	472	241	104	137	0	136	1	0	0	0	136
INDIANA UNIV	123	122	107	41	66	0	64	2	0	3	0	67
INTERAMERICAN/MET	90	90	76	4	72	0	110	4	42	17	0	127
JACKSON STATE UNIV	42	31	23	6	17	0	17	0	0	0	0	17
KEAN UNIV	74	74	49	24	25	0	24	1	0	0	0	24
LOMA LINDA UNIV	25	25	25	4	21	0	21	0	0	0	0	21
LOUISIANA STATE UNIV	105	102	94	27	67	0	65	2	0	0	0	65
LOYOLA UNIV CHICAGO	271	208	161	61	100	0	100	0	0	0	0	100
MARYWOOD UNIV	62	58	52	18	34	0	34	2	2	0	0	34
MICHIGAN STATE UNIV	103	100	89	53	36	0	36	0	0	17	0	53

TABLE 200

Applications for Admission to First-year Status in Full-time Master's Degree Programs During 2000, by Action Taken

Program	Applications			Registered				Withdrawals	Enrollment by 11/1/00			Enrollment First Year/ Full-time
	Total Received	Considered for Admission	Accepted	Accepted But Not Registered	Accepted and Registered	Accepted in Prior Years	Total Newly Enrolled in 2000		Advanced Standing in First Year	Others Still in First Year	In Second Year	
NEW MEXICO HIGHLANDS	76	76	72	25	47	0	43	4	0	0	0	43
NEW MEXICO STATE	80	80	37	19	18	0	16	2	0	0	0	16
NEW YORK UNIV	827	782	637	364	273	0	219	54	0	0	0	219
OHIO STATE UNIV	237	175	142	63	79	0	76	3	0	0	0	76
OUR LADY OF LAKE	*	*	*	*	*	*	*	*	*	*	*	*
PORTLAND STATE UNIV	320	320	231	119	112	0	111	1	0	1	0	112
RADFORD UNIV	66	66	44	23	21	0	21	0	0	0	0	21
RHODE ISLAND COLL	94	94	48	11	37	4	41	0	0	0	0	41
RUTGERS UNIV/NB	326	301	256	156	100	1	97	4	0	0	0	97
SALEM STATE COLL	65	65	45	27	18	0	18	0	0	3	0	21
SAN DIEGO STATE UNIV	244	234	188	86	102	0	97	5	0	0	0	97
SAN FRANCISCO STATE	322	326	79	7	72	0	70	2	0	0	0	70
SAVANNAH STATE UNIV	37	37	23	2	21	0	21	0	0	0	0	21
SIMMONS COLL	309	244	225	138	87	4	116	2	27	0	0	116
SMITH COLL	291	291	235	105	130	0	121	9	0	0	1	120
SOUTHERN CONNECTICUT	218	166	57	7	50	0	50	0	0	0	0	50
SOUTHERN ILL/CAR	22	22	18	10	8	0	8	0	0	0	0	8
SOUTHERN UNIV	121	91	79	13	66	0	66	0	0	0	0	66
SOUTHWEST MISSOURI	35	26	24	12	12	0	12	0	0	0	0	12
SOUTHWEST TEXAS	30	19	17	5	12	0	12	0	0	0	0	12
ST AMBROSE UNIV	40	25	24	8	16	0	16	0	0	0	0	16
ST LOUIS UNIV	118	118	105	79	26	0	26	0	0	0	0	26
SUNY/ALBANY	245	245	187	67	120	7	126	1	0	0	33	93
SUNY/BUFFALO	161	126	106	29	77	0	73	4	0	0	0	73
SYRACUSE UNIV	92	71	61	15	46	0	45	1	0	0	0	45
TEMPLE UNIV	181	172	134	79	55	11	50	16	0	3	0	53
TULANE UNIV	165	150	130	65	65	0	70	2	7	3	0	70
U OF ALABAMA	100	90	62	23	39	1	38	2	0	2	0	40
U OF ALASKA/ANK	41	41	27	15	12	0	11	1	0	0	0	11
U OF ARKANSAS/LR	89	76	52	21	31	1	32	0	0	0	0	32
U OF CALIFORNIA/BERK	412	394	125	30	95	0	92	3	0	0	0	92
U OF CENTRAL FLORIDA	65	65	53	6	47	0	47	0	0	28	0	75
U OF CHICAGO	277	276	232	95	137	4	141	0	0	0	6	135
U OF CINCINNATI	135	105	82	18	64	0	61	3	0	0	14	47
U OF CONNECTICUT	216	205	123	29	94	0	123	3	32	1	0	124
U OF DENVER	213	179	166	96	70	7	89	1	13	1	0	90
U OF GEORGIA	155	129	116	61	55	32	87	2	2	2	32	57
U OF HAWAII	136	131	90	33	57	0	55	2	0	0	0	55
U OF HOUSTON	144	106	83	20	63	2	59	7	1	3	0	62
U OF ILLINOIS/CHI	253	249	191	118	73	0	73	0	0	0	0	73
U OF ILLINOIS/URB	192	182	127	31	96	5	99	2	0	15	0	114
U OF IOWA	57	55	52	27	25	0	35	2	10	0	0	35
U OF KANSAS	187	187	163	65	98	0	63	35	0	23	0	86

TABLE 200

Applications for Admission to First-year Status in Full-time Master's Degree Programs During 2000, by Action Taken

Program	Applications				Registered				Enrollment by 11/1/00			
	Total Received	Considered for Admission	Accepted	Accepted But Not Registered	Accepted and Registered	Accepted in Prior Years	Total Newly Enrolled in 2000	Withdrawals	Advanced Standing in First Year	Others Still in First Year	In Second Year	Enrollment First Year/ Full-time
U OF KENTUCKY	81	60	50	20	30	2	32	0	0	0	7	25
U OF LOUISVILLE	259	231	187	58	129	0	110	19	0	0	0	110
U OF MARYLAND	366	364	289	150	139	0	135	4	0	163	0	298
U OF MICHIGAN	533	513	437	186	251	0	301	2	52	25	0	326
U OF MINNESOTA/DUL	60	60	49	19	30	1	31	0	0	0	0	31
U OF MINNESOTA/TC	185	185	116	37	79	0	79	0	0	1	0	80
U OF MISSOURI/COL	125	111	83	30	53	1	52	3	1	4	25	31
U OF NCGB/NCSU	11	110	40	4	36	0	35	1	0	0	0	35
U OF NEBRASKA/OMA	45	39	37	9	28	0	28	0	0	0	0	28
U OF NEVADA/LV	54	54	44	19	25	0	42	0	17	0	0	42
U OF NEVADA/REN	16	16	14	4	10	0	10	0	0	0	0	10
U OF NEW HAMPSHIRE	87	78	61	28	33	2	35	0	0	0	0	35
U OF NORTH CAR/CH	228	227	100	43	57	4	61	0	0	0	0	61
U OF NORTH DAKOTA	48	48	40	33	7	0	40	0	33	0	0	40
U OF OKLAHOMA	28	25	24	7	17	0	17	0	0	0	0	17
U OF PENNSYLVANIA	274	231	205	121	84	5	89	0	0	0	1	88
U OF PITTSBURGH	312	312	242	99	143	0	143	0	0	33	0	176
U OF PUERTO RICO/RP	90	90	64	10	54	0	52	2	0	19	0	71
U OF SOUTH CAROLINA	360	265	220	109	111	0	107	4	0	0	0	107
U OF SOUTH FLORIDA	105	105	78	31	47	0	43	4	0	0	0	43
U OF SOUTHERN CAL	406	399	319	158	161	0	159	2	0	0	1	158
U OF SOUTHERN IND	43	37	33	14	19	0	19	0	0	0	0	19
U OF SOUTHERN MISS	81	49	39	10	29	0	26	3	0	0	0	26
U OF TENNESSEE/KNX	251	213	176	54	122	0	120	2	0	0	3	117
U OF TEXAS/ARL	219	209	162	33	129	0	136	15	22	10	16	130
U OF TEXAS/AUS	143	143	112	29	83	0	80	3	0	0	0	80
U OF UTAH	275	265	130	1	129	0	129	0	0	0	0	129
U OF VERMONT	61	59	41	26	15	1	18	0	2	0	0	18
U OF WASHINGTON	240	239	158	68	90	0	90	0	0	2	3	89
U OF WISCONSIN/MAD	194	185	155	79	76	0	87	0	11	0	0	87
U OF WISCONSIN/MIL	127	126	91	29	62	0	63	2	3	3	0	66
U OF WYOMING	*	*	*	*	*	*	*	*	*	*	*	*
VALDOSTA STATE UNIV	37	37	27	7	20	0	18	2	0	0	0	18
VIRGINIA COMMONWEAL	289	287	228	112	116	1	117	0	0	0	0	117
WALLA WALLA COLL	69	59	57	9	48	0	43	5	0	3	0	46
WASHBURN UNIV	32	30	24	10	14	0	12	2	0	0	0	12
WASHINGTON UNIV	478	451	397	256	141	18	159	0	0	0	0	159
WAYNE STATE UNIV	166	155	133	47	86	0	85	1	0	0	0	85
WEST VIRGINIA UNIV	112	112	112	64	48	18	66	0	0	0	18	48
WIDENER UNIV	79	77	62	57	5	0	2	3	0	1	0	3
YESHIVA UNIV	392	360	270	173	97	2	96	3	0	0	0	96

* Missing data

TABLE 201

Applications for Admission to First-year Status in Part-time Master's Degree Programs During 2000, by Action Taken

Program	Applications				Registered				Enrollment by 11/1/00		In Second Year	Enrollment First Year/ Part-time
	Total Received	Considered for Admission	Accepted	Accepted But Not Registered	Accepted and Registered	Accepted in Prior Years	Total Newly Enrolled in 2000	Withdrawals	Advanced Standing in First Year	Others Still in First Year		
TOTAL:	9,666	8,822	6,715	1,689	5,026	99	5,028	263	197	1,184	142	6,073
ADELPHI UNIV	330	236	200	32	168	5	170	3	0	0	47	123
ALABAMA A&M UNIV	16	16	16	0	16	0	16	0	0	0	0	16
ANDREWS UNIV	1	1	1	0	1	0	1	0	0	1	0	2
ARIZONA STATE UNIV	103	101	94	13	81	0	81	0	0	45	0	126
AUGSBURG COLL	6	6	6	6	0	3	4	0	1	4	0	8
BARRY UNIV	140	140	126	47	79	0	74	5	0	64	0	138
BOISE STATE UNIV	0	0	0	0	0	0	0	0	0	0	0	0
BOSTON COLL	108	102	91	14	77	3	80	0	0	14	0	94
BOSTON UNIV	121	107	81	29	52	0	45	7	0	8	0	53
BRIGHAM YOUNG/UT	*	*	*	*	*	*	*	*	*	*	*	*
BRYN MAWR COLL	54	47	39	14	25	0	23	2	0	24	0	47
CAL STATE UNIV/FRES	33	33	25	0	25	0	25	0	0	14	0	39
CAL STATE UNIV/LB	*	*	*	*	*	*	*	*	*	*	*	*
CAL STATE UNIV/SB	139	95	41	15	26	0	26	0	0	0	0	26
CAL STATE UNIV/STAN	56	39	33	13	20	1	21	0	0	0	0	21
CASE WESTERN RESERVE	5	5	4	1	3	0	3	0	0	0	0	3
CATHOLIC UNIV/DC	50	30	24	10	14	2	15	1	0	19	0	34
CLARK ATLANTA UNIV	6	6	6	0	6	0	6	0	0	0	0	6
CLEVE ST U/U AKRON	55	55	26	0	26	0	21	2	0	0	0	24
COLL ST CAT/U ST THO	50	47	39	12	27	0	27	0	0	0	0	27
COLORADO STATE UNIV	27	27	21	9	12	0	12	0	0	15	0	27
COLUMBIA UNIV	128	117	79	25	54	0	49	5	0	3	0	52
DELAWARE STATE UNIV	27	27	27	0	27	0	27	0	0	0	0	27
EAST CAROLINA UNIV	24	24	20	8	12	0	13	0	1	0	0	13
EASTERN MICHIGAN	126	107	73	14	59	0	58	1	0	0	0	58
FLORIDA INTERNATL	*	*	*	*	*	*	*	*	*	*	*	*
FLORIDA STATE UNIV	78	74	67	16	51	0	51	0	0	0	0	51
FORDHAM UNIV	945	928	715	308	407	0	407	0	0	0	0	407
GALLAUDET UNIV	9	9	7	2	5	1	4	2	0	0	0	4
GRAMBLING STATE UNIV	10	10	8	1	7	0	4	3	0	0	0	4
GRAND VALLEY STATE	105	97	90	5	85	3	94	4	10	10	62	42
HOWARD UNIV	87	76	56	14	42	5	38	9	0	10	0	48
HUNTER COLL	481	445	228	25	203	0	196	7	0	0	0	196
INDIANA UNIV	256	247	200	36	164	0	154	13	3	38	0	192
INTERAMERICAN/MET	0	0	0	0	0	0	0	0	0	0	0	0
JACKSON STATE UNIV	41	33	24	6	18	2	20	0	0	0	0	20
KEAN UNIV	38	38	32	8	24	0	24	0	0	0	0	24
LOMA LINDA UNIV	15	15	14	2	12	0	12	0	0	0	0	12
LOUISIANA STATE UNIV	23	22	18	2	16	0	16	0	0	0	0	16
LOYOLA UNIV CHICAGO	137	126	108	28	80	0	80	0	0	0	0	80
MARYWOOD UNIV	99	97	85	15	70	2	111	1	40	0	0	111
MICHIGAN STATE UNIV	87	82	77	15	62	0	62	0	0	16	0	78

TABLE 201

Applications for Admission to First-year Status in Part-time Master's Degree Programs During 2000, by Action Taken

Program	Applications				Registered			Withdrawals	Enrollment by 11/1/00			Enrollment First Year/ Part-time
	Total Received	Considered for Admission	Accepted	Accepted But Not Registered	Accepted and Registered	Accepted in Prior Years	Total Newly Enrolled in 2000		Advanced Standing in First Year	Others Still in First Year	In Second Year	
NEW MEXICO HIGHLANDS	86	86	81	13	68	0	67	1	0	0	0	67
NEW MEXICO STATE	28	28	17	3	14	0	9	5	0	0	0	9
NEW YORK UNIV	452	423	335	110	225	0	128	97	0	0	0	128
OHIO STATE UNIV	150	95	84	15	69	0	67	2	0	76	0	143
OUR LADY OF LAKE	*	*	*	*	*	*	*	*	*	*	*	*
PORTLAND STATE UNIV	113	113	62	26	36	0	35	1	0	1	0	36
RADFORD UNIV	0	0	0	0	0	0	0	0	0	0	0	0
RHODE ISLAND COLL	52	52	27	2	25	0	25	0	0	0	0	25
RUTGERS UNIV/NB	274	257	187	35	152	3	154	1	0	0	0	154
SALEM STATE COLL	108	108	74	14	60	0	59	1	0	47	0	106
SAN DIEGO STATE UNIV	82	79	67	25	42	0	40	2	0	0	0	40
SAN FRANCISCO STATE	42	42	17	0	17	0	17	0	0	0	0	17
SAVANNAH STATE UNIV	0	0	0	0	0	0	0	0	0	0	0	0
SIMMONS COLL	59	53	49	18	31	2	33	0	0	7	0	40
SMITH COLL	0	0	0	0	0	0	0	0	0	0	0	0
SOUTHERN CONNECTICUT	81	62	22	2	20	0	20	0	0	0	0	20
SOUTHERN ILL/CAR	11	10	9	2	7	0	7	0	0	3	0	10
SOUTHERN UNIV	123	88	78	20	58	0	57	1	0	0	0	57
SOUTHWEST MISSOURI	40	22	22	3	19	0	19	0	0	1	0	20
SOUTHWEST TEXAS	34	29	27	6	21	1	18	4	0	0	0	18
ST AMBROSE UNIV	26	11	9	0	9	0	9	0	0	10	0	19
ST LOUIS UNIV	117	117	104	69	35	0	35	0	0	0	0	35
SUNY/ALBANY	44	44	32	3	29	5	30	4	0	0	0	30
SUNY/BUFFALO	81	64	56	0	56	0	53	3	0	0	0	53
SYRACUSE UNIV	65	55	50	3	47	0	45	2	0	0	0	45
TEMPLE UNIV	199	174	77	19	58	20	67	11	0	134	0	201
TULANE UNIV	18	18	16	1	15	0	13	2	0	5	0	18
U OF ALABAMA	98	84	56	10	46	0	41	5	0	0	0	41
U OF ALASKA/ANK	11	11	8	0	8	0	8	0	0	0	0	8
U OF ARKANSAS/LR	43	40	34	8	26	0	26	0	0	0	0	26
U OF CALIFORNIA/BERK	*	*	*	*	*	*	*	*	*	*	*	*
U OF CENTRAL FLORIDA	82	82	68	3	65	0	63	2	0	24	2	87
U OF CHICAGO	95	92	55	15	40	0	40	0	0	0	0	38
U OF CINCINNATI	66	50	23	4	19	0	17	2	0	0	0	17
U OF CONNECTICUT	104	94	57	3	54	0	54	0	0	0	0	54
U OF DENVER	20	19	17	6	11	0	13	0	2	11	0	24
U OF GEORGIA	56	55	46	12	34	0	33	1	0	4	0	37
U OF HAWAII	68	65	45	14	31	0	31	0	0	0	0	31
U OF HOUSTON	90	81	73	4	69	0	69	2	2	6	0	75
U OF ILLINOIS/CHI	166	164	125	39	86	0	86	0	0	86	0	86
U OF ILLINOIS/URB	58	57	38	3	35	0	35	0	0	36	0	71
U OF IOWA	64	51	46	1	45	0	56	0	11	0	26	30
U OF KANSAS	77	77	65	19	46	0	34	12	0	115	0	149

TABLE 201

Applications for Admission to First-year Status in Part-time Master's Degree Programs During 2000, by Action Taken

Program	Applications				Registered			Withdrawals	Enrollment by 11/1/00			Enrollment First Year/ Part-time
	Total Received	Considered for Admission	Accepted	Accepted But Not Registered	Accepted and Registered	Accepted in Prior Years	Total Newly Enrolled in 2000		Advanced Standing in First Year	Others Still in First Year	In Second Year	
U OF KENTUCKY	64	56	54	11	43	0	90	0	47	7	0	97
U OF LOUISVILLE	109	58	44	6	38	0	33	5	0	0	0	33
U OF MARYLAND	208	208	160	41	119	0	115	4	0	31	0	146
U OF MICHIGAN	14	14	9	1	8	0	9	0	1	6	0	15
U OF MINNESOTA/DUL	*	*	*	*	*	*	*	*	*	*	*	*
U OF MINNESOTA/TC	112	112	33	6	27	0	27	0	0	12	0	39
U OF MISSOURI/COL	48	46	39	2	37	1	37	2	1	3	1	39
U OF NCGB/NCSU	0	0	0	0	0	0	0	0	0	0	0	0
U OF NEBRASKA/OMA	14	2	11	3	8	0	8	0	0	0	0	8
U OF NEVADA/LV	21	21	19	7	12	0	25	0	13	0	0	25
U OF NEVADA/REN	3	3	1	0	1	0	1	0	0	0	0	1
U OF NEW HAMPSHIRE	42	41	40	20	20	0	19	2	1	19	0	38
U OF NORTH CAR/CH	91	90	59	12	47	0	47	0	0	59	0	106
U OF NORTH DAKOTA	0	0	0	0	0	28	27	0	27	0	0	27
U OF OKLAHOMA	52	50	48	11	37	0	35	2	0	1	0	36
U OF PENNSYLVANIA	58	51	44	13	31	1	32	0	0	0	0	32
U OF PITTSBURGH	92	62	62	7	55	0	55	0	0	81	0	136
U OF PUERTO RICO/RP	*	*	*	*	*	*	*	*	*	*	*	*
U OF SOUTH CAROLINA	89	80	70	4	66	0	63	3	0	0	0	63
U OF SOUTH FLORIDA	0	0	0	0	0	0	0	0	0	0	0	0
U OF SOUTHERN CAL	95	95	75	16	59	0	58	1	0	0	0	58
U OF SOUTHERN IND	2	*	0	0	0	0	0	0	0	10	0	10
U OF SOUTHERN MISS	80	63	33	4	29	0	29	0	0	0	0	29
U OF TENNESSEE/KNX	95	80	71	17	54	0	54	0	0	44	0	98
U OF TEXAS/ARL	125	119	90	27	63	0	84	10	31	31	0	115
U OF TEXAS/AUS	39	39	30	7	23	0	23	0	0	0	0	23
U OF UTAH	*	*	*	*	*	*	*	*	*	*	*	*
U OF VERMONT	19	19	18	1	17	0	17	0	0	1	0	18
U OF WASHINGTON	94	94	69	16	53	0	53	0	0	25	0	78
U OF WISCONSIN/MAD	0	0	0	0	0	0	0	0	0	0	0	0
U OF WISCONSIN/MIL	46	44	33	3	30	0	36	0	6	25	0	61
U OF WYOMING	*	*	*	*	*	*	*	*	*	*	*	*
VALDOSTA STATE UNIV	25	25	17	1	16	0	16	0	0	3	0	19
VIRGINIA COMMONWEAL	151	151	125	11	114	1	115	0	0	0	0	115
WALLA WALLA COLL	10	9	9	0	9	0	8	1	0	3	0	11
WASHBURN UNIV	30	29	24	8	16	0	16	0	0	0	0	16
WASHINGTON UNIV	25	24	23	10	13	3	16	0	0	0	0	16
WAYNE STATE UNIV	100	97	75	14	61	0	60	1	0	58	0	118
WEST VIRGINIA UNIV	77	77	77	64	13	4	17	0	0	0	4	13
WIDENER UNIV	74	73	55	17	38	0	35	3	0	0	0	35
YESHIVA UNIV	163	151	139	54	85	3	85	3	0	0	0	85

* Missing data

TABLE 202

Applications for Admission to Advanced Standing Status in Master's Degree Programs During 2000, by Action Taken

Program	From Baccalaureate Program Under School Auspice			From Other Baccalaureate Social Work Program			On Basis of Other Education			Total Admitted Directly to Adv Standing Enrolled 11/1/00
	Applications Received	Accepted for Admission	Enrolled as of 11/1/00	Applications Received	Accepted for Admission	Enrolled as of 11/1/00	Applications Received	Accepted for Admission	Enrolled as of 11/1/00	
TOTAL:	1,362	1,162	892	4,133	3,232	2,013	235	170	100	3,005
ADELPHI UNIV	36	32	30	47	39	30	*	*	*	60
ALABAMA A&M UNIV	8	8	8	7	7	7	*	*	*	15
ANDREWS UNIV	7	7	6	3	3	2	0	0	0	8
ARIZONA STATE UNIV	*	*	*	*	*	*	*	*	*	*
AUGSBURG COLL	4	4	2	17	15	10	*	*	*	12
BARRY UNIV	*	*	*	*	*	*	*	*	*	0
BOISE STATE UNIV	0	0	0	11	5	4	0	0	0	4
BOSTON COLL	*	*	*	108	29	*	*	*	*	0
BOSTON UNIV	*	*	*	*	*	*	*	*	*	*
BRIGHAM YOUNG/UT	*	*	*	*	*	*	*	*	*	*
BRYN MAWR COLL	*	*	*	*	*	*	*	*	*	*
CAL STATE UNIV/FRES	*	*	*	*	*	*	*	*	*	*
CAL STATE UNIV/LB	*	*	*	*	*	*	*	*	*	*
CAL STATE UNIV/SB	*	*	*	*	*	*	*	*	*	*
CAL STATE UNIV/STAN	*	*	*	*	*	*	*	*	*	*
CASE WESTERN RESERVE	0	0	0	81	72	55	0	0	0	55
CATHOLIC UNIV/DC	*	*	*	12	10	8	2	2	2	10
CLARK ATLANTA UNIV	0	0	0	0	0	0	0	0	0	0
CLEVE ST U/U AKRON	0	0	0	0	0	0	0	0	0	0
COLL ST CAT/U ST THO	14	10	10	43	36	25	*	*	*	35
COLORADO STATE UNIV	3	3	3	3	2	2	*	*	*	5
COLUMBIA UNIV	*	*	*	120	85	43	*	*	*	43
DELAWARE STATE UNIV	4	0	0	0	0	0	0	0	0	0
EAST CAROLINA UNIV	12	9	9	47	34	21	*	*	*	30
EASTERN MICHIGAN	9	5	4	34	25	23	*	*	*	27
FLORIDA INTERNATL	*	*	*	*	*	*	*	*	*	*
FLORIDA STATE UNIV	63	55	50	58	45	34	0	0	0	84
FORDHAM UNIV	3	3	3	430	380	203	10	6	3	209
GALLAUDET UNIV	3	3	3	1	1	2	*	*	*	5
GRAMBLING STATE UNIV	7	4	4	7	4	3	*	*	*	7
GRAND VALLEY STATE	6	4	4	6	3	0	*	*	*	4
HOWARD UNIV	53	42	0	0	0	0	0	0	0	0
HUNTER COLL	*	*	*	*	*	*	*	*	*	*
INDIANA UNIV	18	17	16	27	23	15	3	2	2	33
INTERAMERICAN/MET	0	0	0	0	0	0	0	0	0	0
JACKSON STATE UNIV	9	8	8	15	10	7	*	*	*	15
KEAN UNIV	18	18	12	6	3	2	0	0	0	14
LOMA LINDA UNIV	0	0	0	0	0	0	0	0	0	0
LOUISIANA STATE UNIV	*	*	*	43	32	30	*	*	*	30
LOYOLA UNIV CHICAGO	*	*	*	*	*	*	*	*	*	*
MARYWOOD UNIV	*	*	*	91	85	31	*	*	*	31
MICHIGAN STATE UNIV	9	9	5	28	27	15	*	*	*	20
NEW MEXICO HIGHLANDS	12	12	12	25	25	17	*	*	*	29
NEW MEXICO STATE	8	5	5	11	9	7	13	10	10	22
NEW YORK UNIV	14	14	14	203	148	82	10	7	5	101
OHIO STATE UNIV	18	14	10	55	39	26	*	*	*	36
OUR LADY OF LAKE	*	*	*	*	*	*	*	*	*	*
PORTLAND STATE UNIV	*	*	*	*	*	*	*	*	*	*
RADFORD UNIV	*	*	*	*	*	*	*	*	*	*
RHODE ISLAND COLL	16	6	5	9	5	4	*	*	*	9
RUTGERS UNIV/NB	47	41	37	97	67	38	0	0	0	75
SALEM STATE COLL	8	5	4	19	12	10	*	*	*	14
SAN DIEGO STATE UNIV	*	*	*	*	*	*	*	*	*	*
SAN FRANCISCO STATE	*	*	*	*	*	*	*	*	*	*
SAVANNAH STATE UNIV	0	0	0	*	*	*	*	*	*	0
SIMMONS COLL	*	*	*	*	*	*	*	*	*	*
SMITH COLL	*	*	*	*	*	*	*	*	*	*
SOUTHERN CONNECTICUT	17	6	6	20	12	7	*	*	*	13
SOUTHERN ILL/CAR	31	25	22	5	2	2	0	0	0	24
SOUTHERN UNIV	4	4	4	7	7	5	0	0	0	9
SOUTHWEST MISSOURI	32	24	23	17	9	4	0	0	0	27
SOUTHWEST TEXAS	16	14	8	18	18	12	*	*	*	20
ST AMBROSE UNIV	0	0	0	15	14	9	0	0	0	9
ST LOUIS UNIV	10	10	6	60	58	48	164	140	76	130

TABLE 202

Applications for Admission to Advanced Standing Status in Master's Degree Programs During 2000, by Action Taken

Program	From Baccalaureate Program Under School Auspice			From Other Baccalaureate Social Work Program			On Basis of Other Education			Total Admitted Directly to Adv Standing Enrolled 11/1/00
	Applications Received	Accepted for Admission	Enrolled as of 11/1/00	Applications Received	Accepted for Admission	Enrolled as of 11/1/00	Applications Received	Accepted for Admission	Enrolled as of 11/1/00	
SUNY/ALBANY	12	11	13	40	34	20	0	0	0	33
SUNY/BUFFALO	0	0	0	75	46	30	0	0	0	30
SYRACUSE UNIV	23	23	16	33	23	19	0	0	0	35
TEMPLE UNIV	41	29	27	101	49	41	0	0	0	68
TULANE UNIV	0	0	0	21	19	7	0	0	0	7
U OF ALABAMA	89	66	46	0	0	0	0	0	0	46
U OF ALASKA/ANK	12	9	9	7	5	4	0	0	0	13
U OF ARKANSAS/LR	5	4	6	29	17	15	0	0	0	21
U OF CALIFORNIA/BERK	*	*	*	*	*	*	*	*	*	*
U OF CENTRAL FLORIDA	38	35	32	33	24	24	0	0	0	56
U OF CHICAGO	0	0	0	0	0	0	0	0	0	0
U OF CINCINNATI	1	11	7	3	28	19	0	0	0	26
U OF CONNECTICUT	0	0	0	67	45	32	0	0	0	32
U OF DENVER	0	0	0	122	103	58	0	0	0	58
U OF GEORGIA	19	17	0	30	23	0	0	0	0	0
U OF HAWAII	*	*	*	8	5	3	*	*	*	3
U OF HOUSTON	0	0	0	43	26	20	0	0	0	20
U OF ILLINOIS/CHI	25	18	14	115	78	43	0	0	0	57
U OF ILLINOIS/URB	0	0	0	0	0	0	0	0	0	0
U OF IOWA	6	6	5	26	23	16	0	0	0	21
U OF KANSAS	22	17	17	80	64	50	0	0	0	67
U OF KENTUCKY	29	26	0	41	24	0	0	0	0	0
U OF LOUISVILLE	0	0	0	96	85	58	0	0	0	58
U OF MARYLAND	45	37	34	104	87	73	0	0	0	107
U OF MICHIGAN	0	0	0	110	98	0	3	3	2	2
U OF MINNESOTA/DUL	0	0	0	30	27	19	0	0	0	19
U OF MINNESOTA/TC	0	0	0	81	73	69	0	0	0	69
U OF MISSOURI/COL	6	5	4	28	23	21	0	0	0	25
U OF NCGB/NCSU	0	0	0	0	0	0	0	0	0	0
U OF NEBRASKA/OMA	9	9	9	37	32	28	0	0	0	37
U OF NEVADA/LV	27	24	0	19	16	0	0	0	0	0
U OF NEVADA/REN	19	12	22	4	1	3	0	0	0	25
U OF NEW HAMPSHIRE	6	6	3	4	2	2	0	0	0	5
U OF NORTH CAR/CH	0	0	0	61	29	21	0	0	0	21
U OF NORTH DAKOTA	0	0	0	0	0	0	0	0	0	0
U OF OKLAHOMA	18	17	14	26	17	13	0	0	0	27
U OF PENNSYLVANIA	*	*	*	*	*	*	*	*	*	*
U OF PITTSBURGH	*	*	*	*	*	*	*	*	*	*
U OF PUERTO RICO/RP	0	0	0	0	0	0	0	0	0	0
U OF SOUTH CAROLINA	0	0	0	101	86	55	0	0	0	55
U OF SOUTH FLORIDA	0	0	0	0	0	0	26	0	0	0
U OF SOUTHERN CAL	*	*	*	*	*	*	*	*	*	*
U OF SOUTHERN IND	24	22	20	27	13	9	0	0	0	29
U OF SOUTHERN MISS	*	*	*	*	*	*	*	*	*	*
U OF TENNESSEE/KNX	5	5	5	47	36	26	4	0	0	31
U OF TEXAS/ARI	83	71	38	106	05	33	0	0	0	71
U OF TEXAS/AUS	0	0	0	0	0	0	0	0	0	0
U OF UTAH	*	*	*	*	*	*	*	*	*	*
U OF VERMONT	2	2	0	3	3	0	0	0	0	0
U OF WASHINGTON	25	25	22	23	16	11	0	0	0	33
U OF WISCONSIN/MAD	19	19	19	31	31	31	0	0	0	50
U OF WISCONSIN/MIL	44	34	34	92	85	71	0	0	0	105
U OF WYOMING	*	*	*	*	*	*	*	*	*	*
VALDOSTA STATE UNIV	0	0	0	5	4	3	0	0	0	3
VIRGINIA COMMONWEAL	10	11	9	56	18	13	0	0	0	22
WALLA WALLA COLL	11	11	11	68	67	54	0	0	0	65
WASHBURN UNIV	27	22	16	42	38	23	0	0	0	39
WASHINGTON UNIV	*	*	*	*	*	*	*	*	*	*
WAYNE STATE UNIV	117	113	101	148	129	94	0	0	0	195
WEST VIRGINIA UNIV	18	18	0	47	47	0	0	0	0	0
WIDENER UNIV	6	6	6	30	29	21	0	0	0	27
YESHIVA UNIV	0	0	0	27	19	18	0	0	0	18

* Missing data - in previous years' reports a null cell value was entered as zero

TABLE 203

Full-time Master's Degree Students Enrolled on 11/1/00, by Ethnicity

Program	Total	African American	American Indian	Asian American	Chicano/ Mexican Amer	Puerto Rican	White	Other Minority	Foreign	Unknown
TOTAL:	20,117	3,049	178	740	717	466	13,618	572	308	469
ADELPHI UNIV	284	51	0	8	0	22	195	0	2	6
ALABAMA A&M UNIV	45	34	0	0	0	0	11	0	0	0
ANDREWS UNIV	34	12	0	0	8	0	8	0	6	0
ARIZONA STATE UNIV	272	7	11	0	17	0	232	0	5	0
AUGSBURG COLL	46	4	1	0	0	0	37	0	2	2
BARRY UNIV	164	31	0	1	0	3	105	16	6	2
BOISE STATE UNIV	28	0	0	0	1	0	27	0	0	0
BOSTON COLL	301	16	1	12	9	2	243	9	7	2
BOSTON UNIV	188	13	0	11	5	0	154	2	3	0
BRIGHAM YOUNG/UT	78	0	2	5	3	0	59	3	6	0
BRYN MAWR COLL	125	23	0	1	0	0	94	2	2	3
CAL STATE UNIV/FRES	141	13	1	3	49	0	52	23	0	0
CAL STATE UNIV/LB	138	9	0	18	24	0	62	25	0	0
CAL STATE UNIV/SB	86	16	1	4	18	0	42	1	0	4
CAL STATE UNIV/STAN	59	3	1	7	13	0	25	2	0	8
CASE WESTERN RESERVE	285	59	0	9	0	7	198	6	5	1
CATHOLIC UNIV/DC	82	5	0	1	0	0	72	0	0	4
CLARK ATLANTA UNIV	86	85	0	0	0	0	1	0	0	0
CLEVE ST U/U AKRON	39	7	0	0	0	0	30	0	0	2
COLL ST CAT/U ST THO	124	7	1	3	2	0	109	0	2	0
COLORADO STATE UNIV	62	6	3	0	2	0	51	0	0	0
COLUMBIA UNIV	666	59	1	73	13	15	406	61	15	23
DELAWARE STATE UNIV	84	40	0	0	0	1	43	0	0	0
EAST CAROLINA UNIV	94	10	0	0	0	0	77	1	0	6
EASTERN MICHIGAN	23	6	0	1	0	0	16	0	0	0
FLORIDA INTERNATL	124	25	0	3	0	0	45	48	3	0
FLORIDA STATE UNIV	121	15	1	0	0	0	97	7	1	0
FORDHAM UNIV	934	185	1	32	0	119	477	48	0	72
GALLAUDET UNIV	41	4	0	1	0	1	34	0	1	0
GRAMBLING STATE UNIV	32	19	0	0	0	0	13	0	0	0
GRAND VALLEY STATE	138	10	1	3	2	0	111	0	10	1
HOWARD UNIV	257	234	0	0	4	0	6	0	13	0
HUNTER COLL	406	116	0	19	1	34	184	44	3	5
INDIANA UNIV	260	23	1	2	5	0	224	1	1	3
INTERAMERICAN/MET	*	*	*	*	*	*	*	*	*	*
JACKSON STATE UNIV	41	32	0	0	0	0	8	1	0	0
KEAN UNIV	*	*	*	*	*	*	*	*	*	*
LOMA LINDA UNIV	37	7	0	0	5	0	21	4	0	0
LOUISIANA STATE UNIV	154	16	0	2	1	0	134	0	1	0
LOYOLA UNIV CHICAGO	188	19	0	13	0	3	129	6	0	18
MARYWOOD UNIV	88	2	1	1	0	0	81	0	3	0
MICHIGAN STATE UNIV	126	19	1	3	5	0	96	0	2	0
NEW MEXICO HIGHLANDS	92	5	5	0	26	0	55	1	0	0
NEW MEXICO STATE	42	1	2	1	9	0	28	0	1	0
NEW YORK UNIV	589	84	0	34	0	10	375	71	14	1
OHIO STATE UNIV	194	20	0	3	0	1	161	3	6	0
OUR LADY OF LAKE	92	18	0	1	41	0	29	0	0	3
PORTLAND STATE UNIV	216	8	8	8	5	0	185	1	1	0
RADFORD UNIV	53	7	0	0	1	0	45	0	0	0
RHODE ISLAND COLL	91	5	0	2	0	0	75	8	0	1
RUTGERS UNIV/NB	271	37	0	7	10	6	181	8	1	21
SALEM STATE COLL	48	0	0	0	0	3	45	0	0	0
SAN DIEGO STATE UNIV	238	6	5	27	41	0	157	0	2	0
SAN FRANCISCO STATE	123	18	4	25	20	1	35	14	6	0
SAVANNAH STATE UNIV	41	25	0	0	0	1	14	1	0	0
SIMMONS COLL	213	21	1	10	8	4	158	4	1	6
SMITH COLL	229	13	3	10	4	1	188	3	7	0
SOUTHERN CONNECTICUT	133	16	0	2	0	3	103	9	0	0
SOUTHERN ILL/CAR	40	4	0	1	0	0	35	0	0	0
SOUTHERN UNIV	152	114	0	0	0	0	35	3	0	0
SOUTHWEST MISSOURI	*	*	*	*	*	*	*	*	*	*
SOUTHWEST TEXAS	45	1	0	1	8	0	35	0	0	0
ST AMBROSE UNIV	32	1	0	0	2	0	28	0	1	0

80

TABLE 203

Full-time Master's Degree Students Enrolled on 11/1/00, by Ethnicity

Program	Total	African American	American Indian	Asian American	Chicano/ Mexican Amer	Puerto Rican	White	Other Minority	Foreign	Unknown
ST LOUIS UNIV	148	16	1	9	1	0	119	1	0	1
SUNY/ALBANY	263	22	3	0	0	14	174	0	6	44
SUNY/BUFFALO	168	18	2	2	0	2	110	2	6	26
SYRACUSE UNIV	86	6	0	2	2	0	40	0	0	36
TEMPLE UNIV	129	34	0	4	0	7	74	0	4	6
TULANE UNIV	150	38	2	0	3	0	105	2	0	0
U OF ALABAMA	146	26	1	1	3	0	107	0	8	0
U OF ALASKA/ANK	27	0	4	0	2	0	20	1	0	0
U OF ARKANSAS/LR	120	31	0	0	1	0	88	0	0	0
U OF CALIFORNIA/BERK	183	18	7	19	23	0	116	0	0	0
U OF CENTRAL FLORIDA	106	4	0	4	0	7	83	8	0	0
U OF CHICAGO	251	38	0	22	10	3	165	11	2	0
U OF CINCINNATI	125	30	0	0	2	0	89	1	0	3
U OF CONNECTICUT	207	37	0	2	0	33	135	0	0	0
U OF DENVER	244	8	5	7	16	0	205	0	3	0
U OF GEORGIA	152	21	0	4	4	0	114	3	4	2
U OF HAWAII	118	4	1	48	3	0	37	21	4	0
U OF HOUSTON	124	26	0	6	20	0	68	4	0	0
U OF ILLINOIS/CHI	292	49	1	11	18	7	205	0	1	0
U OF ILLINOIS/URB	224	26	0	3	9	0	184	0	2	0
U OF IOWA	87	5	4	2	2	0	74	0	0	0
U OF KANSAS	237	23	6	4	11	0	157	2	0	34
U OF KENTUCKY	59	2	0	0	1	0	56	0	0	0
U OF LOUISVILLE	259	32	1	2	0	1	219	0	3	1
U OF MARYLAND	662	150	1	13	0	0	477	18	3	0
U OF MICHIGAN	554	63	3	27	9	2	382	15	21	32
U OF MINNESOTA/DUL	62	1	5	0	0	0	54	2	0	0
U OF MINNESOTA/TC	163	12	1	13	1	0	118	1	0	17
U OF MISSOURI/COL	81	11	1	0	0	1	67	0	0	1
U OF NCGB/NCSU	65	28	0	0	0	0	37	0	0	0
U OF NEBRASKA/OMA	95	1	0	1	1	0	92	0	0	0
U OF NEVADA/LV	70	7	1	2	5	0	48	0	1	6
U OF NEVADA/REN	34	2	0	0	2	0	29	1	0	0
U OF NEW HAMPSHIRE	90	1	0	1	2	0	81	0	0	5
U OF NORTH CAR/CH	187	21	2	4	2	0	157	0	1	0
U OF NORTH DAKOTA	24	0	1	0	0	0	13	0	2	8
U OF OKLAHOMA	100	3	12	3	2	0	80	0	0	0
U OF PENNSYLVANIA	194	38	0	12	0	0	133	7	4	0
U OF PITTSBURGH	308	63	0	2	0	0	232	1	10	0
U OF PUERTO RICO/RP	125	0	0	0	0	122	2	0	1	0
U OF SOUTH CAROLINA	323	91	2	10	0	3	216	0	1	0
U OF SOUTH FLORIDA	89	9	0	2	0	5	73	0	0	0
U OF SOUTHERN CAL	329	31	6	41	103	0	145	0	3	0
U OF SOUTHERN IND	45	1	0	0	0	0	41	1	1	1
U OF SOUTHERN MISS	49	12	0	0	0	0	37	0	0	0
U OF TENNESSEE/KNX	246	38	1	2	5	0	199	1	0	0
U OF TEXAS/ARL	297	40	1	7	26	0	222	0	1	0
U OF TEXAS/AUS	199	9	0	11	17	0	151	0	8	3
U OF UTAH	234	6	14	12	9	0	185	0	0	8
U OF VERMONT	39	0	0	0	0	0	38	0	0	1
U OF WASHINGTON	207	8	1	24	4	1	149	4	5	11
U OF WISCONSIN/MAD	183	5	5	2	5	1	156	7	2	0
U OF WISCONSIN/MIL	144	12	4	0	5	0	122	0	1	0
U OF WYOMING	*	*	*	*	*	*	*	*	*	*
VALDOSTA STATE UNIV	50	8	0	0	0	0	41	0	1	0
VIRGINIA COMMONWEAL	259	20	0	6	5	0	216	0	1	11
WALLA WALLA COLL	161	3	6	0	8	0	132	4	2	6
WASHBURN UNIV	63	4	1	0	1	1	53	0	0	3
WASHINGTON UNIV	351	40	11	16	7	0	219	6	52	0
WAYNE STATE UNIV	319	73	2	6	5	2	224	7	0	0
WEST VIRGINIA UNIV	127	4	2	0	0	0	115	3	3	0
WIDENER UNIV	65	24	0	0	0	0	30	2	0	9
YESHIVA UNIV	204	50	0	3	0	17	132	0	2	0

* Missing data

81

TABLE 204

Full-time Master's Degree Students Enrolled on 11/1/00, by Age and Gender

Program	Total	Unknown	Total		25 & under		26 - 30		31 - 40		41 & over	
			Men	Women	Men	Women	Men	Women	Men	Women	Men	Women
TOTAL:												
Number	20,117	117	2,810	17,190	685	7,372	771	4,312	759	2,941	595	2,565
Percent	100.0%	0.6%	14.0%	85.5%	3.4%	36.6%	3.8%	21.4%	3.8%	14.6%	3.0%	12.8%
ADELPHI UNIV	284	0	67	217	18	67	14	53	17	52	18	45
ALABAMA A&M UNIV	45	0	8	37	2	11	0	4	5	10	1	12
ANDREWS UNIV	34	0	6	28	0	13	1	7	2	4	3	4
ARIZONA STATE UNIV	272	0	31	241	2	103	8	58	8	45	13	35
AUGSBURG COLL	46	0	4	42	0	5	3	18	1	11	0	8
BARRY UNIV	164	1	34	129	5	39	8	31	12	32	9	27
BOISE STATE UNIV	28	0	4	24	1	9	2	4	1	5	0	6
BOSTON COLL	301	16	25	260	4	109	10	85	8	31	3	35
BOSTON UNIV	188	0	19	169	7	111	6	43	4	7	2	8
BRIGHAM YOUNG/UT	78	0	26	52	10	31	13	12	2	7	1	2
BRYN MAWR COLL	125	0	14	111	3	37	5	34	3	20	3	20
CAL STATE UNIV/FRES	141	0	29	112	8	37	7	22	7	28	7	25
CAL STATE UNIV/LB	138	0	27	111	5	37	11	41	7	20	4	13
CAL STATE UNIV/SB	86	0	15	71	3	12	2	12	5	23	5	24
CAL STATE UNIV/STAN	59	0	18	41	3	10	8	8	2	13	5	10
CASE WESTERN RESERVE	285	0	30	255	6	99	8	56	8	52	8	48
CATHOLIC UNIV/DC	82	0	9	73	1	26	2	29	4	7	2	11
CLARK ATLANTA UNIV	86	10	5	71	2	25	1	27	1	11	1	8
CLEVE ST U/U AKRON	39	2	8	29	0	7	2	8	1	3	5	11
COLL ST CAT/U ST THO	124	0	13	111	1	31	5	37	6	25	1	18
COLORADO STATE UNIV	62	0	7	55	2	8	4	22	1	12	0	13
COLUMBIA UNIV	666	0	84	582	38	338	17	164	22	48	7	32
DELAWARE STATE UNIV	84	0	21	63	5	17	7	11	5	15	4	20
EAST CAROLINA UNIV	94	0	13	81	3	43	3	19	4	9	3	10
EASTERN MICHIGAN	23	0	3	20	0	1	1	5	1	7	1	7
FLORIDA INTERNATL	124	0	24	100	3	32	5	32	7	18	9	18
FLORIDA STATE UNIV	121	0	21	100	7	57	4	20	6	12	4	11
FORDHAM UNIV	934	9	101	824	13	210	14	168	35	211	39	235
GALLAUDET UNIV	41	0	5	36	1	16	2	11	2	5	0	4
GRAMBLING STATE UNIV	32	0	6	26	1	13	3	4	2	6	0	3
GRAND VALLEY STATE	138	0	13	125	1	51	3	26	5	22	4	26
HOWARD UNIV	257	0	48	209	11	65	15	53	10	55	12	36
HUNTER COLL	406	18	95	293	13	87	26	81	30	75	26	50
INDIANA UNIV	260	0	24	236	5	72	10	80	7	40	2	44
INTERAMERICAN/MET	*	*	*	*	*	*	*	*	*	*	*	*
JACKSON STATE UNIV	41	0	4	37	0	19	3	12	1	3	0	3
KEAN UNIV	*	*	*	*	*	*	*	*	*	*	*	*
LOMA LINDA UNIV	37	0	3	34	1	13	0	3	1	11	1	7
LOUISIANA STATE UNIV	154	0	17	137	8	87	4	23	3	10	2	17
LOYOLA UNIV CHICAGO	188	7	21	160	8	90	7	41	1	23	5	6
MARYWOOD UNIV	88	6	11	71	5	29	2	7	1	12	3	23
MICHIGAN STATE UNIV	126	0	16	110	8	44	3	28	0	16	5	22
NEW MEXICO HIGHLANDS	92	0	25	67	6	17	3	15	4	15	12	20
NEW MEXICO STATE	42	0	9	33	3	6	5	9	1	10	0	8
NEW YORK UNIV	589	0	68	521	30	338	10	56	17	74	11	53
OHIO STATE UNIV	194	0	30	164	12	89	8	27	5	26	5	22
OUR LADY OF LAKE	92	0	18	74	4	26	5	20	5	15	4	13
PORTLAND STATE UNIV	216	0	26	190	4	63	6	51	8	40	8	36
RADFORD UNIV	53	0	5	48	2	21	0	12	1	9	2	6
RHODE ISLAND COLL	91	1	9	81	0	21	2	22	6	22	1	16
RUTGERS UNIV/NB	271	0	27	244	11	116	7	61	6	43	3	24
SALEM STATE COLL	48	0	9	39	0	8	1	18	4	5	4	8
SAN DIEGO STATE UNIV	238	0	34	204	4	88	14	62	10	33	6	21
SAN FRANCISCO STATE	123	0	30	93	3	21	8	29	14	26	5	17
SAVANNAH STATE UNIV	41	0	5	36	0	2	0	9	2	18	3	7
SIMMONS COLL	213	11	15	187	5	104	5	33	3	42	2	8
SMITH COLL	229	0	20	209	9	62	4	78	6	44	1	25
SOUTHERN CONNECTICUT	133	0	22	111	5	34	6	26	5	24	6	27
SOUTHERN ILL/CAR	40	0	8	32	1	18	3	8	2	3	2	3
SOUTHERN UNIV	152	0	16	136	2	59	7	26	5	31	2	20
SOUTHWEST MISSOURI	*	*	*	*	*	*	*	*	*	*	*	*
SOUTHWEST TEXAS	45	0	6	39	1	12	1	18	3	5	1	4

82

TABLE 204

Full-time Master's Degree Students Enrolled on 11/1/00, by Age and Gender

Program	Total	Unknown	Total		25 & under		26 - 30		31 - 40		41 & over	
			Men	Women	Men	Women	Men	Women	Men	Women	Men	Women
ST AMBROSE UNIV	32	0	3	29	3	18	0	5	0	4	0	2
ST LOUIS UNIV	148	0	19	129	3	56	5	43	3	16	8	14
SUNY/ALBANY	263	0	45	218	10	90	12	39	12	43	11	46
SUNY/BUFFALO	168	0	24	144	4	74	8	27	5	26	7	17
SYRACUSE UNIV	86	0	13	73	5	31	1	14	4	16	3	12
TEMPLE UNIV	129	1	25	103	4	44	6	36	9	12	6	11
TULANE UNIV	150	0	12	138	4	78	5	25	3	15	0	20
U OF ALABAMA	146	0	16	130	5	69	3	27	6	18	2	16
U OF ALASKA/ANK	27	0	3	24	0	2	0	6	2	4	1	12
U OF ARKANSAS/LR	120	0	18	102	4	26	3	29	3	22	8	25
U OF CALIFORNIA/BERK	183	0	26	157	1	49	13	65	10	34	2	9
U OF CENTRAL FLORIDA	106	0	19	87	5	45	7	20	3	11	4	11
U OF CHICAGO	251	0	36	215	9	119	12	58	12	24	3	14
U OF CINCINNATI	125	0	15	110	3	18	2	41	3	31	7	20
U OF CONNECTICUT	207	0	40	167	6	26	11	64	8	38	15	39
U OF DENVER	244	0	21	223	2	91	10	74	7	30	2	28
U OF GEORGIA	152	0	14	138	7	70	5	44	2	10	0	14
U OF HAWAII	118	0	15	103	2	42	4	26	7	17	2	18
U OF HOUSTON	124	0	13	111	3	32	1	23	6	31	3	25
U OF ILLINOIS/CHI	292	0	43	249	7	97	10	65	15	47	11	40
U OF ILLINOIS/URB	224	0	28	196	8	109	13	41	5	28	2	18
U OF IOWA	87	4	16	67	5	29	1	17	8	3	2	18
U OF KANSAS	237	0	42	195	6	40	16	57	11	50	9	48
U OF KENTUCKY	59	0	11	48	6	23	1	18	1	4	3	3
U OF LOUISVILLE	259	0	43	216	7	85	12	52	12	32	12	47
U OF MARYLAND	662	0	85	577	12	248	17	142	40	94	16	93
U OF MICHIGAN	554	0	68	486	21	306	26	109	14	34	7	37
U OF MINNESOTA/DUL	62	0	7	55	2	16	2	9	2	16	1	14
U OF MINNESOTA/TC	163	12	18	133	5	46	4	39	4	29	5	19
U OF MISSOURI/COL	81	0	11	70	2	27	1	17	4	13	4	13
U OF NCGB/NCSU	65	0	3	62	0	5	3	48	0	9	0	0
U OF NEBRASKA/OMA	95	0	8	87	2	33	3	32	2	13	1	9
U OF NEVADA/LV	70	0	18	52	4	17	9	20	1	9	4	6
U OF NEVADA/REN	34	0	5	29	0	3	2	13	3	6	0	7
U OF NEW HAMPSHIRE	90	0	5	85	5	79	0	2	0	4	0	0
U OF NORTH CAR/CH	187	0	22	165	2	63	7	54	8	31	5	17
U OF NORTH DAKOTA	24	8	3	13	0	8	0	4	0	1	3	0
U OF OKLAHOMA	100	0	15	85	3	35	7	21	0	16	5	13
U OF PENNSYLVANIA	194	0	21	173	11	121	4	28	2	9	4	15
U OF PITTSBURGH	308	0	54	254	16	133	7	56	18	34	13	31
U OF PUERTO RICO/RP	125	0	13	112	3	64	3	25	3	18	4	5
U OF SOUTH CAROLINA	323	0	34	289	12	185	12	45	3	34	7	25
U OF SOUTH FLORIDA	89	0	13	76	3	23	4	20	4	21	2	12
U OF SOUTHERN CAL	329	0	43	286	17	136	8	89	12	38	6	23
U OF SOUTHERN IND	45	0	5	40	2	19	1	7	2	9	0	5
U OF SOUTHERN MISS	49	0	7	42	3	20	0	11	1	6	3	5
U OF TENNESSEE/KNX	246	0	27	219	10	113	5	54	7	25	5	27
U OF TEXAS/ARL	297	0	55	242	9	60	16	64	18	75	12	43
U OF TEXAS/AUS	199	5	26	168	8	112	10	28	6	19	2	9
U OF UTAH	234	2	68	164	8	41	22	42	19	36	19	45
U OF VERMONT	39	0	7	32	2	9	2	16	2	6	1	1
U OF WASHINGTON	207	0	34	173	5	69	11	69	12	14	6	21
U OF WISCONSIN/MAD	183	0	26	157	8	83	10	44	6	20	2	10
U OF WISCONSIN/MIL	144	0	24	120	18	96	3	13	2	9	1	2
U OF WYOMING	*	*	*	*	*	*	*	*	*	*	*	*
VALDOSTA STATE UNIV	50	0	8	42	1	6	6	9	0	22	1	5
VIRGINIA COMMONWEAL	259	0	23	236	7	143	6	52	7	16	3	25
WALLA WALLA COLL	161	0	30	131	4	21	11	23	7	36	8	51
WASHBURN UNIV	63	0	4	59	0	18	0	12	2	12	2	17
WASHINGTON UNIV	351	0	48	303	14	173	21	89	12	22	1	19
WAYNE STATE UNIV	319	0	25	294	5	115	6	62	6	55	8	62
WEST VIRGINIA UNIV	127	0	27	100	10	58	9	13	5	14	3	15
WIDENER UNIV	65	4	6	55	0	25	2	16	2	7	2	7
YESHIVA UNIV	204	0	43	161	16	64	6	20	11	42	10	35

* Missing data

83

TABLE 205

Master's Degree Students, by Primary Methods Concentration

MO = Methods Only; MC = Methods Combined with Fields of Practice or Social Problem

Program	Total	MO: Direct Practice	MO: Community Organization & Planning	MO: Administration or Management	MO: Combo of Dir Pract w/ CO & Planning or Admin & Man	MO: Combo of CO & Planning w/ Admin & Man	MO: Generic	MO: Other	MO: Not Yet Determined	MC: Direct Practice	MC: Community Organization & Planning	MC: Administration or Management	MC: Combo of Dir Pract w/ CO & Planning or Admin & Man	MC: Combo of CO & Planning w/ Admin & Man	MC: Generic	MC: Other	MC: Not Yet Determined	Fields of Practice Only (No Methods Concentration)
TOTAL:	32,214	5,616	111	426	300	414	1,820	452	1,451	9,838	633	602	1,129	375	2,128	1,184	2,505	3,230
ADELPHI UNIV	694	0	0	0	0	0	0	0	0	0	0	0	0	0	0	0	0	694
ALABAMA A&M UNIV	81	0	0	0	0	0	0	0	0	77	0	0	0	3	0	0	1	0
ANDREWS UNIV	43	17	0	9	0	0	0	0	17	0	0	0	0	0	0	0	0	0
ARIZONA STATE UNIV	443	148	0	0	0	42	253	0	0	0	0	0	0	0	0	0	0	0
AUGSBURG COLL	68	7	0	0	0	0	0	0	0	52	0	0	0	9	0	0	0	0
BARRY UNIV	381	0	0	0	0	0	0	0	0	177	0	0	0	0	0	0	0	204
BOISE STATE UNIV	28	0	0	0	0	0	0	0	0	28	0	0	0	0	0	0	0	0
BOSTON COLL	416	120	0	0	0	20	0	0	0	242	0	0	0	34	0	0	0	0
BOSTON UNIV	378	0	0	0	0	0	0	0	0	273	38	0	0	0	0	67	0	0
BRIGHAM YOUNG/UT	78	0	0	0	0	0	0	0	0	78	0	0	0	0	0	0	0	0
BRYN MAWR COLL	174	112	20	13	0	0	0	0	29	0	0	0	0	0	0	0	0	0
CAL STATE UNIV/FRES	180	0	0	0	0	0	0	0	0	0	0	0	180	0	0	0	0	0
CAL STATE UNIV/LB	*	*	*	*	*	*	*	*	*	*	*	*	*	*	*	*	*	*
CAL STATE UNIV/SB	186	0	0	0	0	0	0	0	0	186	0	0	0	0	0	0	0	0
CAL STATE UNIV/STAN	120	0	0	0	0	0	0	0	60	0	0	0	0	0	0	60	0	0
CASE WESTERN RESERVE	301	0	0	0	0	0	0	0	0	266	13	22	0	0	0	0	0	0
CATHOLIC UNIV/DC	156	0	0	0	0	61	0	0	0	51	0	0	12	0	0	0	32	0
CLARK ATLANTA UNIV	*	*	*	*	*	*	*	*	*	*	*	*	*	*	*	*	*	*
CLEVE ST U/U AKRON	*	*	*	*	*	*	*	*	*	*	*	*	*	*	*	*	*	*
COLL ST CAT/U ST THO	206	0	0	0	0	0	0	206	0	0	0	0	0	0	0	0	0	0
COLORADO STATE UNIV	109	0	0	0	0	0	0	0	0	0	0	0	0	0	0	109	0	0
COLUMBIA UNIV	775	0	0	0	0	0	0	0	0	291	211	24	0	100	33	2	0	114
DELAWARE STATE UNIV	*	*	*	*	*	*	*	*	*	*	*	*	*	*	*	*	*	*
EAST CAROLINA UNIV	129	0	0	0	0	0	0	0	0	82	0	2	42	0	0	0	3	0
EASTERN MICHIGAN	263	0	0	0	0	0	0	0	0	0	0	0	0	0	263	0	0	0
FLORIDA INTERNATL	221	0	0	0	0	0	0	0	0	221	0	0	0	0	0	0	0	0
FLORIDA STATE UNIV	282	191	0	15	0	0	76	0	0	0	0	0	0	0	0	0	0	0
FORDHAM UNIV	1,381	412	0	53	18	0	730	16	0	136	0	6	0	0	0	0	10	0
GALLAUDET UNIV	53	0	0	0	0	0	0	0	0	0	0	0	0	0	0	53	0	0
GRAMBLING STATE UNIV	37	37	0	0	0	0	0	0	0	0	0	0	0	0	0	0	0	0
GRAND VALLEY STATE	368	0	0	0	0	0	0	0	0	0	0	0	0	0	368	0	0	0
HOWARD UNIV	311	0	0	0	0	0	0	0	0	198	25	34	0	0	0	0	0	54
HUNTER COLL	736	0	0	0	0	0	0	0	194	330	47	3	19	7	0	0	0	136
INDIANA UNIV	635	359	0	0	0	0	0	0	0	0	0	0	0	34	0	0	242	0
INTERAMERICAN/MET	*	*	*	*	*	*	*	*	*	*	*	*	*	*	*	*	*	*
JACKSON STATE UNIV	91	0	0	0	0	0	0	0	0	91	0	0	0	0	0	0	0	0
KEAN UNIV	90	0	0	0	0	0	90	0	0	0	0	0	0	0	0	0	0	0
LOMA LINDA UNIV	77	0	0	0	0	0	0	0	0	15	0	1	0	0	0	0	17	41
LOUISIANA STATE UNIV	178	0	0	0	0	0	60	74	0	0	0	0	0	0	29	15	0	0
LOYOLA UNIV CHICAGO	433	0	0	0	0	0	0	0	0	433	0	0	0	0	0	0	0	0
MARYWOOD UNIV	391	151	0	24	0	0	0	0	216	0	0	0	0	0	0	0	0	0
MICHIGAN STATE UNIV	205	60	0	13	0	0	53	0	0	0	0	0	0	0	0	0	0	79

TABLE 205

Master's Degree Students, by Primary Methods Concentration

Program	Total	Methods Only: Direct Practice	Methods Only: Community Organization & Planning	Methods Only: Administration or Management	Methods Only: Combo of Dir Pract w/ CO & Planning or Admin & Man	Methods Only: Combo of CO & Planning w/ Admin & Man	Methods Only: Generic	Methods Only: Other	Methods Only: Not Yet Determined	Combined: Direct Practice	Combined: Community Organization & Planning	Combined: Administration or Management	Combined: Combo of Dir Pract w/ CO & Planning or Admin & Man	Combined: Combo of CO & Planning w/ Admin & Man	Combined: Generic	Combined: Other	Combined: Not Yet Determined	Fields of Practice Only (No Methods Concentration)
NEW MEXICO HIGHLANDS	233	0	0	0	0	0	0	0	0	161	50	0	0	0	0	0	22	0	0
NEW MEXICO STATE	88	0	0	0	0	0	0	0	0	0	0	0	0	0	0	0	88	0	0
NEW YORK UNIV	983	0	0	0	0	0	0	0	0	0	0	0	0	0	0	0	0	0	983
OHIO STATE UNIV	397	0	0	0	0	0	0	0	0	102	0	24	1	0	96	0	0	0	174
OUR LADY OF LAKE	*	*	*	*	*	*	*	*	*	*	*	*	*	*	*	*	*	*	*
PORTLAND STATE UNIV	317	0	0	0	0	0	0	0	38	102	20	10	0	0	147	0	0	0	0
RADFORD UNIV	108	0	0	0	0	0	0	0	0	108	0	0	0	0	0	0	0	0	0
RHODE ISLAND COLL	157	54	0	0	20	17	0	0	0	31	0	20	15	0	0	0	0	0	0
RUTGERS UNIV/NB	690	0	0	0	0	0	0	0	0	493	0	43	0	0	0	0	0	154	0
SALEM STATE COLL	203	0	0	0	0	0	0	0	0	0	0	0	0	0	0	0	203	0	0
SAN DIEGO STATE UNIV	334	110	0	15	0	0	0	0	0	136	0	73	0	0	0	0	0	0	0
SAN FRANCISCO STATE	*	*	*	*	*	*	*	*	*	*	*	*	*	*	*	*	*	*	*
SAVANNAH STATE UNIV	41	16	0	4	0	0	0	0	21	0	0	0	0	0	0	0	0	0	0
SIMMONS COLL	279	279	0	0	0	0	0	0	0	0	0	0	0	0	0	0	0	0	0
SMITH COLL	229	0	0	0	0	0	0	0	0	229	0	0	0	0	0	0	0	0	0
SOUTHERN CONNECTICUT	195	0	0	0	0	0	0	0	0	163	0	32	0	0	0	0	0	0	0
SOUTHERN ILL/CAR	55	0	0	0	0	0	0	0	0	55	0	0	0	0	0	0	0	0	0
SOUTHERN UNIV	256	0	0	0	0	0	0	0	0	72	0	14	0	0	0	0	0	170	0
SOUTHWEST MISSOURI	66	0	0	0	0	0	0	0	0	66	0	0	0	0	0	0	0	0	0
SOUTHWEST TEXAS	84	59	0	25	0	0	0	0	0	0	0	0	0	0	0	0	0	0	0
ST AMBROSE UNIV	66	0	0	0	0	0	0	0	0	0	0	0	66	0	0	0	0	0	0
ST LOUIS UNIV	294	0	0	0	0	0	0	0	0	51	36	0	150	0	57	0	0	0	0
SUNY/ALBANY	360	214	0	23	0	0	0	0	123	0	0	0	0	0	0	0	0	0	0
SUNY/BUFFALO	395	0	0	0	0	0	0	0	0	0	0	0	0	0	148	0	0	0	247
SYRACUSE UNIV	277	0	0	0	0	0	0	0	0	277	0	0	0	0	0	0	0	0	0
TEMPLE UNIV	470	360	0	46	0	0	0	0	64	0	0	0	0	0	0	0	0	0	0
TULANE UNIV	168	0	0	0	0	0	0	0	0	0	0	0	0	0	0	0	168	0	0
U OF ALABAMA	188	0	0	0	0	0	0	0	0	99	0	9	0	0	80	0	0	0	0
U OF ALASKA/ANK	42	0	0	0	0	0	0	0	0	0	0	0	0	0	0	0	0	0	42
U OF ARKANSAS/LR	166	80	0	0	0	8	0	0	78	0	0	0	0	0	0	0	0	0	0
U OF CALIFORNIA/BERK	183	0	0	0	0	0	0	0	0	146	0	37	0	0	0	0	0	0	0
U OF CENTRAL FLORIDA	209	209	0	0	0	0	0	0	0	0	0	0	0	0	0	0	0	0	0
U OF CHICAGO	354	230	0	0	108	0	0	0	16	0	0	0	0	0	0	0	0	0	0
U OF CINCINNATI	195	109	0	25	0	0	0	0	61	0	0	0	0	0	0	0	0	0	0
U OF CONNECTICUT	389	261	37	41	0	0	0	0	0	0	0	0	0	0	0	0	0	0	0
U OF DENVER	308	160	0	0	0	34	0	0	0	0	0	0	0	0	0	0	0	114	0
U OF GEORGIA	239	0	0	0	0	0	0	0	0	91	9	55	84	0	0	0	0	0	0
U OF HAWAII	204	0	0	0	0	0	0	0	0	0	0	0	83	0	0	0	0	121	0
U OF HOUSTON	283	0	0	0	0	0	0	0	0	0	0	0	0	0	283	0	0	0	0
U OF ILLINOIS/CHI	466	0	0	0	0	0	0	0	0	202	0	17	0	0	0	0	0	247	0
U OF ILLINOIS/URB	295	0	0	0	0	0	0	0	0	288	0	0	7	0	0	0	0	0	0
U OF IOWA	*	*	*	*	*	*	*	*	*	*	*	*	*	*	*	*	*	*	*
U OF KANSAS	413	0	0	0	0	0	0	0	0	162	0	17	0	0	127	0	0	0	107

TABLE 205

Master's Degree Students, by Primary Methods Concentration

Program	Total	Methods Only								Methods Combined with Fields of Practice or Social Problem								Fields of Practice Only (No Methods Concentra- tion)
		Direct Practice	Commu- nity Organiza- tion & Planning	Admin- istration or Manage- ment	Combo of Dir Pract w/ CO & Planning or Admin & Man	Combo of CO & Planning w/ Admin & Man	Generic	Other	Not Yet Deter- mined	Direct Practice	Commu- nity Organiza- tion & Planning	Admini- stration or Manage- ment	Combo of Dir Pract w/ CO & Planning or Admin & Man	Combo of CO & Planning w/ Admin & Man	Generic	Other	Not Yet Deter- mined	
U OF KENTUCKY	251	0	0	0	0	0	251	0	0	0	0	0	0	0	0	0	0	0
U OF LOUISVILLE	317	107	0	0	0	39	82	0	89	0	0	0	0	0	0	0	0	0
U OF MARYLAND	865	0	0	0	0	0	0	0	0	306	0	0	0	66	0	0	308	185
U OF MICHIGAN	580	1	0	0	0	0	0	0	0	383	96	59	0	0	0	41	0	0
U OF MINNESOTA/DUL	88	0	0	0	0	0	0	0	0	0	0	0	0	0	0	88	0	0
U OF MINNESOTA/TC	264	0	0	52	0	0	0	0	0	204	0	8	0	0	0	0	0	0
U OF MISSOURI/COL	175	0	0	0	0	0	0	0	0	117	3	11	1	1	0	0	42	0
U OF NCGB/NCSU	65	0	0	0	0	0	0	0	0	0	0	0	0	0	65	0	0	0
U OF NEBRASKA/OMA	178	0	0	0	0	0	0	75	0	0	0	0	0	0	0	0	0	103
U OF NEVADA/LV	140	92	0	0	0	0	0	0	0	0	0	28	0	0	0	20	0	0
U OF NEVADA/REN	35	0	0	0	0	35	0	0	0	0	0	0	0	0	0	0	0	0
U OF NEW HAMPSHIRE	*	*	*	*	*	*	*	*	*	*	*	*	*	*	*	*	*	*
U OF NORTH CAR/CH	293	0	0	0	0	0	0	0	0	111	0	0	0	18	0	0	164	0
U OF NORTH DAKOTA	89	0	0	0	0	0	89	0	0	0	0	0	0	0	0	0	0	0
U OF OKLAHOMA	173	67	0	0	0	16	17	0	73	0	0	0	0	0	0	0	0	0
U OF PENNSYLVANIA	300	0	0	0	0	0	119	0	0	105	0	0	0	0	0	44	32	0
U OF PITTSBURGH	502	427	0	0	0	75	0	0	0	0	0	0	0	0	0	0	0	0
U OF PUERTO RICO/RP	145	0	0	0	0	0	0	0	0	58	6	21	0	0	0	0	60	0
U OF SOUTH CAROLINA	455	0	0	0	0	0	0	0	0	185	43	1	0	0	119	95	12	0
U OF SOUTH FLORIDA	122	122	0	0	0	0	0	0	0	0	0	0	0	0	0	0	0	0
U OF SOUTHERN CAL	485	0	0	0	0	0	0	0	0	357	28	0	10	0	0	90	0	0
U OF SOUTHERN IND	82	72	0	0	0	0	0	0	0	10	0	0	0	0	0	0	0	0
U OF SOUTHERN MISS	127	0	0	0	0	0	0	0	0	127	0	0	0	0	0	0	0	0
U OF TENNESSEE/KNX	388	121	4	12	42	28	0	0	181	0	0	0	0	0	0	0	0	0
U OF TEXAS/ARL	524	107	0	0	0	18	0	0	0	0	0	0	0	0	0	0	399	0
U OF TEXAS/AUS	294	238	0	56	0	0	0	0	0	0	0	0	0	0	0	0	0	0
U OF UTAH	285	0	0	0	0	0	0	0	0	285	0	0	0	0	0	0	0	0
U OF VERMONT	67	0	0	0	0	0	0	0	0	0	0	0	0	0	0	0	0	67
U OF WASHINGTON	328	17	0	0	112	0	0	0	0	101	5	13	9	4	0	0	67	0
U OF WISCONSIN/MAD	183	0	0	0	0	0	0	0	0	0	0	0	0	0	183	0	0	0
U OF WISCONSIN/MIL	318	0	0	0	0	0	0	0	0	264	0	18	36	0	0	0	0	0
U OF WYOMING	*	*	*	*	*	*	*	*	*	*	*	*	*	*	*	*	*	*
VALDOSTA STATE UNIV	81	0	0	0	0	0	0	81	0	0	0	0	0	0	0	0	0	0
VIRGINIA COMMONWEAL	548	259	0	0	0	21	0	0	0	36	0	0	0	0	0	0	232	0
WALLA WALLA COLL	179	3	0	0	0	0	0	0	0	176	0	0	0	0	0	0	0	0
WASHBURN UNIV	116	105	0	0	0	0	0	0	0	11	0	0	0	0	0	0	0	0
WASHINGTON UNIV	414	0	0	0	0	0	0	0	0	0	0	0	414	0	0	0	0	0
WAYNE STATE UNIV	559	123	0	0	0	0	0	0	0	436	0	0	0	0	0	0	0	0
WEST VIRGINIA UNIV	267	0	0	0	0	0	0	0	0	185	0	0	0	80	0	0	2	0
WIDENER UNIV	181	0	0	0	0	0	0	0	181	0	0	0	0	0	0	0	0	0
YESHIVA UNIV	374	0	0	0	0	0	0	0	0	120	0	0	0	19	130	19	86	0

* Missing data

TABLE 206

Master's Degree Students, by Primary Field of Practice or Social Problem Concentration

Program	Total	Aging/ Geron- tological Social Work	Alcohol, Drug or Sub- stance Abuse	Child Welfare	Commu- nity Planning	Correc- tions/ Criminal Justice	Family Services	Group Services	Health	Occupa- tional/ Industrial Social Work	Mental Health or Comm'ity Mental Health	Mental Retarda- tion	Public Assist/ Public Welfare	Rehabili- tation	School Social Work	Other Fields of Practice or Social Problems	Combos	Not Yet Deter- mined	None (Methods Concen- tration Only)
TOTAL:	32,214	556	240	2,388	491	189	2,201	133	1,377	147	3,129	58	41	59	1,011	2,274	758	5,780	11,382
ADELPHI UNIV	694	0	0	0	0	0	0	0	0	0	0	0	0	0	0	0	258	436	0
ALABAMA A&M UNIV	81	0	0	40	0	0	0	0	0	0	37	0	0	0	0	0	0	4	0
ANDREWS UNIV	43	0	0	0	0	0	0	0	0	0	0	0	0	0	0	0	0	0	43
ARIZONA STATE UNIV	443	0	0	0	0	0	0	0	0	0	0	0	0	0	0	0	0	0	443
AUGSBURG COLL	68	2	0	6	9	4	7	2	14	0	6	0	1	0	9	0	0	1	7
BARRY UNIV	381	0	0	0	0	0	98	0	15	0	64	0	0	0	0	0	0	204	0
BOISE STATE UNIV	28	0	0	0	0	0	0	0	0	0	0	0	0	0	0	28	0	0	0
BOSTON COLL	416	2	0	10	0	5	0	0	4	1	0	0	0	0	0	0	0	254	140
BOSTON UNIV	378	4	26	28	38	4	45	11	44	0	85	6	2	0	18	67	0	0	0
BRIGHAM YOUNG/UT	78	0	0	0	0	0	78	0	0	0	0	0	0	0	0	0	0	0	0
BRYN MAWR COLL	174	0	0	0	0	0	0	0	0	0	0	0	0	0	0	0	0	0	174
CAL STATE UNIV/FRES	180	1	1	36	2	3	8	0	11	3	37	0	0	0	27	2	0	49	0
CAL STATE UNIV/LB	*	*	*	*	*	*	*	*	*	*	*	*	*	*	*	*	*	*	*
CAL STATE UNIV/SB	186	0	0	130	0	0	0	0	0	0	39	0	0	0	0	0	0	17	0
CAL STATE UNIV/STAN	120	0	0	0	35	0	0	0	0	0	0	0	0	0	0	25	0	0	60
CASE WESTERN RESERVE	301	4	14	106	35	0	0	0	23	0	78	0	0	0	11	0	2	28	0
CATHOLIC UNIV/DC	156	0	0	0	0	0	0	0	0	0	0	0	0	0	0	51	12	32	61
CLARK ATLANTA UNIV	*	*	*	*	*	*	*	*	*	*	*	*	*	*	*	*	*	*	*
CLEVE ST U/U AKRON	*	*	*	*	*	*	*	*	*	*	*	*	*	*	*	*	*	*	*
COLL ST CAT/U ST THO	206	0	0	0	0	0	0	0	0	0	0	0	0	0	0	0	0	0	206
COLORADO STATE UNIV	109	0	0	0	0	0	0	0	0	0	0	0	0	0	0	109	0	0	0
COLUMBIA UNIV	775	30	0	0	0	0	165	0	243	52	0	0	0	0	63	31	77	114	0
DELAWARE STATE UNIV	*	*	*	*	*	*	*	*	*	*	*	*	*	*	*	*	*	*	*
EAST CAROLINA UNIV	129	0	0	0	0	0	52	0	21	0	49	0	0	0	0	0	0	7	0
EASTERN MICHIGAN	263	34	0	0	0	0	0	0	0	0	0	0	0	0	0	154	75	0	0
FLORIDA INTERNATL	221	12	0	209	0	0	0	0	0	0	0	0	0	0	0	0	0	0	0
FLORIDA STATE UNIV	282	0	0	0	0	0	0	0	0	0	0	0	0	0	0	0	0	0	282
FORDHAM UNIV	1381	0	21	0	0	0	0	0	0	0	0	0	0	0	0	121	0	0	1239
GALLAUDET UNIV	53	0	0	0	0	0	0	0	0	0	0	0	0	0	0	53	0	0	0
GRAMBLING STATE UNIV	37	0	0	0	0	0	0	0	0	0	0	0	0	0	0	0	0	0	37
GRAND VALLEY STATE	368	0	4	25	5	2	10	0	8	3	6	2	0	2	12	0	0	289	0
HOWARD UNIV	311	9	0	0	0	18	143	0	18	0	63	0	0	0	0	6	0	54	0
HUNTER COLL	736	37	16	62	46	19	40	17	37	16	53	15	7	15	26	0	0	0	330
INDIANA UNIV	635	0	0	0	0	0	0	0	0	0	0	0	0	0	0	0	34	242	359
INTERAMERICAN/MET	*	*	*	*	*	*	*	*	*	*	*	*	*	*	*	*	*	*	*
JACKSON STATE UNIV	91	0	0	0	0	0	0	0	0	0	0	0	0	0	0	91	0	0	0
KEAN UNIV	90	0	0	0	0	0	0	0	0	0	0	0	0	0	0	0	0	0	90
LOMA LINDA UNIV	77	0	0	8	0	0	0	0	7	0	1	0	0	0	3	0	0	17	41
LOUISIANA STATE UNIV	178	0	0	0	0	0	0	0	0	0	0	0	0	0	0	0	0	44	134
LOYOLA UNIV CHICAGO	433	8	4	26	0	3	27	0	43	1	122	2	0	1	52	0	0	144	0
MARYWOOD UNIV	391	0	0	0	0	0	0	0	0	0	0	0	0	0	0	0	0	0	391
MICHIGAN STATE UNIV	205	0	0	0	0	0	0	0	0	0	0	0	0	0	0	0	0	0	205
NEW MEXICO HIGHLANDS	233	0	0	0	50	0	0	0	0	0	161	0	0	0	0	22	0	0	0
NEW MEXICO STATE	88	0	0	0	0	0	0	0	0	0	0	0	0	0	0	88	0	0	0
NEW YORK UNIV	983	33	32	50	0	13	120	0	62	7	266	8	1	6	76	6	0	303	0

TABLE 206

Master's Degree Students, by Primary Field of Practice or Social Problem Concentration

Program	Total	Aging/ Gerontological Social Work	Alcohol, Drug or Substance Abuse	Child Welfare	Community Planning	Corrections/ Criminal Justice	Family Services	Group Services	Health	Occupational/ Industrial Social Work	Mental Health or Comm'ity Mental Health	Mental Retardation	Public Assist/ Public Welfare	Rehabilitation	School Social Work	Other Fields of Practice or Social Problems	Combos	Not Yet Determined	None (Methods Concentration Only)
OHIO STATE UNIV	397	10	2	9	2	5	35	0	18	0	34	1	0	0	18	89	0	174	0
OUR LADY OF LAKE	*	*	*	*	*	*	*	*	*	*	*	*	*	*	*	*	*	*	*
PORTLAND STATE UNIV	317	15	10	58	2	26	27	0	17	0	81	2	0	0	29	11	0	1	38
RADFORD UNIV	108	0	0	0	0	0	108	0	0	0	0	0	0	0	0	0	0	0	0
RHODE ISLAND COLL	157	0	0	0	0	0	0	0	0	0	18	0	0	0	0	32	16	0	91
RUTGERS UNIV/NB	690	24	24	27	20	29	81	2	44	1	123	5	5	9	75	16	0	205	0
SALEM STATE COLL	203	34	0	97	0	0	0	0	17	0	72	0	0	0	0	0	0	0	0
SAN DIEGO STATE UNIV	334	18	11	33	0	6	0	0	14	0	32	0	0	2	18	18	17	40	125
SAN FRANCISCO STATE	*	*	*	*	*	*	*	*	*	*	*	*	*	*	*	*	*	*	*
SAVANNAH STATE UNIV	41	0	0	0	0	0	0	0	0	0	0	0	0	0	0	0	0	0	41
SIMMONS COLL	279	0	0	0	0	0	0	0	0	0	0	0	0	0	0	0	0	0	279
SMITH COLL	229	4	3	3	0	3	19	0	9	0	163	0	0	0	23	2	0	0	0
SOUTHERN CONNECTICUT	195	26	0	99	0	0	0	0	19	0	43	0	0	0	0	0	8	0	0
SOUTHERN ILL/CAR	55	0	0	17	0	0	0	0	0	0	22	0	0	0	16	0	0	0	0
SOUTHERN UNIV	256	9	0	25	0	0	0	0	14	0	38	0	0	0	0	0	0	170	0
SOUTHWEST MISSOURI	66	0	0	0	0	0	0	0	0	0	0	0	0	0	0	66	0	0	0
SOUTHWEST TEXAS	84	0	0	0	0	0	0	0	0	0	0	0	0	0	0	0	0	0	84
ST AMBROSE UNIV	66	0	0	0	0	0	0	0	0	0	0	0	0	0	0	66	0	0	0
ST LOUIS UNIV	294	0	0	0	0	0	150	0	51	0	0	0	0	0	0	0	36	57	0
SUNY/ALBANY	360	0	0	0	0	0	0	0	0	0	0	0	0	0	0	0	0	0	360
SUNY/BUFFALO	395	0	9	73	13	0	0	0	0	0	53	0	0	0	0	0	0	0	247
SYRACUSE UNIV	277	8	0	15	0	0	0	0	20	20	48	0	0	0	0	0	0	166	0
TEMPLE UNIV	470	0	0	0	0	0	0	0	0	0	0	0	0	0	0	0	0	0	470
TULANE UNIV	168	0	0	0	0	0	0	0	0	0	0	0	0	0	0	168	0	0	0
U OF ALABAMA	188	5	0	53	0	0	0	0	13	0	28	0	0	0	0	89	0	0	0
U OF ALASKA/ANK	42	0	0	0	0	0	0	0	0	0	0	0	0	0	0	0	0	0	42
U OF ARKANSAS/LR	166	0	0	0	0	0	0	0	0	0	0	0	0	0	0	0	0	0	166
U OF CALIFORNIA/BERK	183	23	0	81	0	0	0	0	36	0	43	0	0	0	0	0	0	0	0
U OF CENTRAL FLORIDA	209	0	0	0	0	0	0	0	0	0	0	0	0	0	0	0	0	0	209
U OF CHICAGO	354	0	0	0	0	0	0	0	0	0	0	0	0	0	0	0	0	0	354
U OF CINCINNATI	195	0	0	0	0	0	0	0	0	0	0	0	0	0	0	0	0	0	195
U OF CONNECTICUT	389	0	0	0	0	0	0	0	0	0	0	0	0	0	0	0	0	0	389
U OF DENVER	308	0	0	0	0	0	0	0	0	0	0	0	0	0	0	0	0	114	194
U OF GEORGIA	239	1	0	0	14	0	199	0	0	0	0	0	0	0	25	0	0	0	0
U OF HAWAII	204	11	0	32	0	0	0	0	7	0	33	0	0	0	0	0	0	121	0
U OF HOUSTON	283	22	0	38	0	0	0	0	26	0	22	0	0	0	0	17	0	158	0
U OF ILLINOIS/CHI	466	0	0	40	0	0	0	0	17	0	56	0	0	0	89	17	0	247	0
U OF ILLINOIS/URB	295	0	0	68	0	0	11	0	30	0	90	0	0	0	88	3	0	5	0
U OF IOWA	*	*	*	*	*	*	*	*	*	*	*	*	*	*	*	*	*	*	*
U OF KANSAS	413	8	0	5	0	0	93	0	23	0	50	0	0	0	0	0	0	234	0
U OF KENTUCKY	251	0	0	0	0	0	0	0	0	0	0	0	0	0	0	0	0	0	251
U OF LOUISVILLE	317	0	0	0	0	0	0	0	0	0	0	0	0	0	0	0	0	0	317
U OF MARYLAND	865	21	12	140	18	0	0	0	42	31	105	0	0	0	0	3	0	308	185
U OF MICHIGAN	580	0	0	260	98	0	0	0	58	0	114	0	0	0	0	49	0	0	1
U OF MINNESOTA/DUL	88	0	0	0	0	0	0	0	0	0	0	0	0	0	0	88	0	0	0

TABLE 206

Master's Degree Students, by Primary Field of Practice or Social Problem Concentration

Program	Total	Aging/Gerontological Social Work	Alcohol, Drug or Substance Abuse	Child Welfare	Community Planning	Corrections/Criminal Justice	Family Services	Group Services	Health	Occupational/Industrial Social Work	Mental Health or Comm'ity Mental Health	Mental Retardation	Public Assist/Public Welfare	Rehabilitation	School Social Work	Other Fields of Practice or Social Problems	Combos	Not Yet Determined	None (Methods Concentration Only)
U OF MINNESOTA/TC	264	0	0	45	3	0	0	0	0	0	164	0	0	0	0	0	0	0	52
U OF MISSOURI/COL	175	2	5	17	1	2	49	0	12	0	17	3	0	2	3	2	0	62	0
U OF NCGB/NCSU	65	0	0	19	0	0	0	0	4	0	7	0	0	0	0	0	0	35	0
U OF NEBRASKA/OMA	178	0	0	0	0	0	0	0	0	0	0	0	0	0	0	15	26	0	137
U OF NEVADA/LV	140	0	0	20	28	0	0	0	0	0	0	0	0	0	0	0	0	0	92
U OF NEVADA/REN	35	0	0	0	0	0	0	0	0	0	0	0	0	0	0	0	0	0	35
U OF NEW HAMPSHIRE	*	*	*	*	*	*	*	*	*	*	*	*	*	*	*	*	*	*	*
U OF NORTH CAR/CH	293	9	0	0	0	0	47	0	18	0	38	0	0	0	0	16	1	164	0
U OF NORTH DAKOTA	89	0	0	0	0	0	0	0	0	0	0	0	0	0	0	0	0	0	89
U OF OKLAHOMA	173	0	0	0	0	0	0	0	0	0	0	0	0	0	0	0	0	0	173
U OF PENNSYLVANIA	300	7	5	30	11	5	12	10	21	1	28	0	0	3	16	0	0	32	119
U OF PITTSBURGH	502	0	0	0	0	0	0	0	0	0	0	0	0	0	0	0	0	0	502
U OF PUERTO RICO/RP	145	9	0	0	6	0	49	0	0	0	0	0	0	0	0	21	0	60	0
U OF SOUTH CAROLINA	455	21	10	30	22	16	21	34	65	0	63	0	0	5	50	95	0	23	0
U OF SOUTH FLORIDA	122	0	0	0	0	0	0	0	0	0	0	0	0	0	0	0	0	0	122
U OF SOUTHERN CAL	485	20	10	25	26	18	97	39	17	10	74	2	16	8	33	0	0	90	0
U OF SOUTHERN IND	82	0	0	0	0	0	0	0	0	0	0	0	0	0	10	0	0	0	72
U OF SOUTHERN MISS	127	0	0	0	0	0	0	0	0	0	0	0	0	0	0	127	0	0	0
U OF TENNESSEE/KNX	388	0	0	0	0	0	0	0	0	0	0	0	0	0	0	0	0	0	388
U OF TEXAS/ARL	524	0	0	0	0	0	0	0	0	0	0	0	0	0	0	0	0	399	125
U OF TEXAS/AUS	294	0	0	0	0	0	0	0	0	0	0	0	0	0	0	0	0	0	294
U OF UTAH	285	0	0	0	0	0	0	0	0	0	0	0	0	0	0	285	0	0	0
U OF VERMONT	67	0	0	0	0	0	0	0	0	0	0	0	0	0	0	0	39	28	0
U OF WASHINGTON	328	0	0	17	0	0	24	0	24	0	25	0	0	0	0	42	0	67	129
U OF WISCONSIN/MAD	183	9	7	47	0	0	0	0	12	0	22	4	0	0	0	0	0	89	0
U OF WISCONSIN/MIL	318	0	0	0	0	0	164	0	61	0	0	0	0	0	85	0	8	0	0
U OF WYOMING	*	*	*	*	*	*	*	*	*	*	*	*	*	*	*	*	*	*	*
VALDOSTA STATE UNIV	81	0	0	0	0	0	0	0	0	0	0	0	0	0	0	0	0	0	81
VIRGINIA COMMONWEAL	548	6	0	0	0	0	0	0	0	0	0	0	0	0	29	1	0	232	280
WALLA WALLA COLL	179	2	7	26	0	8	35	3	19	0	27	3	2	5	8	4	0	27	3
WASHBURN UNIV	116	0	0	0	0	0	0	0	0	0	0	0	0	0	11	0	0	0	105
WASHINGTON UNIV	414	28	0	107	0	0	0	0	22	0	83	0	0	0	0	67	106	1	0
WAYNE STATE UNIV	559	0	0	47	22	0	31	0	23	0	88	1	0	0	80	0	0	144	123
WEST VIRGINIA UNIV	267	0	0	0	0	0	117	0	52	0	96	0	0	0	0	0	0	2	0
WIDENER UNIV	181	0	0	0	0	0	0	0	0	0	0	0	0	0	0	0	0	0	181
YESHIVA UNIV	374	28	16	49	20	0	39	15	19	1	62	4	7	1	8	11	8	86	0

* Missing data

TABLE 207

Master's Degree Students, by Primary Field of Practice in Field Instruction

Program	Total	Aging/ Gerontological Social Work	Alcohol, Drug or Substance Abuse	Child Welfare	Community Planning	Corrections/ Criminal Justice	Family Services	Group Services	Health	Occupational/ Industrial Social Work	Mental Health or Comm'ity Mental Health	Mental Retardation	Public Assist/ Public Welfare	Rehabilitation	School Social Work	Other Fields of Practice or Social Problems	Not Yet Assigned	Not in Field Instruction
TOTAL:	32,255	1,006	784	2,683	752	810	3,006	376	2,503	225	4,727	225	225	182	2,318	979	4,817	6,637
ADELPHI UNIV	694	18	48	37	4	12	35	16	52	7	104	21	13	4	50	2	0	271
ALABAMA A&M UNIV	81	0	0	22	0	0	0	0	0	0	23	0	0	0	0	0	36	0
ANDREWS UNIV	43	0	0	3	11	1	3	6	3	0	0	0	3	0	3	2	4	4
ARIZONA STATE UNIV	443	14	5	47	4	14	34	0	50	1	29	0	0	1	35	33	90	86
AUGSBURG COLL	68	2	0	6	9	4	7	2	14	0	6	0	1	0	9	0	1	7
BARRY UNIV	381	11	3	16	0	0	30	0	30	0	54	1	1	0	33	0	103	99
BOISE STATE UNIV	28	0	0	0	0	1	2	0	5	0	7	0	0	0	3	0	10	0
BOSTON COLL	416	10	4	34	25	17	38	1	22	5	97	3	0	1	57	0	83	19
BOSTON UNIV	378	4	26	28	38	4	45	11	44	0	85	6	2	0	18	0	0	67
BRIGHAM YOUNG/UT	78	2	3	7	0	0	13	0	2	0	10	0	0	0	3	0	38	0
BRYN MAWR COLL	174	6	9	21	9	5	10	13	16	0	37	5	0	1	13	0	0	29
CAL STATE UNIV/FRES	180	1	1	36	2	3	8	0	11	3	37	0	0	0	27	2	49	0
CAL STATE UNIV/LB	*	*	*	*	*	*	*	*	*	*	*	*	*	*	*	*	*	*
CAL STATE UNIV/SB	186	4	0	33	8	0	0	0	14	0	46	2	1	1	29	0	0	49
CAL STATE UNIV/STAN	120	3	1	46	0	3	8	0	6	0	28	1	1	0	4	0	0	19
CASE WESTERN RESERVE	301	16	10	56	15	13	25	0	26	4	52	4	0	0	21	3	35	21
CATHOLIC UNIV/DC	156	6	6	15	2	5	14	0	13	0	33	7	0	0	8	15	0	32
CLARK ATLANTA UNIV	106	3	2	19	0	9	14	0	12	0	7	2	0	0	15	0	23	0
CLEVE ST U/U AKRON	*	*	*	*	*	*	*	*	*	*	*	*	*	*	*	*	*	*
COLL ST CAT/U ST THO	206	6	2	14	2	5	15	0	9	0	28	0	0	0	19	2	1	103
COLORADO STATE UNIV	109	1	1	3	0	2	16	2	9	0	18	0	5	1	4	2	33	12
COLUMBIA UNIV	775	30	0	0	0	77	165	0	243	52	0	0	0	0	63	31	114	0
DELAWARE STATE UNIV	*	*	*	*	*	*	*	*	*	*	*	*	*	*	*	*	*	*
EAST CAROLINA UNIV	129	0	0	9	0	0	18	0	13	0	31	0	0	0	0	0	44	14
EASTERN MICHIGAN	263	7	1	12	0	7	42	0	5	2	11	1	0	0	13	7	31	124
FLORIDA INTERNATL	*	*	*	*	*	*	*	*	*	*	*	*	*	*	*	*	*	*
FLORIDA STATE UNIV	282	4	9	26	2	6	13	1	39	0	17	1	0	3	6	1	154	0
FORDHAM UNIV	1381	59	78	130	14	23	174	19	94	2	240	8	9	5	79	0	0	447
GALLAUDET UNIV	53	3	2	2	6	0	0	0	2	0	7	0	0	0	16	2	3	10
GRAMBLING STATE UNIV	38	1	3	4	0	3	1	0	7	0	5	2	0	0	3	0	0	9
GRAND VALLEY STATE	368	0	4	25	5	2	10	0	8	3	6	2	0	2	12	0	289	0
HOWARD UNIV	311	9	0	0	0	18	143	0	18	0	63	0	0	0	0	6	0	54
HUNTER COLL	736	37	16	62	46	19	40	17	37	16	53	15	7	15	26	15	0	330
INDIANA UNIV	635	6	15	11	11	2	51	9	26	5	62	1	1	1	42	15	189	189
INTERAMERICAN/MET	78	0	0	0	24	0	37	0	0	0	0	0	0	0	0	17	0	0
JACKSON STATE UNIV	91	3	5	25	0	0	10	0	11	0	10	1	0	0	4	0	1	21
KEAN UNIV	*	*	*	*	*	*	*	*	*	*	*	*	*	*	*	*	*	*
LOMA LINDA UNIV	77	0	0	8	0	0	0	0	7	0	1	0	0	0	3	41	0	17
LOUISIANA STATE UNIV	178	4	5	9	8	10	25	3	22	0	28	0	2	1	17	0	28	16
LOYOLA UNIV CHICAGO	433	8	4	26	0	3	27	0	43	1	122	2	0	1	52	0	144	0
MARYWOOD UNIV	391	13	18	21	13	9	37	19	36	3	53	4	6	5	20	18	0	116
MICHIGAN STATE UNIV	205	4	4	16	1	7	13	0	10	0	30	0	1	0	22	17	1	79
NEW MEXICO HIGHLANDS	233	2	5	23	4	9	24	0	16	0	21	0	0	0	13	0	0	116

TABLE 207

Master's Degree Students, by Primary Field of Practice in Field Instruction

Program	Total	Aging/Gerontological Social Work	Alcohol, Drug or Substance Abuse	Child Welfare	Community Planning	Corrections/Criminal Justice	Family Services	Group Services	Health	Occupational/Industrial Social Work	Mental Health or Commnity Mental Health	Mental Retardation	Public Assist/Public Welfare	Rehabilitation	School Social Work	Other Fields of Practice or Social Problems	Not Yet Assigned	Not in Field Instruction
NEW MEXICO STATE	88	3	2	17	0	5	19	0	7	0	24	0	0	1	9	1	0	0
NEW YORK UNIV	983	33	32	50	0	13	120	0	62	7	266	8	1	6	76	6	0	303
OHIO STATE UNIV	397	10	2	9	2	5	35	0	18	0	34	1	0	0	18	89	174	0
OUR LADY OF LAKE	*	*	*	*	*	*	*	*	*	*	*	*	*	*	*	*	*	*
PORTLAND STATE UNIV	317	15	10	58	2	26	27	0	17	0	81	2	0	0	29	11	1	38
RADFORD UNIV	108	2	0	1	0	2	40	0	7	0	34	0	13	0	4	0	0	5
RHODE ISLAND COLL	157	5	7	12	9	7	18	0	7	0	23	5	7	4	9	7	0	37
RUTGERS UNIV/NB	690	24	24	27	20	29	81	2	44	1	123	5	5	9	75	16	0	205
SALEM STATE COLL	203	14	2	19	5	2	8	4	3	0	24	2	0	5	8	6	37	64
SAN DIEGO STATE UNIV	334	18	18	59	9	14	22	6	25	2	46	10	0	13	18	18	40	16
SAN FRANCISCO STATE	*	*	*	*	*	*	*	*	*	*	*	*	*	*	*	*	*	*
SAVANNAH STATE UNIV	41	0	0	1	1	1	1	1	6	0	5	0	0	0	3	1	21	0
SIMMONS COLL	279	10	6	12	0	8	10	0	33	0	58	0	2	5	51	61	12	11
SMITH COLL	229	4	3	3	0	3	19	0	9	0	163	0	0	0	23	2	0	0
SOUTHERN CONNECTICUT	195	8	14	7	10	1	20	2	12	0	14	0	0	1	15	3	0	88
SOUTHERN ILL/CAR	55	1	2	11	0	1	7	0	3	0	13	0	0	0	10	0	2	5
SOUTHERN UNIV	256	9	0	25	0	0	0	0	14	38	0	0	0	0	0	113	0	57
SOUTHWEST MISSOURI	66	2	8	15	1	6	5	1	3	0	11	1	1	1	10	1	0	0
SOUTHWEST TEXAS	*	*	*	*	*	*	*	*	*	*	*	*	*	*	*	*	*	*
ST AMBROSE UNIV	66	2	0	6	4	2	6	2	10	2	8	1	2	2	8	1	0	10
ST LOUIS UNIV	294	6	0	4	8	5	19	0	16	0	36	0	0	2	24	5	0	169
SUNY/ALBANY	360	33	23	41	3	5	27	21	24	1	59	4	12	6	46	7	0	48
SUNY/BUFFALO	395	16	18	31	0	10	42	0	17	1	54	7	0	6	38	26	58	71
SYRACUSE UNIV	277	13	14	29	4	7	17	0	17	5	60	2	1	0	16	0	45	47
TEMPLE UNIV	470	28	6	72	7	21	10	1	33	0	61	8	0	3	32	32	0	156
TULANE UNIV	168	2	1	4	0	3	13	0	13	0	26	1	0	1	7	9	88	0
U OF ALABAMA	188	7	1	23	8	16	14	8	19	3	28	1	0	4	7	0	49	0
U OF ALASKA/ANK	42	1	1	3	0	1	8	0	2	0	8	0	0	0	0	5	0	13
U OF ARKANSAS/LR	166	10	3	8	0	8	22	0	22	0	39	0	2	0	8	5	0	39
U OF CALIFORNIA/BERK	183	23	0	81	0	0	0	0	36	0	43	0	0	0	0	2	0	0
U OF CENTRAL FLORIDA	209	4	6	8	0	3	19	0	17	0	10	0	0	0	7	2	133	0
U OF CHICAGO	354	18	10	61	11	17	29	4	28	1	68	2	10	4	45	16	16	14
U OF CINCINNATI	195	3	4	24	4	2	9	0	15	0	14	0	2	2	0	0	55	61
U OF CONNECTICUT	389	14	14	25	24	21	43	24	26	0	32	0	13	3	33	11	0	106
U OF DENVER	308	13	3	49	6	17	60	7	24	1	50	0	1	3	36	2	20	16
U OF GEORGIA	239	4	5	4	4	10	24	4	16	2	6	4	11	2	24	2	94	23
U OF HAWAII	204	13	1	17	4	6	30	0	29	0	25	0	0	0	3	16	15	45
U OF HOUSTON	283	13	0	8	6	1	6	0	18	0	14	0	1	0	6	9	85	116
U OF ILLINOIS/CHI	466	8	5	26	14	3	71	0	17	0	56	2	2	0	89	0	87	86
U OF ILLINOIS/URB	295	0	0	18	0	0	0	0	11	1	32	0	0	1	50	0	29	155
U OF IOWA	204	1	1	5	3	1	16	4	10	2	8	1	0	1	9	2	142	0
U OF KANSAS	413	16	5	24	2	3	137	0	33	0	75	0	1	0	8	2	0	107
U OF KENTUCKY	251	6	15	20	7	10	12	14	7	0	30	1	3	5	2	0	119	0
U OF LOUISVILLE	317	9	8	45	11	8	39	0	18	0	61	6	0	0	23	0	6	83

TABLE 207

Master's Degree Students, by Primary Field of Practice in Field Instruction

Program	Total	Aging/ Gerontological Social Work	Alcohol, Drug or Substance Abuse	Child Welfare	Community Planning	Corrections/ Criminal Justice	Family Services	Group Services	Health	Occupational/ Industrial Social Work	Mental Health or Comm'ity Mental Health	Mental Retardation	Public Assist/ Public Welfare	Rehabilitation	School Social Work	Other Fields of Practice or Social Problems	Not Yet Assigned	Not in Field Instruction
U OF MARYLAND	865	21	12	140	18	0	0	0	42	31	105	0	0	0	0	3	308	185
U OF MICHIGAN	580	24	35	42	51	14	53	0	44	0	92	5	2	0	46	0	148	24
U OF MINNESOTA/DUL	88	1	1	13	3	0	6	0	2	0	2	0	0	0	5	0	15	40
U OF MINNESOTA/TC	264	8	1	29	0	2	18	0	10	0	17	1	0	0	19	8	0	151
U OF MISSOURI/COL	175	4	5	19	9	3	17	0	21	0	18	3	0	3	9	2	21	41
U OF NCGB/NCSU	65	0	0	19	0	0	0	0	4	0	7	0	0	0	0	0	35	0
U OF NEBRASKA/OMA	178	3	0	1	1	1	15	0	4	0	14	0	0	0	3	0	113	23
U OF NEVADA/LV	140	3	6	11	10	6	7	4	7	0	10	0	4	0	15	4	0	53
U OF NEVADA/REN	35	0	0	0	0	0	0	0	0	0	0	0	0	0	0	35	0	0
U OF NEW HAMPSHIRE	136	4	1	0	3	0	24	5	16	0	12	0	0	1	21	4	0	43
U OF NORTH CAR/CH	293	10	8	23	10	2	16	0	40	1	60	0	2	2	22	19	31	47
U OF NORTH DAKOTA	*	*	*	*	*	*	*	*	*	*	*	*	*	*	*	*	*	*
U OF OKLAHOMA	173	3	1	0	1	0	6	1	1	0	4	0	0	0	0	0	83	73
U OF PENNSYLVANIA	300	13	12	61	9	7	25	12	30	3	52	5	0	4	35	0	32	0
U OF PITTSBURGH	502	18	16	11	8	10	24	1	28	0	75	4	2	4	20	14	212	55
U OF PUERTO RICO/RP	145	0	0	6	10	2	10	0	6	2	7	0	0	0	4	0	43	55
U OF SOUTH CAROLINA	455	21	10	30	21	16	21	35	64	0	64	0	0	5	50	0	23	95
U OF SOUTH FLORIDA	122	1	2	16	0	0	9	0	25	0	20	0	0	0	11	6	32	0
U OF SOUTHERN CAL	485	20	10	25	26	18	97	39	17	10	74	2	16	8	33	0	90	0
U OF SOUTHERN IND	82	0	1	2	0	1	4	0	2	0	12	0	0	2	10	0	29	19
U OF SOUTHERN MISS	127	6	3	10	5	1	7	3	12	0	10	1	0	1	2	3	45	18
U OF TENNESSEE/KNX	388	17	11	42	8	14	31	3	47	2	99	1	4	1	28	16	0	64
U OF TEXAS/ARL	524	0	0	14	5	5	48	0	20	0	20	0	0	0	13	0	153	246
U OF TEXAS/AUS	294	3	0	13	0	20	5	4	22	0	11	2	0	3	19	0	149	43
U OF UTAH	285	10	12	21	1	17	44	0	27	0	106	2	6	0	29	0	9	1
U OF VERMONT	67	1	2	9	0	2	11	0	8	0	4	1	2	0	4	0	2	21
U OF WASHINGTON	328	11	7	21	14	15	29	0	53	0	43	0	3	1	22	42	13	54
U OF WISCONSIN/MAD	183	8	13	15	10	5	10	0	12	0	19	9	15	0	21	8	35	3
U OF WISCONSIN/MIL	318	6	7	52	4	12	9	0	17	1	49	0	2	0	31	0	16	112
U OF WYOMING	*	*	*	*	*	*	*	*	*	*	*	*	*	*	*	*	*	*
VALDOSTA STATE UNIV	81	3	2	15	0	5	0	0	6	3	20	0	1	0	15	3	0	8
VIRGINIA COMMONWEAL	548	23	7	27	7	12	36	11	49	2	84	9	14	5	35	41	8	178
WALLA WALLA COLL	179	2	7	26	0	8	35	3	19	0	27	3	2	5	8	4	27	3
WASHBURN UNIV	116	1	2	10	0	2	5	0	14	0	17	0	0	0	11	2	23	29
WASHINGTON UNIV	414	7	3	6	17	7	27	6	30	0	48	1	2	5	26	39	190	0
WAYNE STATE UNIV	559	5	2	72	22	3	44	10	29	0	118	2	0	0	107	1	100	44
WEST VIRGINIA UNIV	267	0	1	8	7	0	6	0	13	0	25	2	0	0	3	2	0	200
WIDENER UNIV	181	3	4	11	0	2	14	0	20	1	37	3	0	0	12	3	0	71
YESHIVA UNIV	374	28	16	49	20	2	39	15	19	1	62	4	7	1	8	19	0	84

*Missing data

TABLE 208

Full-time Master's Students Receiving Financial Aid Not Tied to Current Field Instruction, by Source of Funds

Program	Total Full-time Students	Child Welfare	Office of Aging	NIAAA	NIDA	NIMH	VA	FCWSP	Other	State or Local Gov't	Veterans Benefits	Social Welfare Agencies	Founda-tions or Other	School or University	Foreign Gov't	Formal Loan Programs	Work Study	Research or Graduate Assists	Other	Total From All Sources
TOTAL:	20,369	596	1	3	2	0	15	1,166	408	812	74	187	664	5,542	612	9,660	416	964	366	21,488
ADELPHI UNIV	284	0	0	0	0	0	0	0	0	0	0	0	0	237	0	0	0	0	0	237
ALABAMA A&M UNIV	45	6	0	0	0	0	1	0	5	0	0	0	0	0	0	25	0	4	0	41
ANDREWS UNIV	34	0	0	0	0	0	0	0	1	19	0	0	11	14	0	28	2	0	0	75
ARIZONA STATE UNIV	272	0	0	0	0	0	0	7	5	0	3	0	8	45	0	143	0	0	0	211
AUGSBURG COLL	46	0	0	0	0	0	0	0	0	1	0	0	1	6	0	48	0	0	0	56
BARRY UNIV	164	0	0	0	0	0	0	0	0	19	0	0	0	120	0	128	0	5	0	272
BOISE STATE UNIV	28	0	0	0	0	0	0	0	0	0	0	0	0	0	0	13	0	5	1	19
BOSTON COLL	301	0	0	0	0	0	0	120	0	0	0	0	0	86	0	409	2	37	0	654
BOSTON UNIV	188	0	0	0	0	0	0	29	71	0	0	0	0	109	0	0	0	0	0	209
BRIGHAM YOUNG/UT	78	0	0	0	0	0	0	0	0	0	0	2	0	3	0	0	0	19	0	24
BRYN MAWR COLL	125	0	0	0	0	0	0	0	0	8	0	0	2	101	0	77	0	0	0	188
CAL STATE UNIV/FRES	141	40	0	0	0	0	0	0	113	0	0	0	0	51	0	0	0	0	45	249
CAL STATE UNIV/LB	138	0	0	0	0	0	0	0	0	0	0	0	0	0	0	0	0	0	0	0
CAL STATE UNIV/SB	86	*	*	*	*	*	*	*	*	*	*	*	*	*	*	*	*	*	*	*
CAL STATE UNIV/STAN	59	27	0	0	0	0	0	0	0	0	0	0	1	12	0	18	0	0	0	58
CASE WESTERN RESERVE	285	0	0	0	0	0	1	0	0	2	1	17	0	218	3	240	150	0	0	631
CATHOLIC UNIV/DC	82	0	0	0	0	0	0	0	2	0	0	0	2	36	0	70	0	0	1	111
CLARK ATLANTA UNIV	86	0	0	0	0	0	0	0	0	0	0	0	0	41	0	69	0	0	2	112
CLEVE ST U/U AKRON	39	0	0	0	0	0	0	0	0	3	0	1	0	13	0	0	0	8	0	25
COLL ST CAT/U ST THO	124	0	0	0	0	0	0	0	0	0	0	0	0	10	0	91	6	14	0	121
COLORADO STATE UNIV	62	0	0	0	0	0	0	0	0	0	0	0	0	0	0	0	8	0	0	8
COLUMBIA UNIV	666	0	0	0	0	0	0	0	0	53	0	0	0	281	0	1183	0	0	47	1564
DELAWARE STATE UNIV	84	0	0	0	0	0	0	0	0	0	0	0	0	0	0	0	0	5	0	5
EAST CAROLINA UNIV	94	0	0	0	0	0	0	1	0	1	0	0	0	49	0	73	0	18	2	145
EASTERN MICHIGAN	23	0	0	0	0	0	0	0	0	0	0	0	0	0	0	11	0	7	0	18
FLORIDA INTERNATL	124	0	0	0	0	0	0	14	0	107	0	0	0	190	169	0	0	0	0	480
FLORIDA STATE UNIV	121	0	0	0	0	0	0	0	0	2	0	0	0	0	0	0	0	32	0	34
FORDHAM UNIV	934	0	0	0	0	0	0	0	0	0	0	0	0	0	0	0	0	0	0	0
GALLAUDET UNIV	41	0	0	0	0	0	0	12	11	1	0	0	16	12	8	22	0	1	0	83
GRAMBLING STATE UNIV	32	0	0	0	0	0	0	0	0	0	0	0	0	0	0	20	0	4	0	24
GRAND VALLEY STATE	138	0	0	0	0	0	0	1	0	3	0	0	1	5	0	120	0	23	3	156
HOWARD UNIV	257	0	1	0	0	0	0	0	8	9	0	1	0	46	0	120	0	32	0	217
HUNTER COLL	406	0	0	0	0	0	0	0	0	3	0	0	195	0	0	0	0	0	0	198
INDIANA UNIV	260	0	0	0	0	0	2	4	0	4	0	4	1	48	0	286	0	4	0	355
INTERAMERICAN/MET	78	*	*	*	*	*	*	*	*	*	*	*	*	*	*	*	*	*	*	*
JACKSON STATE UNIV	41	0	0	0	0	0	0	0	0	0	0	0	0	11	0	0	0	1	1	13
KEAN UNIV	66	0	0	0	0	0	0	4	0	0	0	0	0	0	0	43	0	17	0	64
LOMA LINDA UNIV	37	19	0	0	0	0	0	16	0	0	0	0	0	5	0	0	0	0	0	40
LOUISIANA STATE UNIV	154	0	0	0	0	0	0	0	0	9	0	0	6	6	0	75	0	25	0	121
LOYOLA UNIV CHICAGO	188	0	0	0	0	0	0	0	0	0	0	0	2	12	0	0	0	0	18	32
MARYWOOD UNIV	88	6	0	0	0	0	1	0	0	0	4	0	0	37	0	60	0	2	2	112
MICHIGAN STATE UNIV	126	0	0	0	0	0	0	0	0	0	0	0	0	27	0	0	24	7	0	58
NEW MEXICO HIGHLANDS	92	0	0	0	0	0	0	0	0	0	0	0	0	0	0	67	0	0	0	67

TABLE 208

Full-time Master's Students Receiving Financial Aid Not Tied to Current Field Instruction, by Source of Funds

Program	Total Full-time Students	Public Funds — Federal Govt: Child Welfare	Office of Aging	NIAAA	NIDA	NIMH	VA	FCWSP	Other	State or Local Govt	Veterans Benefits	Voluntary Funds: Social Welfare Agencies	Foundations or Other	School or University	Foreign Govt	Formal Loan Programs	Work Study	Research or Graduate Assists	Other	Total From All Sources
NEW MEXICO STATE	42	10	0	0	0	0	0	0	0	1	5	0	0	0	0	18	0	8	0	42
NEW YORK UNIV	589	0	0	0	0	0	0	28	5	52	0	0	14	443	0	629	0	0	5	1176
OHIO STATE UNIV	194	0	0	0	0	0	0	0	21	3	0	0	3	48	2	0	0	0	40	114
OUR LADY OF LAKE	92	0	0	0	0	0	0	0	4	46	8	0	3	6	0	87	1	0	0	155
PORTLAND STATE UNIV	216	0	0	0	0	0	0	0	0	0	0	0	0	0	0	0	0	0	0	0
RADFORD UNIV	53	0	0	0	0	0	0	3	0	0	0	18	8	3	0	122	12	13	0	179
RHODE ISLAND COLL	91	0	0	0	0	0	0	22	0	0	0	0	0	0	0	0	0	10	0	32
RUTGERS UNIV/NB	271	0	0	0	0	0	0	0	0	0	0	0	0	0	0	0	0	0	0	0
SALEM STATE COLL	48	0	0	0	0	0	0	3	0	6	0	0	0	5	0	25	0	4	0	43
SAN DIEGO STATE UNIV	238	33	0	3	0	0	0	0	11	7	3	0	2	15	1	117	0	9	6	207
SAN FRANCISCO STATE	123	43	0	0	0	0	0	0	0	0	0	0	0	0	0	0	0	0	0	43
SAVANNAH STATE UNIV	41	0	0	0	0	0	0	0	0	0	1	0	1	4	14	0	0	2	0	22
SIMMONS COLL	213	0	0	0	0	0	0	99	0	0	0	0	6	119	0	200	0	0	0	424
SMITH COLL	229	0	0	0	0	0	0	0	0	0	0	0	0	99	0	89	0	4	0	188
SOUTHERN CONNECTICUT	133	15	0	0	0	0	0	0	0	0	0	1	0	0	0	45	0	4	1	64
SOUTHERN ILL/CAR	40	0	0	0	0	0	0	0	1	1	0	0	0	1	0	10	0	4	0	19
SOUTHERN UNIV	152	0	0	0	0	0	0	0	0	0	0	0	0	0	0	0	0	0	0	0
SOUTHWEST MISSOURI	36	0	0	0	0	0	0	0	0	0	0	0	0	0	0	0	0	4	0	4
SOUTHWEST TEXAS	45	0	0	0	0	0	0	0	0	0	0	0	0	0	0	34	0	6	0	34
ST AMBROSE UNIV	32	0	0	0	0	0	0	0	0	0	0	0	0	5	0	66	1	6	0	77
ST LOUIS UNIV	148	0	0	0	0	0	0	0	0	0	0	2	0	133	0	0	0	0	0	136
SUNY/ALBANY	263	0	0	0	0	0	0	0	0	72	0	0	0	0	0	0	0	0	0	72
SUNY/BUFFALO	168	1	0	0	0	0	0	2	1	3	2	0	0	5	0	25	0	3	4	44
SYRACUSE UNIV	86	0	0	0	0	0	1	1	4	33	2	0	0	0	0	86	0	36	12	175
TEMPLE UNIV	129	0	0	0	0	0	0	6	0	0	0	0	0	25	0	0	0	0	0	31
TULANE UNIV	150	0	0	0	0	0	0	64	0	0	0	0	0	53	0	130	0	0	17	264
U OF ALABAMA	146	0	0	0	0	0	0	0	0	2	0	0	0	0	0	0	0	0	0	2
U OF ALASKA/ANK	27	0	0	0	0	0	0	0	0	0	0	0	0	0	0	0	0	2	6	8
U OF ARKANSAS/LR	120	2	0	0	0	0	0	0	0	0	0	0	0	6	0	37	0	6	0	51
U OF CALIFORNIA/BERK	183	0	0	0	0	0	0	25	3	35	0	1	5	54	0	111	1	31	0	265
U OF CENTRAL FLORIDA	106	0	0	0	0	0	0	0	0	0	0	0	0	23	0	90	1	16	0	130
U OF CHICAGO	251	0	0	0	0	0	0	0	0	2	0	0	93	224	0	230	0	0	0	549
U OF CINCINNATI	125	0	0	0	0	0	0	63	0	15	0	0	0	67	0	0	0	5	0	87
U OF CONNECTICUT	207	0	0	0	0	0	0	22	3	0	6	0	6	191	0	260	0	2	25	556
U OF DENVER	244	25	0	0	0	0	0	0	0	35	1	0	10	234	0	288	2	25	0	615
U OF GEORGIA	152	0	0	0	0	0	0	0	0	0	0	0	1	2	0	0	2	2	0	30
U OF HAWAII	118	15	0	0	0	0	1	0	1	1	0	0	2	12	0	8	0	0	2	44
U OF HOUSTON	124	4	0	0	0	0	0	0	0	0	0	0	0	3	0	0	0	6	0	13
U OF ILLINOIS/CHI	292	0	0	0	0	0	0	0	0	0	0	0	5	22	0	185	69	21	0	302
U OF ILLINOIS/URB	224	0	0	0	0	0	0	0	2	0	2	0	0	24	0	112	0	42	0	194
U OF IOWA	87	0	0	0	0	0	0	0	0	0	0	0	0	0	0	41	2	12	0	55
U OF KANSAS	237	0	0	0	0	0	0	0	0	0	0	0	3	65	0	0	0	4	0	72
U OF KENTUCKY	59	0	0	0	0	0	0	0	0	21	0	0	7	18	0	0	0	5	0	51
U OF LOUISVILLE	259	0	0	0	0	0	0	0	0	0	0	55	0	0	0	0	0	0	0	55

TABLE 208

Full-time Master's Students Receiving Financial Aid Not Tied to Current Field Instruction, by Source of Funds

Program	Total Full-time Students	Public Funds										Voluntary Funds		School or University	Foreign Gov't	Formal Loan Programs	Work Study	Research or Graduate Assists	Other	Total From All Sources
		Federal Government								State or Local Gov't	Veterans Benefits	Social Welfare Agencies	Foundations or Other							
		Child Welfare	Office of Aging	NIAAA	NIDA	NIMH	VA	FCWSP	Other											
U OF MARYLAND	662	0	0	0	0	0	0	10	4	31	13	0	0	101	0	667	82	2	0	910
U OF MICHIGAN	554	0	0	0	0	0	0	149	4	1	3	6	14	315	1	399	30	37	4	963
U OF MINNESOTA/DUL	62	45	0	0	0	0	0	0	0	0	0	0	0	12	0	0	0	9	0	66
U OF MINNESOTA/TC	163	0	0	0	0	0	0	0	0	40	0	0	10	8	0	0	0	20	0	78
U OF MISSOURI/COL	81	16	0	0	0	0	0	0	3	0	0	0	1	17	0	12	4	23	3	79
U OF NCGB/NCSU	65	12	0	0	0	0	4	0	0	0	0	0	0	10	0	0	0	10	0	36
U OF NEBRASKA/OMA	95	0	0	0	0	0	0	0	0	0	0	2	2	41	0	31	0	0	2	78
U OF NEVADA/LV	70	8	0	0	0	0	0	35	0	0	0	0	0	0	0	0	0	0	0	43
U OF NEVADA/REN	34	6	0	0	0	0	0	0	0	0	0	0	0	0	0	0	0	7	0	13
U OF NEW HAMPSHIRE	90	0	0	0	0	0	0	0	0	0	0	0	0	0	0	0	0	6	4	10
U OF NORTH CAR/CH	187	0	0	0	0	0	0	3	0	0	0	0	0	112	0	92	0	26	35	268
U OF NORTH DAKOTA	58	0	0	0	0	0	2	2	0	8	0	1	0	3	0	13	0	0	3	32
U OF OKLAHOMA	100	7	0	0	0	0	0	0	44	17	2	0	0	18	0	0	0	6	0	94
U OF PENNSYLVANIA	194	23	0	0	0	0	0	60	0	0	1	0	8	0	0	252	0	2	0	346
U OF PITTSBURGH	308	38	0	0	0	0	0	0	0	0	0	0	1	77	0	2	0	4	0	120
U OF PUERTO RICO/RP	125	0	0	0	0	0	0	0	1	14	0	3	0	41	0	2	0	7	1	69
U OF SOUTH CAROLINA	323	0	0	0	0	0	0	5	19	3	11	4	5	22	0	38	0	60	0	167
U OF SOUTH FLORIDA	89	0	0	0	0	0	0	0	0	0	0	0	0	1	0	60	0	13	0	74
U OF SOUTHERN CAL	329	0	0	0	0	0	0	189	0	29	0	65	94	1	416	0	0	9	0	803
U OF SOUTHERN IND	45	2	0	0	0	0	0	0	1	0	0	0	4	0	0	34	0	4	0	41
U OF SOUTHERN MISS	49	0	0	0	0	0	0	10	0	0	0	0	0	21	0	34	0	0	0	69
U OF TENNESSEE/KNX	246	0	0	0	0	0	0	2	7	0	1	0	1	15	0	142	0	5	25	198
U OF TEXAS/ARL	297	51	0	0	0	0	0	0	0	0	0	0	0	15	0	0	0	19	0	85
U OF TEXAS/AUS	199	0	0	0	0	0	0	0	0	0	0	0	0	10	0	0	0	105	0	115
U OF UTAH	234	45	0	0	0	0	0	0	0	1	0	0	38	0	0	0	0	4	0	84
U OF VERMONT	39	0	0	0	0	0	0	15	24	0	0	2	2	0	0	1	0	4	4	46
U OF WASHINGTON	207	0	0	0	0	0	2	0	27	0	0	2	2	33	0	183	0	10	4	263
U OF WISCONSIN/MAD	183	20	0	0	0	0	0	0	0	0	0	0	0	24	0	0	0	1	0	45
U OF WISCONSIN/MIL	144	23	0	0	0	0	0	0	0	23	0	0	0	4	0	0	0	10	0	60
U OF WYOMING	38	*	*	*	*	*	*	*	*	*	*	*	*	*	*	*	*	*	*	*
VALDOSTA STATE UNIV	50	2	0	0	0	0	0	2	0	0	0	0	1	4	0	11	0	1	0	21
VIRGINIA COMMONWEAL	259	26	0	0	0	0	0	9	2	50	0	0	30	5	0	189	0	0	5	311
WALLA WALLA COLL	161	26	0	0	0	0	0	3	0	0	2	0	0	252	0	290	15	0	0	593
WASHBURN UNIV	63	0	0	0	0	0	0	0	0	0	2	0	0	4	0	43	4	0	0	53
WASHINGTON UNIV	351	0	0	0	0	0	0	126	0	4	0	7	7	328	6	265	0	0	0	736
WAYNE STATE UNIV	319	0	0	0	0	0	0	0	0	0	0	0	0	51	0	17	0	7	32	100
WEST VIRGINIA UNIV	127	0	0	0	0	0	0	0	0	0	0	0	0	24	0	0	0	7	0	31
WIDENER UNIV	65	0	0	0	0	0	0	0	0	0	0	0	1	7	0	61	0	2	0	71
YESHIVA UNIV	204	0	0	0	0	0	0	0	0	0	3	0	33	226	0	340	1	3	0	606

*Missing data

TABLE 209

Full-time Master's Students Receiving Financial Aid Paid Directly by Field Instruction Agency, by Source of Funds

Program	Total Full-time Students	Public Funds — Federal Government: Child Welfare	Office of Aging	NIAAA	NIDA	NIMH	VA	FCWSP	Other	State or Local Gov't	Veterans Benefits	Voluntary Funds: Social Welfare Agencies	Foundations or Other	School or University	Foreign Gov't	Formal Loan Programs	Work Study	Research or Graduate Assists	Other	Total From All Sources
TOTAL:	20,369	220	3	0	0	7	149	358	151	535	14	523	351	90	48	1	180	32	49	2,711
ADELPHI UNIV	284	0	0	0	0	0	0	0	0	0	0	0	0	0	0	0	0	0	0	0
ALABAMA A&M UNIV	45	0	0	0	0	0	0	0	0	0	0	0	0	0	0	0	0	0	2	2
ANDREWS UNIV	34	0	0	0	0	0	0	0	0	0	0	0	0	0	0	0	0	0	0	0
ARIZONA STATE UNIV	272	0	0	0	0	0	7	48	0	0	0	4	1	0	0	0	0	0	0	60
AUGSBURG COLL	46	0	0	0	0	0	0	0	0	0	0	0	0	0	0	0	0	0	0	0
BARRY UNIV	164	0	0	0	0	0	0	0	0	0	0	0	33	0	0	0	0	0	0	33
BOISE STATE UNIV	28	0	0	0	0	0	3	0	0	0	0	5	0	0	0	0	0	0	0	8
BOSTON COLL	301	0	0	0	0	0	0	0	0	2	0	0	0	0	0	0	0	0	0	2
BOSTON UNIV	188	0	0	0	0	0	0	0	0	0	0	0	0	0	0	0	0	0	0	0
BRIGHAM YOUNG/UT	78	1	0	0	0	0	1	0	0	18	0	19	0	0	0	0	0	0	0	39
BRYN MAWR COLL	125	0	0	0	0	0	0	0	0	0	0	0	0	0	0	0	0	0	0	0
CAL STATE UNIV/FRES	141	0	0	0	0	0	0	0	0	9	0	0	0	0	0	0	0	0	0	9
CAL STATE UNIV/LB	138	24	2	0	0	0	2	0	3	15	0	8	3	0	0	0	0	0	0	57
CAL STATE UNIV/SB	86	0	0	0	0	0	2	0	0	47	0	22	0	0	0	0	0	0	0	71
CAL STATE UNIV/STAN	59	0	0	0	0	0	0	0	4	0	0	0	0	0	0	0	0	0	0	4
CASE WESTERN RESERVE	285	0	0	0	0	0	0	0	0	0	0	0	0	0	0	0	0	0	0	0
CATHOLIC UNIV/DC	82	0	0	0	0	0	0	0	0	0	0	0	0	0	0	0	0	0	0	0
CLARK ATLANTA UNIV	86	0	0	0	0	0	2	0	0	0	0	5	0	0	0	0	0	0	7	14
CLEVE ST U/U AKRON	39	0	0	0	0	0	0	0	0	0	0	0	0	0	0	0	0	0	0	0
COLL ST CAT/U ST THO	124	0	0	0	0	0	0	0	0	0	0	0	0	0	0	0	0	0	0	0
COLORADO STATE UNIV	62	0	0	0	0	0	0	0	7	0	0	0	0	0	0	0	0	0	0	7
COLUMBIA UNIV	666	0	0	0	0	0	0	275	0	0	0	33	0	0	0	0	0	0	0	308
DELAWARE STATE UNIV	84	0	0	0	0	0	0	0	0	0	0	0	0	0	0	0	0	3	0	3
EAST CAROLINA UNIV	94	9	0	0	0	3	0	0	0	0	0	0	0	0	0	0	0	0	0	12
EASTERN MICHIGAN	23	0	0	0	0	0	0	0	0	0	0	0	0	0	0	0	0	0	0	0
FLORIDA INTERNATL	124	0	0	0	0	0	0	0	0	0	0	0	0	0	0	0	0	0	0	0
FLORIDA STATE UNIV	121	0	0	0	0	0	0	0	0	2	0	0	0	0	0	0	0	0	0	2
FORDHAM UNIV	934	0	0	0	0	0	0	0	0	0	0	0	0	0	0	0	0	0	0	0
GALLAUDET UNIV	41	0	0	0	0	0	0	1	0	0	0	0	0	0	0	0	0	0	0	1
GRAMBLING STATE UNIV	32	4	0	0	0	0	0	0	0	0	0	0	0	0	0	0	0	0	0	4
GRAND VALLEY STATE	138	0	0	0	0	0	0	0	0	0	0	0	0	0	0	0	0	0	0	0
HOWARD UNIV	257	0	0	0	0	0	0	0	0	17	0	9	0	0	0	0	0	0	0	26
HUNTER COLL	406	0	0	0	0	0	0	0	0	90	0	49	0	0	0	0	0	0	0	139
INDIANA UNIV	260	0	0	0	0	0	8	0	0	0	0	0	0	0	0	0	0	0	0	8
INTERAMERICAN/MET	78	*	*	*	*	*	*	*	*	*	*	*	*	*	*	*	*	*	*	*
JACKSON STATE UNIV	41	0	0	0	0	0	2	0	0	15	0	0	0	0	0	0	0	0	0	17
KEAN UNIV	66	0	0	0	0	0	0	0	0	0	0	0	0	0	0	0	0	0	0	0
LOMA LINDA UNIV	37	0	0	0	0	0	1	0	0	7	0	0	0	0	0	0	0	0	18	26
LOUISIANA STATE UNIV	154	6	0	0	0	0	4	14	0	0	0	0	0	0	0	0	0	5	0	29
LOYOLA UNIV CHICAGO	188	11	0	0	0	4	0	0	52	0	0	0	0	0	0	0	0	0	0	67
MARYWOOD UNIV	88	0	0	0	0	0	0	0	0	0	0	0	0	0	0	0	0	0	0	0
MICHIGAN STATE UNIV	126	0	0	0	0	0	0	0	0	0	0	0	0	0	0	0	0	0	0	0
NEW MEXICO HIGHLANDS	92	17	0	0	0	0	4	0	0	0	1	0	0	0	0	0	0	6	4	32

TABLE 209

Full-time Master's Students Receiving Financial Aid Paid Directly by Field Instruction Agency, by Source of Funds

Program	Total Full-time Students	Child Welfare	Office of Aging	NIAAA	NIDA	NIMH	VA	FCWSP	Other (Federal)	State or Local Gov't	Veterans Benefits	Social Welfare Agencies	Foundations or Other	School or University	Foreign Gov't	Formal Loan Programs	Work Study	Research or Graduate Assists	Other	Total From All Sources
NEW MEXICO STATE	42	0	0	0	0	0	0	0	0	0	0	0	0	0	0	0	0	0	0	0
NEW YORK UNIV	589	0	0	0	0	0	0	0	0	0	0	0	0	0	0	0	0	0	0	0
OHIO STATE UNIV	194	0	0	0	0	0	0	0	0	0	4	14	0	0	0	0	11	0	0	29
OUR LADY OF LAKE	92	0	0	0	0	0	0	0	0	0	0	0	0	0	0	0	0	0	0	0
PORTLAND STATE UNIV	216	0	0	0	0	0	0	0	0	0	0	0	0	0	0	0	0	0	0	0
RADFORD UNIV	53	0	0	0	0	0	0	0	0	0	0	0	0	0	0	0	0	0	0	0
RHODE ISLAND COLL	91	0	0	0	0	0	1	0	0	0	0	0	4	0	0	0	0	0	3	8
RUTGERS UNIV/NB	271	0	0	0	0	0	0	0	0	0	0	0	0	0	0	0	0	0	0	0
SALEM STATE COLL	48	0	0	0	0	0	3	0	0	0	0	1	3	0	0	0	4	0	0	11
SAN DIEGO STATE UNIV	238	5	0	0	0	0	4	0	0	0	0	17	0	0	0	0	0	0	0	26
SAN FRANCISCO STATE	123	0	0	0	0	0	2	4	0	8	0	51	10	0	0	0	0	0	0	75
SAVANNAH STATE UNIV	41	0	0	0	0	0	0	0	0	0	0	0	0	0	0	0	0	0	0	0
SIMMONS COLL	213	0	0	0	0	0	0	0	0	0	0	0	0	0	0	0	0	0	0	0
SMITH COLL	229	0	0	0	0	0	0	0	0	0	0	0	16	0	0	0	0	0	0	16
SOUTHERN CONNECTICUT	133	0	0	0	0	0	0	0	0	0	0	0	0	0	0	0	0	0	0	0
SOUTHERN ILL/CAR	40	0	0	0	0	0	1	0	1	2	0	0	0	0	0	0	0	0	0	4
SOUTHERN UNIV	152	0	0	0	0	0	0	0	0	0	0	0	0	0	0	0	0	0	0	0
SOUTHWEST MISSOURI	36	2	0	0	0	0	0	0	0	0	0	0	0	0	0	0	0	0	0	2
SOUTHWEST TEXAS	45	0	0	0	0	0	0	0	0	0	0	0	0	0	0	0	0	0	0	0
ST AMBROSE UNIV	32	2	0	0	0	0	0	0	6	0	0	0	0	0	0	0	0	0	0	8
ST LOUIS UNIV	148	0	0	0	0	0	0	0	0	0	0	0	0	11	0	0	0	0	0	11
SUNY/ALBANY	263	0	0	0	0	0	5	0	0	3	0	2	0	0	0	0	0	0	0	10
SUNY/BUFFALO	168	0	0	0	0	0	0	0	0	0	0	0	0	0	0	1	0	0	1	2
SYRACUSE UNIV	86	0	0	0	0	0	6	0	13	0	0	0	0	0	0	1	44	0	1	65
TEMPLE UNIV	129	5	1	0	0	0	0	0	0	5	0	2	0	2	0	0	0	0	0	15
TULANE UNIV	150	0	0	0	0	0	0	0	0	0	0	0	0	0	0	0	0	0	0	0
U OF ALABAMA	146	0	0	0	0	0	0	0	0	16	0	0	0	0	0	0	0	0	0	16
U OF ALASKA/ANK	27	0	0	0	0	0	0	0	0	0	0	0	0	0	0	0	0	0	0	0
U OF ARKANSAS/LR	120	7	0	0	0	0	13	0	12	0	0	0	0	0	0	0	0	0	0	32
U OF CALIFORNIA/BERK	183	0	0	0	0	0	1	11	0	1	0	15	4	1	0	0	6	0	0	39
U OF CENTRAL FLORIDA	106	0	0	0	0	0	0	0	12	7	0	0	0	0	0	0	0	0	0	19
U OF CHICAGO	251	0	0	0	0	0	0	0	0	0	0	0	0	0	0	0	0	0	0	0
U OF CINCINNATI	125	0	0	0	0	0	0	0	0	0	0	2	0	0	0	0	0	0	0	2
U OF CONNECTICUT	207	0	0	0	0	0	0	0	0	0	0	0	0	0	0	0	0	0	0	0
U OF DENVER	244	0	0	0	0	0	5	0	0	0	0	24	1	15	0	0	0	0	0	45
U OF GEORGIA	152	0	0	0	0	0	0	0	0	0	0	0	0	0	0	0	0	0	0	0
U OF HAWAII	118	0	0	0	0	0	1	0	4	13	0	0	9	0	0	0	0	5	0	32
U OF HOUSTON	124	5	0	0	0	0	5	0	0	0	0	7	4	1	0	0	0	0	0	22
U OF ILLINOIS/CHI	292	0	0	0	0	0	0	0	0	0	0	0	114	0	0	0	0	0	0	114
U OF ILLINOIS/URB	224	0	0	0	0	0	2	0	0	4	0	7	0	49	0	0	0	0	0	62
U OF IOWA	87	*	*	*	*	*	*	*	*	*	*	*	*	*	*	*	*	*	*	*
U OF KANSAS	237	0	0	0	0	0	11	0	0	0	0	0	0	0	0	0	92	0	0	103
U OF KENTUCKY	59	0	0	0	0	0	0	0	0	0	0	0	0	0	0	0	0	0	0	0
U OF LOUISVILLE	259	0	0	0	0	0	0	0	0	0	0	0	0	0	0	0	0	0	0	0

TABLE 209

Full-time Master's Students Receiving Financial Aid Paid Directly by Field Instruction Agency, by Source of Funds

Program	Total Full-time Students	Public Funds — Federal Government								Public Funds — State or Local Gov't	Public Funds — Veterans Benefits	Voluntary Funds — Social Welfare Agencies	Voluntary Funds — Foundations or Other	School or University	Foreign Gov't	Formal Loan Programs	Work Study	Research or Graduate Assists	Other	Total From All Sources
		Child Welfare	Office of Aging	NIAAA	NIDA	NIMH	VA	FCWSP	Other											
U OF MARYLAND	662	5	0	0	0	0	0	0	0	103	5	55	0	0	0	0	0	0	2	170
U OF MICHIGAN	554	0	0	0	0	0	0	0	0	0	0	16	0	0	0	0	0	0	0	16
U OF MINNESOTA/DUL	62	*	*	*	*	*	*	*	*	*	*	*	*	*	*	*	*	*	*	*
U OF MINNESOTA/TC	163	0	0	0	0	0	0	0	0	0	0	9	0	2	0	0	0	0	0	11
U OF MISSOURI/COL	81	11	0	0	0	0	0	0	0	0	0	0	0	0	0	0	0	0	11	22
U OF NCGB/NCSU	65	0	0	0	0	0	0	0	0	0	0	0	0	0	0	0	0	0	0	0
U OF NEBRASKA/OMA	95	*	*	*	*	*	*	*	*	*	*	*	*	*	*	*	*	*	*	*
U OF NEVADA/LV	70	0	0	0	0	0	0	0	0	0	0	0	0	0	0	0	0	0	0	0
U OF NEVADA/REN	34	*	*	*	*	*	*	*	*	*	*	*	*	*	*	*	*	*	*	*
U OF NEW HAMPSHIRE	90	*	*	*	*	*	*	*	*	*	*	*	*	*	*	*	*	*	*	*
U OF NORTH CAR/CH	187	0	0	0	0	0	0	0	0	16	0	7	0	0	0	0	0	0	0	23
U OF NORTH DAKOTA	58	0	0	0	0	0	0	0	0	0	0	0	0	0	0	0	0	0	0	0
U OF OKLAHOMA	100	*	*	*	*	*	*	*	*	*	*	*	*	*	*	*	*	*	*	*
U OF PENNSYLVANIA	194	0	0	0	0	0	0	0	0	3	0	14	0	0	0	0	0	0	0	17
U OF PITTSBURGH	308	0	0	0	0	0	7	0	0	0	0	11	1	0	0	0	0	0	0	19
U OF PUERTO RICO/RP	125	0	0	0	0	0	0	0	1	0	4	0	0	0	0	0	0	0	0	5
U OF SOUTH CAROLINA	323	26	0	0	0	0	9	0	1	74	0	14	8	0	19	0	19	0	0	170
U OF SOUTH FLORIDA	89	0	0	0	0	0	5	0	0	0	0	4	1	0	0	0	0	0	0	10
U OF SOUTHERN CAL	329	0	0	0	0	0	8	5	0	20	0	0	0	0	0	0	0	0	0	33
U OF SOUTHERN IND	45	*	*	*	*	*	*	*	*	*	*	*	*	*	*	*	*	*	*	*
U OF SOUTHERN MISS	49	*	*	*	*	*	*	*	*	*	*	*	*	*	*	*	*	*	*	*
U OF TENNESSEE/KNX	246	0	0	0	0	0	4	0	0	0	0	7	0	0	0	0	0	0	0	7
U OF TEXAS/ARL	297	26	0	0	0	0	4	0	14	26	0	0	0	0	29	0	0	0	0	99
U OF TEXAS/AUS	199	0	0	0	0	0	0	0	0	0	0	17	0	0	0	0	0	0	0	17
U OF UTAH	234	0	0	0	0	0	1	0	2	1	0	0	128	0	0	0	0	0	0	129
U OF VERMONT	39	22	0	0	0	0	1	0	2	0	0	0	0	0	0	0	0	0	0	25
U OF WASHINGTON	207	0	0	0	0	0	0	0	0	0	0	0	0	0	0	0	0	0	0	0
U OF WISCONSIN/MAD	183	7	0	0	0	0	7	0	0	0	0	0	9	0	0	0	0	0	0	23
U OF WISCONSIN/MIL	144	0	0	0	0	0	5	5	0	0	0	0	0	0	0	0	0	0	0	5
U OF WYOMING	38	*	*	*	*	*	*	*	*	*	*	*	*	*	*	*	*	*	*	*
VALDOSTA STATE UNIV	50	2	0	0	0	0	0	0	0	0	0	0	0	0	0	0	0	0	0	2
VIRGINIA COMMONWEAL	259	0	0	0	0	0	6	0	0	0	0	0	0	0	0	0	0	0	0	6
WALLA WALLA COLL	161	*	*	*	*	*	*	*	*	*	*	*	*	*	*	*	*	*	*	*
WASHBURN UNIV	63	*	*	*	*	*	*	*	*	*	*	*	*	*	*	*	*	*	*	*
WASHINGTON UNIV	351	0	0	0	0	0	0	0	19	4	0	32	2	5	0	0	4	8	0	74
WAYNE STATE UNIV	319	0	0	0	0	0	0	0	0	0	0	18	0	5	0	0	0	5	0	18
WEST VIRGINIA UNIV	127	0	0	0	0	0	0	0	0	4	0	3	0	3	0	0	0	5	0	15
WIDENER UNIV	65	0	0	0	0	0	0	0	0	3	0	3	0	3	0	0	0	0	0	6
YESHIVA UNIV	204	23	0	0	0	0	1	0	0	0	0	17	0	0	0	0	0	0	0	41

* Missing data

TABLE 210

Unduplicated Count of Full-time Master's Degree Students Receiving Financial Aid From All Sources and Number of Grants Awarded

Program	Total Full-time Students	Students Receiving	Total Number of Grants Awarded	Program	Total Full-time Students	Students Receiving	Total Number of Grants Awarded
TOTAL:	20,369	11,040	24,199	ST LOUIS UNIV	148	131	147
				SUNY/ALBANY	263	72	82
ADELPHI UNIV	284	237	237				
ALABAMA A&M UNIV	45	*	43	SUNY/BUFFALO	168	46	46
ANDREWS UNIV	34	34	75	SYRACUSE UNIV	86	82	240
ARIZONA STATE UNIV	272	180	271	TEMPLE UNIV	129	46	46
AUGSBURG COLL	46	42	56	TULANE UNIV	150	127	264
				U OF ALABAMA	146	18	18
BARRY UNIV	164	*	305				
BOISE STATE UNIV	28	27	27	U OF ALASKA/ANK	27	8	8
BOSTON COLL	301	234	656	U OF ARKANSAS/LR	120	83	83
BOSTON UNIV	188	99	209	U OF CALIFORNIA/BERK	183	155	304
BRIGHAM YOUNG/UT	78	*	63	U OF CENTRAL FLORIDA	106	*	149
				U OF CHICAGO	251	249	549
BRYN MAWR COLL	125	107	188				
CAL STATE UNIV/FRES	141	110	258	U OF CINCINNATI	125	61	89
CAL STATE UNIV/LB	138	*	57	U OF CONNECTICUT	207	191	556
CAL STATE UNIV/SB	86	34	71	U OF DENVER	244	237	660
CAL STATE UNIV/STAN	59	36	62	U OF GEORGIA	152	30	30
				U OF HAWAII	118	56	76
CASE WESTERN RESERVE	285	240	631				
CATHOLIC UNIV/DC	82	72	111	U OF HOUSTON	124	25	35
CLARK ATLANTA UNIV	86	45	126	U OF ILLINOIS/CHI	292	*	416
CLEVE ST U/U AKRON	39	25	25	U OF ILLINOIS/URB	224	119	256
COLL ST CAT/U ST THO	124	95	121	U OF IOWA	87	3	55
				U OF KANSAS	237	83	175
COLORADO STATE UNIV	62	8	15				
COLUMBIA UNIV	666	508	1,872	U OF KENTUCKY	59	51	51
DELAWARE STATE UNIV	84	5	8	U OF LOUISVILLE	259	55	55
EAST CAROLINA UNIV	94	78	157	U OF MARYLAND	662	359	1,080
EASTERN MICHIGAN	23	14	18	U OF MICHIGAN	554	443	979
				U OF MINNESOTA/DUL	62	58	66
FLORIDA INTERNATL	124	101	480				
FLORIDA STATE UNIV	121	34	36	U OF MINNESOTA/TC	163	89	89
FORDHAM UNIV	934	*	0	U OF MISSOURI/COL	81	65	101
GALLAUDET UNIV	41	30	84	U OF NCGB/NCSU	65	36	36
GRAMBLING STATE UNIV	32	*	28	U OF NEBRASKA/OMA	95	72	78
				U OF NEVADA/LV	70	43	43
GRAND VALLEY STATE	138	101	156				
HOWARD UNIV	257	224	243	U OF NEVADA/REN	34	12	13
HUNTER COLL	406	245	337	U OF NEW HAMPSHIRE	90	10	10
INDIANA UNIV	260	*	363	U OF NORTH CAR/CH	107	107	291
INTERAMERICAN/MET	78	*	*	U OF NORTH DAKOTA	58	14	32
				U OF OKLAHOMA	100	48	94
JACKSON STATE UNIV	41	13	30				
KEAN UNIV	66	53	64	U OF PENNSYLVANIA	194	169	363
LOMA LINDA UNIV	37	18	66	U OF PITTSBURGH	308	83	139
LOUISIANA STATE UNIV	154	122	150	U OF PUERTO RICO/RP	125	68	74
LOYOLA UNIV CHICAGO	188	99	99	U OF SOUTH CAROLINA	323	*	337
				U OF SOUTH FLORIDA	89	71	84
MARYWOOD UNIV	88	67	112				
MICHIGAN STATE UNIV	126	43	58	U OF SOUTHERN CAL	329	293	836
NEW MEXICO HIGHLANDS	92	23	99	U OF SOUTHERN IND	45	36	41
NEW MEXICO STATE	42	42	42	U OF SOUTHERN MISS	49	41	69
NEW YORK UNIV	589	480	1,176	U OF TENNESSEE/KNX	246	149	205
				U OF TEXAS/ARL	297	182	184
OHIO STATE UNIV	184	143	143				
OUR LADY OF LAKE	92	91	155	U OF TEXAS/AUS	199	*	132
PORTLAND STATE UNIV	216	*	0	U OF UTAH	234	65	213
RADFORD UNIV	53	53	179	U OF VERMONT	39	37	71
RHODE ISLAND COLL	91	24	40	U OF WASHINGTON	207	183	263
				U OF WISCONSIN/MAD	183	25	68
RUTGERS UNIV/NB	271	232	0				
SALEM STATE COLL	48	30	54	U OF WISCONSIN/MIL	144	40	65
SAN DIEGO STATE UNIV	238	233	233	U OF WYOMING	38	*	*
SAN FRANCISCO STATE	123	41	118	VALDOSTA STATE UNIV	50	23	23
SAVANNAH STATE UNIV	41	20	22	VIRGINIA COMMONWEAL	259	193	317
				WALLA WALLA COLL	161	155	593
SIMMONS COLL	213	181	424				
SMITH COLL	229	111	204	WASHBURN UNIV	63	46	53
SOUTHERN CONNECTICUT	133	*	64	WASHINGTON UNIV	351	304	810
SOUTHERN ILL/CAR	40	18	23	WAYNE STATE UNIV	319	118	118
SOUTHERN UNIV	152	*	0	WEST VIRGINIA UNIV	127	46	46
				WIDENER UNIV	65	54	77
SOUTHWEST MISSOURI	36	4	6				
SOUTHWEST TEXAS	45	33	34	YESHIVA UNIV	204	204	647
ST AMBROSE UNIV	32	32	85	* Missing data			

99

TABLE 300

Number of Faculty Assigned 50 Percent or More Time to Social Work Program,
by Percentage of Time Assigned to Doctoral Program

Program	Percentage of Time to Doctoral Program				Total Number of Full-time Faculty
	0%	1% - 24%	25% - 49%	50% and Over	
TOTAL:					
Number	1,415	306	176	109	2,006
Percent	70.5%	15.3%	8.8%	5.4%	100.0%
ADELPHI UNIV	17	3	5	2	27
ARIZONA STATE UNIV	28	3	2	0	33
BARRY UNIV	18	8	2	1	29
BOSTON COLL	16	11	0	4	31
BOSTON UNIV	36	1	0	0	37
BRYN MAWR COLL	9	10	2	0	21
CASE WESTERN RESERVE	19	9	3	0	31
CATHOLIC UNIV/DC	11	0	2	4	17
CLARK ATLANTA UNIV	12	0	0	3	15
COLUMBIA UNIV	34	6	4	0	44
FLORIDA INTERNATL	19	0	2	3	24
FLORIDA STATE UNIV	26	1	7	4	38
HOWARD UNIV	6	13	3	1	23
HUNTER COLL	34	4	0	3	41
INDIANA UNIV	27	1	1	3	32
JACKSON STATE UNIV	10	0	2	4	16
LOUISIANA STATE UNIV	16	0	2	3	21
LOYOLA UNIV CHICAGO	22	9	2	0	33
MARYWOOD UNIV	27	0	0	0	27
MICHIGAN STATE UNIV	42	1	1	2	46
NEW YORK UNIV	37	13	3	7	60
OHIO STATE UNIV	24	0	6	1	31
PORTLAND STATE UNIV	23	6	1	0	30
RUTGERS UNIV/NB	23	1	5	1	30
SIMMONS COLL	18	4	2	1	25
SMITH COLL	5	5	2	3	15
SUNY/ALBANY	14	12	2	1	29
SUNY/BUFFALO	13	1	5	1	20
TULANE UNIV	10	6	0	2	18
U OF ALABAMA	23	0	2	3	28
U OF CALIFORNIA/BERK	18	1	12	0	31
U OF CHICAGO	18	11	0	0	29
U OF CONNECTICUT	30	0	0	0	30
U OF DENVER	24	5	4	0	33
U OF GEORGIA	19	4	5	1	29
U OF HAWAII	28	1	4	1	34
U OF HOUSTON	19	0	4	2	25
U OF ILLINOIS/CHI	25	3	4	1	33
U OF ILLINOIS/URB	12	2	5	0	19
U OF IOWA	13	1	3	0	17
U OF KANSAS	25	1	1	4	31
U OF KENTUCKY	39	1	2	2	44
U OF LOUISVILLE	14	3	2	1	20
U OF MARYLAND	80	4	2	2	88
U OF MICHIGAN	6	31	4	3	44
U OF MINNESOTA/TC	26	1	6	2	35
U OF MISSOURI/COL	23	1	0	1	25
U OF NORTH CAR/CH	71	7	2	0	80
U OF OKLAHOMA	19	0	0	0	19
U OF PENNSYLVANIA	23	6	0	5	34
U OF PITTSBURGH	21	9	1	2	33
U OF SOUTH CAROLINA	13	23	2	1	39
U OF TENNESSEE/KNX	29	0	3	4	36
U OF TEXAS/ARL	12	8	8	4	32
U OF TEXAS/AUS	40	0	0	7	47
U OF UTAH	15	7	0	2	24
U OF WASHINGTON	37	8	2	3	50
U OF WISCONSIN/MAD	6	9	9	0	24
VIRGINIA COMMONWEAL	21	8	6	2	37
WASHINGTON UNIV	6	14	11	1	32
WAYNE STATE UNIV	37	0	0	0	37
YESHIVA UNIV	27	9	6	1	43

TABLE 301

Full-time Doctoral Students Enrolled on 11/1/00, by Ethnicity

Program	Taking Coursework										Completed Coursework									
	African Amer	Amer Indian	Asian Amer	Chicano/ Mexican Amer	Puerto Rican	White	Other Minority	Foreign	Unk	Total	African Amer	Amer Indian	Asian Amer	Chicano/ Mexican Amer	Puerto Rican	White	Other Minority	Foreign	Unk	Total
TOTAL:																				
Number	119	13	31	12	6	444	17	98	9	749	69	3	16	13	6	349	7	56	11	530
Percent	15.9%	1.7%	4.1%	1.6%	0.8%	59.3%	2.3%	13.1%	1.2%	100.0%	13.0%	0.6%	3.0%	2.5%	1.1%	65.8%	1.3%	10.6%	2.1%	100.0%
ADELPHI UNIV	10	0	0	1	0	17	2	2	0	32	0	0	0	0	0	0	0	0	0	0
ARIZONA STATE UNIV	0	0	0	1	0	4	2	0	0	5	0	0	0	0	0	1	0	0	0	1
BARRY UNIV	0	0	0	0	0	0	0	0	0	0	0	0	0	0	0	0	0	0	0	0
BOSTON COLL	0	0	0	0	0	1	0	0	0	1	0	0	0	0	0	0	0	0	0	0
BOSTON UNIV	0	0	0	0	0	0	0	0	0	0	0	0	0	0	0	1	0	0	0	1
BRYN MAWR COLL	0	0	1	0	0	7	0	1	0	9	0	0	0	0	1	8	0	2	0	11
CASE WESTERN RESERVE	1	0	0	0	0	4	0	1	0	6	1	0	0	0	0	21	0	10	0	32
CATHOLIC UNIV/DC	3	0	0	1	0	9	1	1	0	15	6	0	0	1	1	24	0	0	0	32
COLUMBIA UNIV	2	1	7	0	2	19	1	0	0	32	4	0	8	2	0	24	5	7	0	50
FLORIDA INTERNATL	0	0	0	0	0	5	0	1	0	6	0	0	0	0	0	0	0	0	0	0
FORDHAM UNIV	4	0	2	1	0	19	0	1	0	27	9	0	0	2	0	27	0	0	0	38
HOWARD UNIV	13	0	0	0	0	1	0	1	0	15	0	0	0	0	0	0	0	0	0	0
HUNTER COLL	7	0	2	0	2	19	5	1	4	40	3	0	0	0	1	12	0	0	7	23
INDIANA UNIV	1	0	0	0	0	8	0	0	0	9	1	0	0	0	0	3	0	0	0	4
JACKSON STATE UNIV	10	0	1	0	0	3	0	0	0	14	13	0	0	0	0	2	0	0	0	15
LOMA LINDA UNIV	0	0	0	0	0	0	0	0	0	0	0	0	0	0	0	0	0	0	0	0
LOUISIANA STATE UNIV	0	0	1	0	0	2	0	0	0	3	0	0	0	0	0	1	0	0	0	1
LOYOLA UNIV CHICAGO	1	0	0	1	0	10	0	0	0	12	0	0	0	0	0	0	0	0	0	0
MARYWOOD UNIV	0	0	0	0	0	0	0	0	0	0	0	0	0	0	0	0	0	0	0	0
MICHIGAN STATE UNIV	2	0	0	0	0	3	0	0	0	5	0	0	0	0	0	5	0	0	0	5
NEW YORK UNIV	0	0	1	0	0	21	0	3	0	25	0	0	0	0	0	0	0	0	0	0
OHIO STATE UNIV	7	0	0	0	0	20	0	4	0	31	3	0	0	1	0	8	0	3	0	15
PORTLAND STATE UNIV	0	0	1	1	0	10	0	0	0	12	1	0	0	1	0	2	0	0	0	4
RUTGERS UNIV/NB	0	0	0	0	0	5	0	0	2	7	1	0	0	0	1	1	0	0	0	3
SIMMONS COLL	0	0	0	0	0	0	0	0	0	0	0	0	0	0	0	0	0	0	0	0
SMITH COLL	1	2	0	0	0	11	1	2	0	17	0	0	0	0	0	0	0	0	0	0
SUNY/ALBANY	3	0	1	0	0	9	1	2	0	16	0	0	0	0	0	0	0	0	0	0
SUNY/STONY BROOK	3	0	0	0	1	12	1	1	0	17	0	0	0	0	0	2	0	0	0	2
TULANE UNIV	1	0	0	0	0	7	1	0	0	9	0	0	0	0	0	0	0	0	0	0
U OF ALABAMA	1	1	0	0	0	5	0	3	0	10	2	0	0	0	0	3	1	3	0	8
U OF CHICAGO	5	0	1	0	0	14	2	2	0	23	3	1	1	1	0	38	0	3	0	47
U OF DENVER	1	0	1	0	0	8	0	4	0	14	0	0	0	0	0	0	0	0	0	0
U OF GEORGIA	4	0	0	0	0	20	1	4	0	29	1	0	0	0	0	13	0	2	0	16
U OF HAWAII	0	0	1	0	0	0	0	0	0	1	0	0	0	0	0	0	0	0	0	0
U OF ILLINOIS/CHI	3	0	1	0	1	8	0	1	0	14	5	0	2	0	0	11	1	2	0	21
U OF ILLINOIS/URB	2	0	0	0	0	4	0	6	0	12	0	0	0	0	0	1	0	2	0	3
U OF IOWA	0	0	0	0	0	8	0	1	0	9	0	0	0	0	0	1	0	1	0	2
U OF KANSAS	1	1	1	0	0	3	0	0	1	7	0	0	1	1	0	8	0	0	0	10
U OF KENTUCKY	0	0	0	0	0	4	0	0	0	4	0	0	0	0	0	0	0	0	0	0
U OF LOUISVILLE	0	1	0	0	0	9	0	1	0	11	0	0	0	0	0	3	0	0	0	3

TABLE 301

Full-time Doctoral Students Enrolled on 11/1/00, by Ethnicity

Program	Taking Coursework										Completed Coursework									
	African Amer	Amer Indian	Asian Amer	Chicano/ Mexican Amer	Puerto Rican	White	Other Minority	Foreign	Unk	Total	African Amer	Amer Indian	Asian Amer	Chicano/ Mexican Amer	Puerto Rican	White	Other Minority	Foreign	Unk	Total
U OF MARYLAND	5	0	3	0	0	6	0	0	0	14	1	0	0	0	0	21	0	0	0	22
U OF MINNESOTA/TC	0	0	0	0	0	5	0	5	0	10	1	0	1	0	0	3	0	1	0	6
U OF MISSOURI/COL	0	0	0	0	0	0	0	0	0	0	0	0	0	0	0	0	0	0	0	0
U OF PENNSYLVANIA	0	0	0	0	0	5	0	5	0	10	4	0	1	0	1	36	0	9	0	51
U OF PITTSBURGH	4	1	0	0	0	8	0	4	0	17	3	0	0	0	0	10	0	1	0	14
U OF SOUTH CAROLINA	6	0	0	0	0	3	0	4	0	13	0	0	0	0	0	0	0	0	0	0
U OF TENNESSEE/KNX	4	1	0	0	0	20	1	1	0	27	4	1	0	0	0	20	1	1	0	27
U OF TEXAS/AUS	2	0	1	3	0	13	0	11	0	30	1	0	0	3	0	13	0	0	0	17
U OF UTAH	3	1	0	3	0	24	0	1	0	32	0	0	0	1	0	6	0	0	0	7
U OF WASHINGTON	0	0	4	0	0	13	0	2	1	20	0	1	1	0	0	1	0	1	0	4
U OF WISCONSIN/MAD	1	2	2	0	0	19	1	7	0	32	2	0	0	0	0	7	0	0	4	13
VIRGINIA COMMONWEAL	2	0	0	0	0	6	0	1	1	10	0	0	0	0	0	0	0	0	0	0
WASHINGTON UNIV	6	2	0	0	0	13	0	14	0	35	0	0	1	0	1	12	0	8	0	22

* Missing data

102

TABLE 302

Full-time Doctoral Students Enrolled on 11/1/00, by Age and Gender

Program	Taking Coursework				Completed Coursework			
	Number		Mean Age		Number		Mean Age	
	Men	Women	Men	Women	Men	Women	Men	Women
TOTAL:								
Number	195	554	39.1	37.8	151	379	40.9	40.3
Percent	26.0%	74.0%			28.5%	71.5%		
ADELPHI UNIV	4	28	38	33	0	0	*	*
ARIZONA STATE UNIV	2	3	44	41	0	1	*	38
BARRY UNIV	0	0	*	*	0	0	*	*
BOSTON COLL	0	1	*	26	0	0	*	*
BOSTON UNIV	0	0	*	*	0	1	*	33
BRYN MAWR COLL	3	6	36	36	2	9	35	40
CASE WESTERN RESERVE	1	5	49	36	12	20	37	41
CATHOLIC UNIV/DC	5	10	37	36	10	22	42	54
COLUMBIA UNIV	8	24	32	30	17	33	*	*
FLORIDA INTERNATL	3	3	*	*	0	0	*	*
FORDHAM UNIV	4	23	32	35	8	30	36	37
HOWARD UNIV	4	11	36	34	0	0	*	*
HUNTER COLL	10	30	39	41	1	22	46	49
INDIANA UNIV	3	6	45	41	4	0	44	*
JACKSON STATE UNIV	4	10	47	45	5	10	43	42
LOMA LINDA UNIV	0	0	*	*	0	0	*	*
LOUISIANA STATE UNIV	1	2	52	42	0	1	*	31
LOYOLA UNIV CHICAGO	2	10	45	42	0	0	*	*
MARYWOOD UNIV	0	0	*	*	0	0	*	*
MICHIGAN STATE UNIV	2	3	37	41	1	4	47	51
NEW YORK UNIV	5	20	43	39	0	0	*	*
OHIO STATE UNIV	8	23	39	39	4	11	37	41
PORTLAND STATE UNIV	1	11	33	37	0	4	*	41
RUTGERS UNIV/NB	4	3	*	*	1	2	48	48
SIMMONS COLL	0	0	*	*	0	0	*	*
SMITH COLL	3	14	*	*	0	0	*	*
SUNY/ALBANY	2	14	46	39	0	0	*	*
SUNY/STONY BROOK	4	13	47	38	1	1	34	33
TULANE UNIV	3	6	38	41	0	0	*	*
U OF ALABAMA	6	4	41	36	0	8	*	33
U OF CHICAGO	8	15	*	*	12	35	*	*
U OF DENVER	2	12	31	41	0	0	*	*
U OF GEORGIA	5	24	38	38	8	8	42	38
U OF HAWAII	0	1	*	46	0	0	*	*
U OF ILLINOIS/CHI	2	12	36	36	6	15	48	45
U OF ILLINOIS/URB	2	10	40	36	2	1	33	37
U OF IOWA	5	4	40	44	0	2	*	34
U OF KANSAS	2	5	38	35	1	9	49	43
U OF KENTUCKY	2	2	40	45	0	0	*	*
U OF LOUISVILLE	4	7	48	44	0	3	*	*
U OF MARYLAND	1	13	*	*	7	15	*	*
U OF MINNESOTA/TC	1	9	36	35	1	5	38	40
U OF MISSOURI/COL	0	0	*	*	0	0	*	*
U OF PENNSYLVANIA	1	9	36	35	14	37	37	39
U OF PITTSBURGH	6	11	33	42	5	9	37	44
U OF SOUTH CAROLINA	2	11	35	36	0	0	*	*
U OF TENNESSEE/KNX	9	18	38	37	9	18	38	37
U OF TEXAS/AUS	5	25	35	35	4	13	46	45
U OF UTAH	11	21	38	40	1	6	31	43
U OF WASHINGTON	7	13	36	32	2	2	44	35
U OF WISCONSIN/MAD	14	18	36	33	4	9	45	39
VIRGINIA COMMONWEAL	3	7	39	36	0	0	*	*
WASHINGTON UNIV	11	24	35	32	9	13	44	38

* Missing data

103

TABLE 303

Applications for Admission to Doctoral Degree Programs During 2000, by Action Taken

Program	Completed Applications			Enrollment				
	Received	Received and Considered	Accepted	Accepted and Enrolled	Accepted in Prior Years	Newly Enrolled in 2000	Withdrawals by 11/1/00	Enrolled for the First Time on 11/1/00
TOTAL:	1,846	1,152	565	402	6	408	17	391
ADELPHI UNIV	25	25	10	12	0	12	1	11
ARIZONA STATE UNIV	12	12	6	4	0	4	0	4
BARRY UNIV	12	12	11	8	0	8	1	7
BOSTON COLL	23	23	12	7	1	8	1	7
BOSTON UNIV	0	0	0	0	0	0	0	0
BRYN MAWR COLL	15	15	10	8	0	8	0	8
CASE WESTERN RESERVE	670	33	11	11	0	11	0	11
CATHOLIC UNIV/DC	16	14	9	7	0	7	0	7
COLUMBIA UNIV	52	52	24	14	0	14	0	14
FLORIDA INTERNATL	11	11	6	5	0	5	0	5
FORDHAM UNIV	58	28	13	7	1	8	0	8
HOWARD UNIV	18	18	8	7	0	7	0	7
HUNTER COLL	53	53	15	15	0	15	1	14
INDIANA UNIV	11	8	4	4	0	4	0	4
JACKSON STATE UNIV	19	19	12	9	0	9	0	9
LOMA LINDA UNIV	6	6	3	3	0	3	3	0
LOUISIANA STATE UNIV	7	7	6	4	0	4	0	4
LOYOLA UNIV CHICAGO	8	8	7	6	0	6	0	6
MARYWOOD UNIV	7	7	4	4	0	4	0	4
MICHIGAN STATE UNIV	12	9	8	3	1	4	0	4
NEW YORK UNIV	38	35	23	18	0	18	0	18
OHIO STATE UNIV	25	25	16	10	0	10	0	10
PORTLAND STATE UNIV	24	24	10	10	0	10	0	10
RUTGERS UNIV/NB	13	9	5	5	0	5	0	5
SIMMONS COLL	15	15	12	10	0	10	0	10
SMITH COLL	17	17	10	8	0	8	0	8
SUNY/ALBANY	34	34	17	12	0	12	0	12
SUNY/STONY BROOK	21	21	9	6	0	6	0	6
TULANE UNIV	10	9	6	4	0	4	0	4
U OF ALABAMA	12	12	7	4	0	4	0	4
U OF CHICAGO	68	68	10	9	0	9	0	9
U OF DENVER	21	21	16	6	2	8	0	8
U OF GEORGIA	24	24	15	15	0	15	2	13
U OF HAWAII	5	5	4	1	0	1	0	1
U OF ILLINOIS/CHI	21	21	12	11	0	11	0	11
U OF ILLINOIS/URB	35	35	13	6	0	6	1	5
U OF IOWA	3	3	2	2	0	2	0	2
U OF KANSAS	7	7	5	5	0	5	0	5
U OF KENTUCKY	17	17	6	5	0	5	0	5
U OF LOUISVILLE	15	15	10	10	0	10	1	9
U OF MARYLAND	24	21	14	9	0	9	0	9
U OF MINNESOTA/TC	25	25	12	6	0	6	0	6
U OF MISSOURI/COL	13	13	3	1	0	1	0	1
U OF PENNSYLVANIA	41	38	10	9	0	9	0	9
U OF PITTSBURGH	38	34	16	10	0	10	0	10
U OF SOUTH CAROLINA	15	15	12	7	1	8	1	7
U OF TENNESSEE/KNX	10	10	6	5	0	5	5	0
U OF TEXAS/AUS	33	33	17	7	0	7	0	7
U OF UTAH	46	46	26	19	0	19	0	19
U OF WASHINGTON	34	34	11	4	0	4	0	4
U OF WISCONSIN/MAD	40	40	18	7	0	7	0	7
VIRGINIA COMMONWEAL	22	21	13	9	0	9	0	9
WASHINGTON UNIV	45	45	20	14	0	14	0	14

TABLE 400

Full-time Master's and Doctoral Students Enrolled in Social Work Programs**, 1991 through 2000

Program	1991	1992	1993	1994	1995	1996	1997	1998	1999	2000	% Change 99-00
TOTAL:	20,369	21,671	22,055	22,702	22,077	23,966	24,603	21,536	23,441	21,629	-7.7%
ADELPHI UNIV	491	576	597	535	497	450	367	308	309	316	2.3%
ALABAMA A & M UNIV	---	---	---	---	---	---	---	28	19	45	136.8%
ANDREWS UNIV	---	---	---	---	---	---	---	---	31	34	9.7%
ARIZONA STATE UNIV	186	231	282	291	349	383	413	384	309	278	-10.0%
AUGSBURG COLL	---	---	---	---	63	50	40	58	62	46	-25.8%
AURORA UNIV	61	90	88	81	68	104	105	160	144	*	*
BARRY UNIV	232	293	169	222	*	200	193	186	191	164	-14.1%
BOISE STATE UNIV	---	---	---	---	33	30	38	49	35	28	-20.0%
BOSTON COLL	297	345	357	379	391	432	418	367	352	302	-14.2%
BOSTON UNIV	291	316	314	352	344	334	323	318	258	189	-26.7%
BRIGHAM YOUNG/UT	45	45	42	50	61	68	71	71	76	78	2.6%
BRYN MAWR COLL	209	211	219	216	235	257	230	203	200	145	-27.5%
CAL STATE UNIV/FRES	90	113	127	122	122	116	107	107	121	141	16.5%
CAL STATE UNIV/LA	---	---	---	---	---	---	---	---	---	*	*
CAL STATE UNIV/LB	82	71	86	106	134	138	122	*	133	138	3.8%
CAL STATE UNIV/SAC	222	235	213	*	237	300	*	296	286	*	*
CAL STATE UNIV/SB	---	49	60	53	51	49	44	77	89	86	-3.4%
CAL STATE UNIV/STAN	---	---	---	---	---	---	---	47	48	59	22.9%
CASE WESTERN RESERVE	352	405	465	498	431	450	460	391	328	323	-1.5%
CATHOLIC UNIV/DC	164	166	192	192	183	185	165	136	133	129	-3.0%
CLARK ATLANTA UNIV	83	105	143	147	*	127	143	113	136	86	-36.8%
CLEVE ST U/U AKRON	---	---	---	---	---	---	---	---	*	39	*
COLL ST CATH/UNIV ST THOM	---	30	40	38	45	99	105	106	104	124	19.2%
COLORADO STATE UNIV	47	39	68	57	72	54	53	79	77	62	-19.5%
COLUMBIA UNIV	649	647	647	695	693	706	702	719	745	748	0.4%
DELAWARE STATE UNIV	*	46	51	*	*	*	76	75	80	84	5.0%
EAST CAROLINA UNIV	68	75	77	96	79	131	113	102	125	94	-24.8%
EASTERN MICHIGAN	---	---	---	---	---	40	58	*	17	23	35.3%
EASTERN WASHINGTON	79	76	84	83	85	87	98	134	*	*	*
FLORIDA INTERNATL	107	*	168	*	193	216	203	206	186	130	-30.1%
FLORIDA STATE UNIV	240	316	238	168	151	178	172	219	230	121	-47.4%
FORDHAM UNIV	616	637	763	942	972	1,044	993	*	1,011	999	-1.2%
GALLAUDET UNIV	---	---	---	---	25	31	41	*	33	41	24.2%
GRAMBLING STATE	*	134	154	107	126	---	---	---	---	32	---
GRAND VALLEY STATE	106	150	120	165	160	179	141	150	126	138	9.5%
HOWARD UNIV	121	164	206	237	283	284	324	*	297	272	-8.4%
HUNTER COLL	560	513	515	547	504	498	535	556	484	469	-3.1%
INDIANA UNIV	263	256	235	248	303	326	277	259	260	273	5.0%
INTERAMERICAN/MET	---	---	---	---	---	---	---	---	---	78	---
JACKSON STATE UNIV	---	---	---	---	---	---	---	57	56	70	25.0%
KEAN UNIV	---	---	---	---	---	---	---	---	64	66	3.1%
LOMA LINDA UNIV	---	---	---	---	---	---	51	58	37	37	0.0%
LOUISIANA STATE UNIV	165	183	172	164	179	173	196	173	146	158	8.2%
LOYOLA UNIV CHICAGO	243	254	236	254	282	253	218	193	222	200	-9.9%
MARYWOOD UNIV	157	155	200	227	197	177	223	*	200	88	-56.0%
MICHIGAN STATE UNIV	150	130	128	143	135	144	204	149	129	136	5.4%
NEW MEXICO HIGHLANDS	101	93	92	104	110	106	98	127	72	92	27.8%
NEW MEXICO STATE	---	---	71	74	54	65	*	80	45	42	-6.7%
NEW YORK UNIV	549	612	599	619	638	654	635	634	685	614	-10.4%
NORFOLK STATE UNIV	129	158	138	127	120	103	84	92	100	*	*
OHIO STATE UNIV	260	278	264	220	198	226	256	244	241	240	-0.4%
OUR LADY OF LAKE	151	179	175	142	123	147	135	130	89	92	3.4%
PORTLAND STATE UNIV	152	166	180	169	188	199	207	217	230	232	0.9%
RADFORD UNIV	---	---	---	---	---	---	59	43	50	53	6.0%
RHODE ISLAND COLLEGE	114	95	99	92	92	106	116	*	86	91	5.8%
ROBERTS WESLEYAN	---	---	---	---	---	---	99	*	69	*	*
RUTGERS UNIV/NB	330	282	219	261	*	279	286	325	288	281	-2.4%
SALEM STATE COLL	*	52	60	59	*	65	67	76	65	48	-26.2%
SAN DIEGO STATE UNIV	190	190	204	*	211	230	204	207	238	238	0.0%
SAN FRANCISCO STATE	113	73	94	132	*	137	154	105	108	123	13.9%
SAN JOSE STATE UNIV	122	207	170	170	189	141	145	178	*	*	*
SAVANNAH STATE UNIV	---	---	---	---	---	---	---	---	---	41	---
SIMMONS COLL	201	210	100	194	247	220	212	205	210	210	-1.4%

105

TABLE 400

Full-time Master's and Doctoral Students Enrolled in Social Work Programs**, 1991 through 2000

Program	1991	1992	1993	1994	1995	1996	1997	1998	1999	2000	% Change 99-00
SMITH COLL	256	252	260	251	266	279	291	290	272	246	-9.6%
SOUTHERN BAPTIST	105	110	109	107	61	11	---	---	---	---	---
SOUTHERN CONN STATE	104	96	92	96	113	104	86	94	111	133	19.8%
SOUTHERN ILL/CAR	38	49	53	65	46	46	53	51	39	40	2.6%
SOUTHERN UNIV	*	94	134	157	*	193	167	183	179	152	-15.1%
SOUTHWEST MISSOURI	---	---	---	---	---	---	---	---	46	36	-21.7%
SOUTHWEST TEXAS	---	---	---	---	---	---	---	---	---	45	---
SPRINGFIELD COLL	---	---	*	*	*	*	*	*	*	*	*
ST AMBROSE UNIV	---	---	---	---	---	---	---	---	---	32	---
ST LOUIS UNIV	98	123	122	105	143	126	148	143	164	148	-9.8%
SUNY/ALBANY	261	251	293	313	261	286	287	272	305	279	-8.5%
SUNY/BUFFALO	172	163	183	191	278	257	184	152	179	168	-6.1%
SUNY/STONY BROOK	287	278	*	*	*	*	*	*	4	*	*
SYRACUSE UNIV	148	242	277	297	302	162	163	168	161	86	-46.6%
TEMPLE UNIV	139	162	192	197	188	178	173	146	117	129	10.3%
TULANE UNIV	219	237	253	257	244	236	233	212	171	159	-7.0%
U OF ALABAMA	226	207	181	174	167	176	168	171	174	164	-5.7%
U OF ALASKA/ANK	---	---	---	---	---	---	---	---	30	27	-10.0%
U OF ARKANSAS/LR	82	95	121	*	111	142	120	127	126	120	-4.8%
U OF CALIFORNIA/BERK	218	195	206	240	235	228	233	232	193	183	-5.2%
U OF CALIFORNIA/LA	178	172	*	220	*	*	232	*	178	*	*
U OF CENTRAL FLA	---	---	---	---	---	---	130	137	112	106	-5.4%
U OF CHICAGO	203	206	228	218	308	336	330	367	278	321	15.5%
U OF CINCINNATI	97	78	99	115	108	117	126	119	120	125	4.2%
U OF CONNECTICUT	193	231	273	263	253	260	249	249	233	207	-11.2%
U OF DENVER	279	251	267	305	334	347	311	314	271	258	-4.8%
U OF GEORGIA	194	161	164	171	169	169	172	172	188	197	4.8%
U OF HAWAII	138	144	125	153	181	118	120	151	142	119	-16.2%
U OF HOUSTON	156	138	171	154	169	189	213	173	198	124	-37.4%
U OF ILLINOIS/CHI	393	376	*	389	386	384	343	306	344	327	-4.9%
U OF ILLINOIS/URB	208	231	236	241	224	245	248	242	244	239	-2.0%
U OF IOWA	111	128	126	117	98	96	114	112	111	98	-11.7%
U OF KANSAS	292	335	339	334	344	363	423	397	334	254	-24.0%
U OF KENTUCKY	312	373	374	393	*	323	331	*	272	63	-76.8%
U OF LOUISVILLE	142	185	201	219	262	294	316	280	244	273	11.9%
U OF MAINE/OR	22	30	31	24	*	29	27	28	29	*	*
U OF MARYLAND/BAL	727	674	660	592	749	735	747	701	706	698	-1.1%
U OF MICHIGAN	566	565	525	636	622	622	661	661	641	554	-13.6%
U OF MINNESOTA/DUL	18	46	58	48	44	43	38	34	70	62	-11.4%
U OF MINNESOTA/TC	154	146	132	197	214	147	137	133	131	179	36.6%
U OF MISSOURI/COL	95	80	76	76	88	81	80	82	88	81	-8.0%
U OF NEBRASKA/OMA	97	97	100	109	133	128	126	109	102	95	-6.9%
U OF NEVADA/LV	---	---	---	67	88	33	22	55	68	70	2.9%
U OF NEVADA/REN	---	---	---	32	29	33	25	31	37	34	-8.1%
U OF NEW ENGLAND	47	71	75	115	102	97	144	144	125	*	*
U OF NEW HAMPSHIRE	---	---	---	---	---	---	---	70	68	90	32.4%
U OF NORTH CAROLINA/CH	151	143	167	161	192	156	201	193	194	187	-3.6%
U OF NCGB/NCSU	---	---	---	---	---	---	---	---	---	65	---
U OF NORTH DAKOTA	---	---	---	30	39	28	24	26	34	58	70.6%
U OF OKLAHOMA	69	77	79	93	94	91	99	98	104	100	-3.8%
U OF PENNSYLVANIA	198	271	279	319	334	349	336	247	223	255	14.3%
U OF PITTSBURGH	217	228	268	257	277	308	324	336	352	339	-3.7%
U OF PUERTO RICO/RP	168	177	145	116	138	114	111	*	125	125	0.0%
U OF SOUTH CAROLINA	254	298	299	277	323	316	347	402	366	336	-8.2%
U OF SOUTH FLORIDA	54	68	70	72	67	95	109	97	111	89	-19.8%
U OF SOUTHERN CAL	282	282	284	315	309	333	351	*	329	329	0.0%
U OF SOUTHERN IND	---	---	---	---	---	---	---	47	44	45	2.3%
U OF SOUTHERN MISS	85	76	67	68	64	61	61	52	31	49	58.1%
U OF TENNESSEE/KNX	228	264	292	325	249	276	258	252	297	300	1.0%
U OF TEXAS/ARL	362	354	377	445	*	383	395	341	320	297	-7.2%
U OF TEXAS/AUS	173	204	158	177	188	206	302	290	237	246	3.8%
U OF UTAH	157	159	161	162	173	165	232	197	209	273	30.6%
U OF VERMONT	---	---	48	63	49	53	51	33	36	39	8.3%
U OF WASHINGTON	218	217	242	236	235	223	245	*	229	231	0.9%

TABLE 400

Full-time Master's and Doctoral Students Enrolled in Social Work Programs**, 1991 through 2000

Program	1991	1992	1993	1994	1995	1996	1997	1998	1999	2000	% Change 99-00
U OF WISCONSIN/MAD	185	229	258	234	228	244	252	242	223	228	2.2%
U OF WISCONSIN/MIL	183	129	180	201	201	185	194	184	147	144	-2.0%
U OF WYOMING	---	---	---	---	---	---	---	---	---	38	---
VALDOSTA STATE UNIV	---	---	---	---	---	---	---	50	54	50	-7.4%
VIRGINIA COMMONWEAL	342	332	391	361	289	290	382	368	291	269	-7.6%
WALLA WALLA COLL	---	*	118	117	108	125	121	160	176	161	-8.5%
WASHBURN UNIV	---	---	---	---	---	---	---	52	48	63	31.3%
WASHINGTON UNIV	321	332	368	406	430	453	445	429	424	408	-3.8%
WAYNE STATE UNIV	276	276	317	284	362	356	390	338	299	319	6.7%
WEST VIRGINIA UNIV	117	103	117	121	93	111	105	113	122	127	4.1%
WESTERN MICHIGAN	108	123	107	92	94	105	108	107	112	*	*
WIDENER UNIV	---	---	---	---	69	82	79	94	*	65	*
YESHIVA UNIV	458	406	518	354	299	274	331	283	228	204	-10.5%

* Missing data
** Some entries may include only master's students or only doctoral students

TABLE 401

Students Enrolled on 11/1/00, by Type of Enrollment

Program	Total	Total Master's and Doctoral**	Full-time			Part-time			Total Other	Undergrad as Part of Undergrad/ Grad Continuum	Not Working Toward Social Work Degree
			Total	Master's	Doctoral**	Total	Master's	Doctoral**			
TOTAL:	39,233	35,944	21,629	20,369	1,260	14,315	13,446	869	3,289	144	3,145
ADELPHI UNIV	803	726	316	284	32	410	410	0	77	39	38
ALABAMA A&M UNIV	83	81	45	45	0	36	36	0	2	0	2
ANDREWS UNIV	47	43	34	34	0	9	9	0	4	0	4
ARIZONA STATE UNIV	521	463	278	272	6	185	171	14	58	11	47
AUGSBURG COLL	68	68	46	46	0	22	22	0	0	0	0
BARRY UNIV	408	404	164	164	0	240	217	23	4	0	4
BOISE STATE UNIV	28	28	28	28	0	0	0	0	0	0	0
BOSTON COLL	504	466	302	301	1	164	115	49	38	5	33
BOSTON UNIV	415	393	189	188	1	204	190	14	22	0	22
BRIGHAM YOUNG/UT	111	78	78	78	0	0	0	0	33	33	0
BRYN MAWR COLL	221	220	145	125	20	75	49	26	1	0	1
CAL STATE UNIV/FRES	180	180	141	141	0	39	39	0	0	0	*
CAL STATE UNIV/LB	560	560	138	138	0	422	422	0	*	*	*
CAL STATE UNIV/SB	197	186	86	86	0	100	100	0	11	0	11
CAL STATE UNIV/STAN	120	120	59	59	0	61	61	0	0	0	0
CASE WESTERN RESERVE	378	370	323	285	38	47	16	31	8	4	4
CATHOLIC UNIV/DC	228	223	129	82	47	94	74	20	5	0	5
CLARK ATLANTA UNIV	106	106	86	86	*	20	20	*	0	0	0
CLEVE ST U/U AKRON	64	63	39	39	0	24	24	0	1	0	1
COLL ST CAT/U ST THO	214	206	124	124	0	82	82	0	8	0	8
COLORADO STATE UNIV	113	109	62	62	0	47	47	0	4	0	4
COLUMBIA UNIV	877	857	748	666	82	109	109	0	20	0	20
DELAWARE STATE UNIV	116	111	84	84	0	27	27	0	5	2	3
EAST CAROLINA UNIV	136	129	94	94	0	35	35	0	7	0	7
EASTERN MICHIGAN	277	263	23	23	0	240	240	0	14	0	14
FLORIDA INTERNATL	244	244	130	124	6	114	97	17	0	0	0
FLORIDA STATE UNIV	424	282	121	121	*	161	161	*	142	0	142
FORDHAM UNIV	1,642	1,468	999	934	65	469	447	22	174	10	164
GALLAUDET UNIV	53	53	41	41	0	12	12	0	0	0	0
GRAMBLING STATE UNIV	37	37	32	32	0	5	5	0	0	0	0
GRAND VALLEY STATE	403	368	138	138	0	230	230	0	35	5	30
HOWARD UNIV	352	352	272	257	15	80	54	26	0	0	0
HUNTER COLL	1,044	803	469	406	63	334	330	4	241	0	241
INDIANA UNIV	666	656	273	260	13	383	375	8	10	0	10
INTERAMERICAN/MET	78	78	78	78	0	0	0	0	0	0	0
JACKSON STATE UNIV	122	120	70	41	29	50	50	0	2	0	2
KEAN UNIV	90	90	66	66	0	24	24	0	0	0	0
LOMA LINDA UNIV	93	80	37	37	0	43	40	3	13	13	0
LOUISIANA STATE UNIV	199	198	158	154	4	40	24	16	1	0	1
LOYOLA UNIV CHICAGO	478	468	200	188	12	268	245	23	10	0	10
MARYWOOD UNIV	413	405	88	88	0	317	303	14	8	0	8
MICHIGAN STATE UNIV	232	227	136	126	10	91	79	12	5	0	5
NEW MEXICO HIGHLANDS	233	233	92	92	0	141	141	0	0	0	0
NEW MEXICO STATE	96	88	42	42	0	46	46	0	8	0	8
NEW YORK UNIV	1,203	1,078	614	589	25	464	394	70	125	1	124
OHIO STATE UNIV	443	443	240	194	46	203	203	0	0	0	0
OUR LADY OF LAKE	139	139	92	92	0	47	47	0	0	0	0
PORTLAND STATE UNIV	378	355	232	216	16	123	101	22	23	0	23
RADFORD UNIV	196	108	53	53	0	55	55	0	88	0	88
RHODE ISLAND COLL	224	157	91	91	0	66	66	0	67	0	67
RUTGERS UNIV/NB	970	743	281	271	10	462	419	43	227	0	227
SALEM STATE COLL	263	203	48	48	0	155	155	0	60	0	60
SAN DIEGO STATE UNIV	334	334	238	238	0	96	96	0	0	0	0
SAN FRANCISCO STATE	192	166	123	123	0	43	43	0	26	0	26
SAVANNAH STATE UNIV	41	41	41	41	0	0	0	0	0	0	0
SIMMONS COLL	324	315	213	213	0	102	66	36	9	0	9
SMITH COLL	287	287	246	229	17	41	0	41	0	0	0
SOUTHERN CONNECTICUT	240	195	133	133	0	62	62	0	45	0	45
SOUTHERN ILL/CAR	59	55	40	40	0	15	15	0	4	0	4

TABLE 401

Students Enrolled on 11/1/00, by Type of Enrollment

Program	Total	Social Work Students							Other Students Taking Graduate Courses		
		Total Master's and Doctoral**	Full-time			Part-time			Total Other	Undergrad as Part of Undergrad/Grad Continuum	Not Working Toward Social Work Degree
			Total	Master's	Doctoral**	Total	Master's	Doctoral**			
SOUTHERN UNIV	256	256	152	152	0	104	104	0	0	0	0
SOUTHWEST MISSOURI	66	66	36	36	0	30	30	0	0	0	0
SOUTHWEST TEXAS	84	84	45	45	0	39	39	0	0	0	0
ST AMBROSE UNIV	71	66	32	32	0	34	34	0	5	0	5
ST LOUIS UNIV	299	294	148	148	0	146	146	0	5	0	5
SUNY/ALBANY	499	432	279	263	16	153	97	56	67	0	67
SUNY/BUFFALO	431	395	168	168	0	227	227	0	36	0	36
SYRACUSE UNIV	280	277	86	86	0	191	191	0	3	0	3
TEMPLE UNIV	485	470	129	129	0	341	341	0	15	0	15
TULANE UNIV	210	210	159	150	9	51	18	33	0	0	0
U OF ALABAMA	215	215	164	146	18	51	42	9	0	0	0
U OF ALASKA/ANK	48	42	27	27	0	15	15	0	6	0	6
U OF ARKANSAS/LR	181	166	120	120	0	46	46	0	15	0	15
U OF CALIFORNIA/BERK	183	183	183	183	*	0	0	*	0	0	0
U OF CENTRAL FLORIDA	219	209	106	106	0	103	103	0	10	0	10
U OF CHICAGO	447	424	321	251	70	103	103	0	23	0	23
U OF CINCINNATI	195	195	125	125	0	70	70	0	0	0	0
U OF CONNECTICUT	626	389	207	207	*	182	182	*	237	0	237
U OF DENVER	365	354	258	244	14	96	64	32	11	0	11
U OF GEORGIA	287	284	197	152	45	87	87	0	3	0	3
U OF HAWAII	246	216	119	118	1	97	86	11	30	0	30
U OF HOUSTON	288	283	124	124	*	159	159	*	5	0	5
U OF ILLINOIS/CHI	535	508	327	292	35	181	174	7	27	0	27
U OF ILLINOIS/URB	473	315	239	224	15	76	71	5	158	0	158
U OF IOWA	349	215	98	87	11	117	117	0	134	0	134
U OF KANSAS	447	447	254	237	17	193	176	17	0	0	0
U OF KENTUCKY	292	274	63	59	4	211	192	19	18	0	18
U OF LOUISVILLE	370	344	273	259	14	71	58	13	26	0	26
U OF MARYLAND	911	908	698	662	36	210	203	7	3	0	3
U OF MICHIGAN	685	580	554	554	0	26	26	0	105	0	105
U OF MINNESOTA/DUL	99	88	62	62	0	26	26	0	11	0	11
U OF MINNESOTA/TC	555	305	179	163	16	126	101	25	250	0	250
U OF MISSOURI/COL	182	176	81	81	0	95	94	1	6	2	4
U OF NCGB/NCSU	65	65	65	65	0	0	0	0	0	0	0
U OF NEBRASKA/OMA	187	178	95	95	0	83	83	0	9	7	2
U OF NEVADA/LV	140	140	70	70	0	70	70	0	0	0	0
U OF NEVADA/REN	40	35	34	34	0	1	1	0	5	0	5
U OF NEW HAMPSHIRE	158	136	90	90	0	46	46	0	22	0	22
U OF NORTH CAR/CH	359	293	187	187	*	106	106	*	66	0	66
U OF NORTH DAKOTA	96	89	58	58	0	31	31	0	7	1	6
U OF OKLAHOMA	174	173	100	100	*	73	73	*	1	0	1
U OF PENNSYLVANIA	368	367	255	194	61	112	106	6	1	0	1
U OF PITTSBURGH	586	555	339	308	31	216	194	22	31	0	31
U OF PUERTO RICO/RP	146	145	125	125	0	20	20	0	1	0	1
U OF SOUTH CAROLINA	509	490	336	323	13	154	132	22	19	0	19
U OF SOUTH FLORIDA	132	122	89	89	0	33	33	0	10	0	10
U OF SOUTHERN CAL	485	485	329	329	*	156	156	*	0	0	0
U OF SOUTHERN IND	89	82	45	45	0	37	37	0	7	0	7
U OF SOUTHERN MISS	128	127	49	49	0	78	78	0	1	0	1
U OF TENNESSEE/KNX	443	442	300	246	54	142	142	0	1	0	1
U OF TEXAS/ARL	533	524	297	297	*	227	227	*	9	0	9
U OF TEXAS/AUS	370	345	246	199	47	99	95	4	25	0	25
U OF UTAH	333	333	273	234	39	60	51	9	0	0	0
U OF VERMONT	93	67	39	39	0	28	28	0	26	3	23
U OF WASHINGTON	383	360	231	207	24	129	121	8	23	0	23
U OF WISCONSIN/MAD	233	228	228	183	45	0	0	0	5	0	5
U OF WISCONSIN/MIL	380	318	144	144	0	174	174	0	62	0	62
U OF WYOMING	38	38	38	38	0	0	0	0	0	0	0
VALDOSTA STATE UNIV	81	81	50	50	0	31	31	0	0	0	0
VIRGINIA COMMONWEAL	589	583	269	259	10	314	289	25	6	0	6

TABLE 401

Students Enrolled on 11/1/00, by Type of Enrollment

Program	Total	Social Work Students							Other Students Taking Graduate Courses		
		Total Master's and Doctoral**	Full-time			Part-time			Total Other	Undergrad as Part of Undergrad/ Grad Continuum	Not Working Toward Social Work Degree
			Total	Master's	Doctoral**	Total	Master's	Doctoral**			
WALLA WALLA COLL	179	179	161	161	0	18	18	0	0	0	0
WASHBURN UNIV	135	116	63	63	0	53	53	0	19	0	19
WASHINGTON UNIV	481	475	408	351	57	67	63	4	6	0	6
WAYNE STATE UNIV	621	559	319	319	*	240	240	*	62	7	55
WEST VIRGINIA UNIV	267	267	127	127	0	140	140	0	0	0	0
WIDENER UNIV	192	181	65	65	0	116	116	0	11	1	10
YESHIVA UNIV	374	374	204	204	*	170	170	*	0	0	0

* Missing data

**Includes doctoral students who are taking coursework and who have finished coursework

TABLE 402

Students Receiving Degrees During Academic Year 1999-2000 by Degree and Gender

Program	Master's Degree				Doctoral Degree		
	Total	Men	Women	Unknown	Total	Men	Women
TOTAL:	15,016	2,302	12,701	13	229	63	166
ADELPHI UNIV	259	35	224	0	6	1	5
ALABAMA A&M UNIV	22	3	19	0	0	0	0
ANDREWS UNIV	17	4	13	0	0	0	0
ARIZONA STATE UNIV	165	24	141	0	4	0	4
AUGSBURG COLL	44	9	35	0	0	0	0
BARRY UNIV	159	33	126	0	10	1	9
BOISE STATE UNIV	23	5	18	0	0	0	0
BOSTON COLL	177	28	149	0	2	1	1
BOSTON UNIV	222	23	196	3	2	0	2
BRIGHAM YOUNG/UT	36	6	30	0	0	0	0
BRYN MAWR COLL	90	13	77	0	3	0	3
CAL STATE UNIV/FRES	49	13	36	0	0	0	0
CAL STATE UNIV/LB	180	28	152	0	0	0	0
CAL STATE UNIV/SB	95	19	76	0	0	0	0
CAL STATE UNIV/STAN	44	11	33	0	0	0	0
CASE WESTERN RESERVE	176	23	153	0	6	2	4
CATHOLIC UNIV/DC	88	7	81	0	4	2	2
CLARK ATLANTA UNIV	49	4	43	2	*	*	*
CLEVE ST U/U AKRON	20	7	13	0	0	0	0
COLL ST CAT/U ST THO	56	5	51	0	0	0	0
COLORADO STATE UNIV	44	10	34	0	0	0	0
COLUMBIA UNIV	370	42	328	0	17	10	7
DELAWARE STATE UNIV	37	9	27	1	0	0	0
EAST CAROLINA UNIV	100	11	89	0	0	0	0
EASTERN MICHIGAN	71	9	62	0	0	0	0
FLORIDA INTERNATL	155	24	131	0	1	1	0
FLORIDA STATE UNIV	205	35	170	0	*	*	*
FORDHAM UNIV	631	98	533	0	7	0	7
GALLAUDET UNIV	15	0	15	0	0	0	0
GRAMBLING STATE UNIV	15	1	14	0	0	0	0
GRAND VALLEY STATE	116	19	97	0	0	0	0
HOWARD UNIV	152	26	126	0	0	0	0
HUNTER COLL	243	67	176	0	7	3	4
INDIANA UNIV	197	20	177	0	1	0	1
INTERAMERICAN/MET	78	6	72	0	0	0	0
JACKSON STATE UNIV	44	4	40	0	0	0	0
KEAN UNIV	*	*	*	*	0	0	0
LOMA LINDA UNIV	29	7	22	0	0	0	0
LOUISIANA STATE UNIV	91	8	83	0	1	0	1
LOYOLA UNIV CHICAGO	194	33	160	1	3	0	3
MARYWOOD UNIV	131	19	106	6	2	0	2
MICHIGAN STATE UNIV	112	16	96	0	4	2	2
NEW MEXICO HIGHLANDS	81	18	63	0	0	0	0
NEW MEXICO STATE	36	7	29	0	0	0	0
NEW YORK UNIV	565	88	477	0	19	4	15
OHIO STATE UNIV	183	27	156	0	8	5	3
OUR LADY OF LAKE	75	13	62	0	0	0	0
PORTLAND STATE UNIV	197	42	155	0	1	0	1
RADFORD UNIV	36	7	29	0	0	0	0
RHODE ISLAND COLL	48	9	39	0	0	0	0
RUTGERS UNIV/NB	258	36	222	0	4	1	3
SALEM STATE COLL	65	10	55	0	0	0	0
SAN DIEGO STATE UNIV	129	19	110	0	0	0	0
SAN FRANCISCO STATE	53	14	39	0	0	0	0
SAVANNAH STATE UNIV	18	3	15	0	0	0	0
SIMMONS COLL	138	15	123	0	0	0	0
SMITH COLL	132	14	118	0	10	2	8
SOUTHERN CONNECTICUT	44	6	38	0	0	0	0
SOUTHERN ILL/CAR	33	3	30	0	0	0	0
SOUTHERN UNIV	104	19	85	0	0	0	0
SOUTHWEST MISSOURI	29	5	24	0	0	0	0
SOUTHWEST TEXAS	84	13	71	0	0	0	0
ST AMBROSE UNIV	30	5	20	0	0	0	0
ST LOUIS UNIV	122	20	102	0	0	0	0
SUNY/ALBANY	158	25	133	0	5	1	4

TABLE 402

Students Receiving Degrees During Academic Year 1999-2000 by Degree and Gender

Program	Master's Degree				Doctoral Degree		
	Total	Men	Women	Unknown	Total	Men	Women
SUNY/BUFFALO	121	22	99	0	0	0	0
SUNY/STONY BROOK	*	*	*	*	0	0	0
SYRACUSE UNIV	129	21	108	0	0	0	0
TEMPLE UNIV	151	28	123	0	0	0	0
TULANE UNIV	97	8	89	0	2	1	1
U OF ALABAMA	111	12	99	0	2	1	1
U OF ALASKA/ANK	16	1	15	0	0	0	0
U OF ARKANSAS/LR	76	8	68	0	0	0	0
U OF CALIFORNIA/BERK	90	15	75	0	*	*	*
U OF CENTRAL FLORIDA	72	9	63	0	0	0	0
U OF CHICAGO	180	31	149	0	11	1	10
U OF CINCINNATI	78	10	68	0	0	0	0
U OF CONNECTICUT	152	26	126	0	*	*	*
U OF DENVER	169	15	154	0	5	3	2
U OF GEORGIA	95	7	88	0	11	5	6
U OF HAWAII	100	16	84	0	2	1	1
U OF HOUSTON	150	21	129	0	*	*	*
U OF ILLINOIS/CHI	221	36	185	0	1	0	1
U OF ILLINOIS/URB	127	19	108	0	5	0	5
U OF IOWA	95	17	78	0	0	0	0
U OF KANSAS	211	34	177	0	2	0	2
U OF KENTUCKY	126	13	113	0	0	0	0
U OF LOUISVILLE	142	26	116	0	0	0	0
U OF MARYLAND	389	49	340	0	12	0	12
U OF MICHIGAN	326	44	282	0	0	0	0
U OF MINNESOTA/DUL	45	11	34	0	0	0	0
U OF MINNESOTA/TC	55	9	46	0	7	3	4
U OF MISSOURI/COL	65	12	53	0	0	0	0
U OF NCGB/NCSU	20	3	17	0	0	0	0
U OF NEBRASKA/OMA	62	8	54	0	0	0	0
U OF NEVADA/LV	31	9	22	0	0	0	0
U OF NEVADA/REN	24	2	22	0	0	0	0
U OF NEW HAMPSHIRE	39	8	31	0	0	0	0
U OF NORTH CAR/CH	117	26	91	0	*	*	*
U OF NORTH DAKOTA	40	4	36	0	0	0	0
U OF OKLAHOMA	81	6	75	0	*	*	*
U OF PENNSYLVANIA	130	23	107	0	5	2	3
U OF PITTSBURGH	218	32	186	0	6	1	5
U OF PUERTO RICO/RP	25	3	22	0	0	0	0
U OF SOUTH CAROLINA	238	29	209	0	5	1	4
U OF SOUTH FLORIDA	50	5	45	0	0	0	0
U OF SOUTHERN CAL	197	23	174	0	*	*	*
U OF SOUTHERN IND	46	8	38	0	0	0	0
U OF SOUTHERN MISS	23	3	20	0	0	0	0
U OF TENNESSEE/KNX	211	34	177	0	4	1	3
U OF TEXAS/ARL	192	19	173	0	*	*	*
U OF TEXAS/AUS	136	19	117	0	4	1	3
U OF UTAH	285	81	204	0	0	0	0
U OF VERMONT	22	3	19	0	0	0	0
U OF WASHINGTON	129	27	102	0	7	3	4
U OF WISCONSIN/MAD	112	12	100	0	4	2	2
U OF WISCONSIN/MIL	150	20	130	0	0	0	0
U OF WYOMING	*	*	*	*	0	0	0
VALDOSTA STATE UNIV	25	7	18	0	0	0	0
VIRGINIA COMMONWEAL	229	21	208	0	3	1	2
WALLA WALLA COLL	140	38	102	0	0	0	0
WASHBURN UNIV	44	4	40	0	0	0	0
WASHINGTON UNIV	206	29	177	0	4	0	4
WAYNE STATE UNIV	257	35	222	0	*	*	*
WEST VIRGINIA UNIV	111	19	92	0	0	0	0
WIDENER UNIV	75	10	65	0	0	0	0
YESHIVA UNIV	140	30	110	0	*	*	*

* Missing data

TABLE 403

Number of Full-time Non-Administrative Graduate Faculty Assigned 50 Percent or More Time to Social Work Program, by Gender, Type of Appointment, and Academic Responsibility

Program	Total	Total Men	Total Women	Class Men	Class Women	Class & Field Men	Class & Field Women	Field Men	Field Women	Other Men	Other Women	Prof Men	Prof Women	Assoc Prof Men	Assoc Prof Women	Asst Prof Men	Asst Prof Women	Other Faculty Men	Other Faculty Women
TOTAL: Number	2,040	762	1,278	548	795	13	30	46	166	155	287	228	194	197	316	184	384	151	383
Percent	100.0%	37.2%	62.5%	26.8%	38.9%	0.6%	1.5%	2.2%	8.1%	7.6%	14.0%	11.2%	9.5%	9.6%	15.5%	9.0%	18.8%	7.4%	18.7%
ADELPHI UNIV	22	10	12	9	9	0	0	0	1	1	2	5	2	3	6	1	2	1	2
ALABAMA A&M UNIV	9	2	7	2	5	0	0	0	1	0	1	0	2	1	2	1	3	0	0
ARIZONA STATE UNIV	25	11	14	1	2	0	0	0	0	10	12	4	2	4	5	1	6	2	1
AUGSBURG COLL	11	3	8	2	6	1	0	0	0	0	2	0	1	1	2	0	5	2	0
BARRY UNIV	18	6	12	6	11	0	0	0	0	0	1	2	4	3	6	1	2	0	0
BOSTON COLL	24	15	9	10	5	0	0	2	0	3	4	3	1	7	3	1	1	4	4
BOSTON UNIV	29	4	25	4	25	0	0	0	0	0	0	3	3	1	4	0	11	0	7
BRYN MAWR COLL	15	6	9	3	8	0	0	0	1	3	0	4	4	2	1	0	3	0	1
CAL STATE UNIV/FRES	12	3	9	2	6	0	0	0	0	1	3	0	5	0	0	0	2	3	2
CAL STATE UNIV/LB	22	6	16	3	14	1	0	1	1	1	1	3	10	0	1	0	1	3	4
CAL STATE UNIV/SB	10	4	6	1	3	0	0	1	2	2	1	1	1	0	2	0	1	3	2
CASE WESTERN RESERVE	22	10	12	8	9	0	0	0	0	2	3	6	1	2	6	1	1	1	4
CATHOLIC UNIV/DC	12	1	11	1	11	0	0	0	0	0	0	1	3	0	5	0	3	0	0
CLARK ATLANTA UNIV	8	6	2	5	1	0	0	0	0	1	1	0	0	4	2	2	0	0	0
COLL ST CAT/U ST THO	19	8	11	3	8	0	0	5	1	0	2	0	2	1	3	3	5	4	1
COLORADO STATE UNIV	11	5	6	5	4	0	0	0	1	0	1	1	2	2	0	2	2	0	2
COLUMBIA UNIV	44	17	27	13	15	0	0	0	0	4	12	7	4	3	15	7	8	0	0
DELAWARE STATE UNIV	8	3	5	3	3	0	0	0	1	0	1	0	0	3	3	0	1	0	1
EAST CAROLINA UNIV	19	6	13	4	6	2	4	0	0	0	3	2	0	1	3	2	2	1	8
EASTERN MICHIGAN	15	4	11	3	2	0	1	1	4	0	4	2	5	0	3	1	1	1	2
EDINBORO UNIV	5	4	1	4	1	0	0	0	0	0	0	1	0	1	1	2	0	0	0
FLORIDA ATLANTIC	14	9	5	9	4	0	0	0	1	0	0	1	0	2	2	6	0	0	3
FLORIDA GULF COAST	3	1	2	1	2	0	0	0	0	0	0	0	0	0	0	0	2	1	0
FLORIDA INTERNATL	18	11	7	3	0	0	0	1	2	7	5	2	1	4	2	3	1	2	3
GALLAUDET UNIV	8	0	8	0	7	0	0	0	1	0	0	0	1	0	2	0	3	0	2
GRAMBLING STATE UNIV	6	1	5	0	4	1	1	0	0	0	0	0	1	1	0	0	4	0	0
GRAND VALLEY STATE	22	8	14	7	7	1	4	0	1	0	2	3	3	0	0	1	4	4	7
GREATER ROCHESTER	2	1	1	1	1	0	0	0	0	0	0	0	1	0	0	1	0	0	0
HOWARD UNIV	18	6	12	5	9	0	0	0	2	1	1	2	1	3	6	1	5	0	0
HUNTER COLL	35	11	24	11	23	0	0	0	0	0	1	7	5	2	13	2	5	0	1
INDIANA UNIV	27	7	20	2	9	0	0	0	2	5	9	3	1	1	8	1	2	2	9
JACKSON STATE UNIV	12	2	10	2	8	0	0	0	1	0	1	0	1	1	0	1	4	0	5
LOMA LINDA UNIV	8	6	2	1	1	0	0	0	0	5	1	2	0	1	0	1	1	2	1
LOUISIANA STATE UNIV	13	4	9	3	7	1	0	0	0	0	2	3	0	0	2	1	5	0	2
LOYOLA UNIV CHICAGO	18	5	13	5	13	0	0	0	0	0	0	1	1	1	3	1	6	2	3
MARYWOOD UNIV	21	8	13	8	9	0	0	0	4	0	0	0	0	3	3	3	6	2	4
MICHIGAN STATE UNIV	37	12	25	8	8	0	0	1	9	3	8	0	1	3	1	2	7	7	16
MONMOUTH UNIV	14	6	8	6	8	0	0	0	0	0	0	0	0	1	1	3	3	2	4
NEW MEXICO STATE	13	9	4	7	2	1	0	1	1	0	1	0	0	1	0	4	2	4	2
NEW YORK UNIV	47	8	39	2	5	0	2	1	12	5	20	2	4	2	18	1	12	3	5
OHIO STATE UNIV	26	9	17	9	13	0	0	0	3	0	1	5	2	2	5	2	7	0	3

113

TABLE 403

Number of Full-time Non-Administrative Graduate Faculty Assigned 50 Percent or More Time to Social Work Program, by Gender, Type of Appointment, and Academic Responsibility

Program	Total	Total		Major Responsibility								Academic Rank							
		Total Men	Total Women	Class Men	Class Women	Class and Field Men	Class and Field Women	Field Men	Field Women	Other Men	Other Women	Professor Men	Professor Women	Associate Professor Men	Associate Professor Women	Assistant Professor Men	Assistant Professor Women	Other Faculty Men	Other Faculty Women
OHIO UNIV	9	3	6	3	6	0	0	0	0	0	0	0	0	1	1	2	5	0	0
OUR LADY OF LAKE	8	4	4	3	2	0	0	0	2	1	0	2	0	2	1	1	1	0	2
PORTLAND STATE UNIV	25	8	17	6	10	0	0	0	3	2	4	1	4	3	5	3	4	1	4
RADFORD UNIV	23	4	19	2	15	0	0	1	3	1	1	0	0	0	0	1	4	3	15
RHODE ISLAND COLL	13	4	9	4	8	0	1	0	0	0	0	2	3	0	3	2	3	0	0
RUTGERS UNIV/NB	23	11	12	10	12	0	0	0	0	1	0	3	1	3	2	4	5	0	3
SALEM STATE COLL	12	6	6	6	5	0	0	0	0	0	1	2	3	2	1	2	2	0	0
SAN FRANCISCO STATE	13	4	9	4	5	0	0	0	4	0	0	3	2	0	1	0	1	1	5
SAVANNAH STATE UNIV	4	2	2	2	2	0	0	0	0	0	0	1	0	1	2	0	0	0	0
SHIPPENSBURG UNIV	2	1	1	1	1	0	0	0	0	0	0	0	0	1	0	0	1	0	0
SIMMONS COLL	25	4	21	3	14	0	0	0	6	1	1	2	5	1	10	0	5	1	1
SMITH COLL	14	6	8	1	4	0	0	2	0	3	4	1	3	3	4	2	1	0	0
SOUTHERN CONNECTICUT	14	7	7	5	6	1	1	0	0	1	0	4	2	3	3	0	2	0	0
SOUTHERN ILL/EDW	5	3	2	3	1	0	0	0	1	0	0	0	0	1	0	2	1	0	1
SOUTHERN UNIV	19	8	11	5	8	0	0	2	3	1	0	1	0	3	4	4	6	0	1
SOUTHWEST MISSOURI	3	1	2	1	2	0	0	0	0	0	0	0	0	1	1	0	0	0	1
SOUTHWEST TEXAS	12	4	8	2	5	0	1	1	1	1	1	0	0	1	2	0	2	3	4
SPALDING UNIV	7	2	5	2	3	0	2	0	0	0	0	0	0	1	1	1	3	0	1
ST AMBROSE UNIV	5	3	2	3	2	0	0	0	0	0	0	2	0	1	2	0	0	0	0
STEPHEN F AUSTIN	7	2	5	2	4	0	0	0	1	0	0	1	0	0	0	1	3	0	2
SUNY/ALBANY	16	8	8	7	7	0	0	0	0	1	1	3	3	2	2	3	3	0	0
TEMPLE UNIV	21	9	12	9	12	0	0	0	0	0	0	2	5	4	2	3	5	0	0
TEXAS A&M UNIV/COM	6	2	4	2	2	0	0	1	1	1	1	1	0	0	1	2	0	1	1
TULANE UNIV	11	7	4	6	3	0	0	1	1	0	0	1	0	1	2	2	0	3	2
U OF ALABAMA	20	10	10	5	7	0	0	0	1	5	2	5	1	1	0	2	4	2	5
U OF ALASKA/ANK	5	3	2	3	2	0	0	0	0	0	0	0	0	2	0	0	0	0	0
U OF ARKANSAS/LR	12	4	8	4	6	0	0	0	0	0	1	2	1	1	1	1	4	0	2
U OF CENTRAL FLORIDA	11	7	4	6	3	1	0	0	1	0	0	0	1	3	0	1	1	3	2
U OF CHICAGO	25	9	16	0	0	0	0	0	0	9	16	3	8	1	5	3	2	2	1
U OF CONNECTICUT	27	12	15	11	13	0	0	0	0	1	2	6	6	2	4	0	5	4	0
U OF DENVER	24	7	17	5	12	0	1	1	1	1	3	1	2	3	4	1	6	2	5
U OF GEORGIA	17	11	6	8	6	0	0	0	0	3	0	5	1	2	1	4	3	0	1
U OF HAWAII	26	6	20	4	5	0	0	0	3	2	12	2	2	0	2	1	4	3	12
U OF ILLINOIS/CHI	30	8	22	5	14	0	0	1	4	2	4	1	3	1	4	5	10	1	5
U OF ILLINOIS/URB	15	7	8	5	6	0	0	1	0	1	2	0	1	3	1	4	5	0	1
U OF IOWA	9	3	6	0	3	0	0	0	0	3	3	0	0	0	2	1	3	0	1
U OF KENTUCKY	42	14	28	8	13	3	3	2	10	2	2	2	1	3	4	1	10	8	17
U OF LOUISVILLE	20	7	13	1	0	0	0	0	0	6	13	3	2	2	4	2	5	1	2
U OF MARYLAND	67	27	40	22	20	0	0	3	13	2	7	8	4	10	7	5	11	4	18
U OF MICHIGAN	40	23	17	22	14	0	0	0	3	1	3	11	2	7	10	4	5	1	0
U OF MINNESOTA/DUL	9	3	6	2	4	0	0	1	0	0	2	1	1	1	3	1	0	0	2
U OF MISSOURI/COL	15	4	11	4	11	0	0	0	0	0	0	0	1	3	2	0	4	1	4
U OF MISSOURI/KC	3	0	3	0	3	0	0	0	0	0	0	0	1	0	0	0	2	0	0
U OF MISSOURI/STL	13	3	10	3	6	0	2	0	1	0	1	0	0	1	0	0	4	2	6

114

TABLE 403

Number of Full-time Non-Administrative Graduate Faculty Assigned 50 Percent or More Time to Social Work Program, by Gender, Type of Appointment, and Academic Responsibility

Program	Total	Total		Major Responsibility								Academic Rank							
				Class		Class and Field		Field		Other		Professor		Associate Professor		Assistant Professor		Other Faculty	
		Men	Women	Men	Women	Men	Women	Men	Women	Men	Women	Men	Women	Men	Women	Men	Women	Men	Women
U OF NEBRASKA/OMA	11	2	9	2	7	0	0	0	1	0	1	1	5	1	2	0	0	0	2
U OF NEVADA/LV	15	5	10	5	8	0	0	0	1	0	1	2	0	0	3	1	5	1	2
U OF NEVADA/REN	5	1	4	1	4	0	0	0	0	0	0	0	0	1	1	0	3	0	0
U OF NEW HAMPSHIRE	9	3	6	3	5	0	0	0	0	0	1	1	0	0	0	2	4	0	2
U OF NORTH CAR/CH	70	24	46	4	8	0	0	1	1	19	37	9	3	0	4	1	3	13	36
U OF NORTH CAR/CHT	4	2	2	2	2	0	0	0	0	0	0	1	0	1	0	0	2	0	0
U OF NORTH CAR/GRB	6	1	5	0	5	0	0	0	0	1	0	1	0	0	1	0	2	0	2
U OF NORTH DAKOTA	9	4	5	3	2	0	0	1	1	0	2	0	0	2	1	2	3	0	1
U OF NORTHERN IOWA	11	7	4	6	3	0	0	1	0	0	1	1	2	4	1	4	0	1	1
U OF PENNSYLVANIA	25	12	13	5	7	0	0	0	0	7	6	2	3	5	1	1	3	4	6
U OF PITTSBURGH	25	9	16	7	10	0	0	0	0	2	6	4	2	2	3	0	3	3	8
U OF PUERTO RICO/RP	17	3	14	3	9	0	0	0	0	0	5	2	10	1	3	0	1	0	0
U OF SACRED HEART	2	0	2	0	2	0	0	0	0	0	0	0	2	0	0	0	0	0	0
U OF SOUTH CAROLINA	36	18	18	15	14	0	0	2	4	1	0	5	2	2	4	5	6	6	6
U OF SOUTH FLORIDA	16	6	10	4	4	0	2	0	2	2	2	1	1	2	2	3	1	0	6
U OF SOUTHERN IND	11	9	2	5	2	1	0	3	0	0	0	0	0	1	0	4	1	4	1
U OF TENNESSEE/KNX	26	16	10	12	9	0	0	0	0	4	1	4	1	7	3	4	6	1	0
U OF TEXAS/AUS	39	12	27	12	13	0	0	0	11	0	3	6	3	0	4	2	3	4	17
U OF TEXAS/PAN	4	2	2	2	1	0	0	0	1	0	0	0	0	0	0	2	1	0	1
U OF UTAH	15	9	6	5	5	0	1	3	0	1	0	2	1	1	2	1	2	5	1
U OF WASHINGTON	38	14	24	11	13	0	0	2	4	1	7	4	3	3	10	5	6	2	5
U OF WISCONSIN/MAD	18	5	13	3	8	0	3	1	1	1	1	1	4	2	0	2	3	0	6
U OF WISCONSIN/MIL	24	9	15	5	1	0	0	1	6	3	8	6	1	2	8	1	6	0	0
U OF WYOMING	4	2	2	2	2	0	0	0	0	0	0	0	1	0	0	2	0	0	1
VALDOSTA STATE UNIV	5	3	2	3	2	0	0	0	0	0	0	0	0	1	0	2	2	0	0
VIRGINIA COMMONWEAL	29	5	24	2	9	0	0	0	13	3	2	2	2	1	6	2	3	0	13
WALLA WALLA COLL	11	2	9	2	9	0	0	0	0	0	0	1	3	1	2	0	3	0	1
WAYNE STATE UNIV	35	11	24	8	14	0	0	0	4	3	6	2	1	2	5	3	5	4	13
WEST CHESTER UNIV	5	1	4	1	4	0	0	0	0	0	0	0	0	1	0	0	4	0	0
WEST VIRGINIA UNIV	11	4	7	3	6	0	0	0	0	1	1	1	1	1	1	1	3	1	2
WESTERN MICHIGAN	15	7	8	6	6	0	0	0	0	1	2	3	1	2	1	1	3	1	3
WICHITA STATE UNIV	6	3	3	3	3	0	0	0	0	0	0	0	0	0	0	3	0	0	3
YESHIVA UNIV	34	12	22	12	17	0	0	0	4	0	1	5	0	3	8	1	8	3	6

115

TABLE 404

Ethnic Characteristics of Full-time and Part-time Graduate Faculty

Program	At Least 50 Percent in Social Work Program								Less Than 50 Percent in Social Work Program							
	Total	African American	Amerian Indian	Asian American	Chic/Mex American	Puerto Rican	White	Other	Total	African American	Amerian Indian	Asian American	Chic/Mex American	Puerto Rican	White	Other
TOTAL: Number / Percent	2,639 / 100.0%	402 / 15.2%	25 / 0.9%	80 / 3.0%	52 / 2.0%	53 / 2.0%	1,974 / 74.8%	53 / 2.0%	1,232 / 100.0%	155 / 12.6%	8 / 0.6%	15 / 1.2%	24 / 1.9%	15 / 1.2%	1,002 / 81.3%	13 / 1.1%
ADELPHI UNIV	26	2	0	1	0	1	22	0	57	4	0	1	0	3	49	0
ALABAMA A&M UNIV	11	7	1	0	0	0	2	1	0	0	0	0	0	0	0	0
ARIZONA STATE UNIV	33	2	1	1	3	2	22	2	0	3	0	0	0	0	0	0
AUGSBURG COLL	16	2	0	2	0	1	11	1	9	3	0	0	0	0	6	0
BARRY UNIV	29	5	0	0	1	0	23	0	0	0	0	0	0	0	0	0
BOSTON COLL	31	4	0	1	0	0	26	0	46	8	0	0	0	2	35	1
BOSTON UNIV	37	3	0	1	0	1	32	0	23	2	0	0	0	0	20	0
BRIGHAM YOUNG/UT	0	0	0	0	0	0	0	0	6	0	1	1	1	0	4	0
BRYN MAWR COLL	21	3	1	0	0	0	17	0	15	1	0	0	0	0	13	1
CAL STATE UNIV/BAK	1	0	0	1	0	0	0	0	0	0	0	0	0	0	0	0
CAL STATE UNIV/FRES	15	2	0	1	3	0	9	0	14	3	0	1	1	0	8	1
CAL STATE UNIV/LB	22	3	1	1	2	0	15	0	33	2	0	0	5	0	23	3
CAL STATE UNIV/SB	10	2	0	2	0	0	6	0	0	0	0	0	0	0	0	0
CASE WESTERN RESERVE	31	4	0	1	0	0	25	1	0	0	0	0	0	0	0	0
CATHOLIC UNIV/DC	17	3	0	0	0	1	13	0	0	0	0	0	0	0	0	0
CLARK ATLANTA UNIV	15	15	0	0	0	0	0	0	6	5	0	0	0	0	1	0
COLL ST CAT/U ST THO	24	2	0	0	0	0	22	0	8	0	0	0	1	0	7	0
COLORADO STATE UNIV	16	0	0	0	2	0	14	0	3	0	0	0	0	0	2	1
COLUMBIA UNIV	44	4	1	3	0	0	33	3	0	0	0	0	0	0	0	0
DELAWARE STATE UNIV	13	9	0	0	0	0	3	1	0	0	0	0	0	0	0	0
EAST CAROLINA UNIV	24	5	0	0	0	0	19	0	3	1	0	0	0	0	2	0
EASTERN MICHIGAN	20	5	1	0	1	0	13	0	15	3	0	0	1	0	11	0
EDINBORO UNIV	8	0	0	0	0	1	7	0	0	0	0	0	0	0	0	0
FLORIDA ATLANTIC	15	0	1	1	1	0	10	2	0	0	0	0	0	0	0	0
FLORIDA GULF COAST	6	1	0	0	0	0	4	1	0	0	0	0	0	0	0	0
FLORIDA INTERNATL	23	2	0	1	0	0	16	4	21	1	0	0	0	0	18	2
GALLAUDET UNIV	11	2	1	0	0	0	8	0	0	0	0	0	0	0	0	0
GRAMBLING STATE UNIV	10	6	1	0	0	0	2	1	0	0	0	0	0	0	0	0
GRAND VALLEY STATE	27	5	0	1	2	2	18	0	2	0	0	0	1	0	0	0
GREATER ROCHESTER	4	2	0	0	0	0	2	0	1	0	0	0	0	0	1	0
HOWARD UNIV	23	20	0	1	0	0	2	0	24	22	0	1	0	0	1	0
HUNTER COLL	41	6	1	1	0	4	29	0	0	0	0	0	0	0	0	0
INDIANA UNIV	32	5	0	0	0	0	26	1	0	0	0	0	0	0	0	0
JACKSON STATE UNIV	16	11	0	0	0	0	5	0	5	5	0	0	0	0	0	0
LOMA LINDA UNIV	12	2	0	0	0	1	9	1	0	0	0	0	0	0	0	0
LOUISIANA STATE UNIV	21	1	0	1	0	0	19	0	20	3	0	0	0	0	17	0
LOYOLA UNIV CHICAGO	33	3	0	1	2	0	27	0	33	6	0	0	1	0	26	0
MARYWOOD UNIV	27	0	0	0	0	1	26	0	35	1	0	0	1	0	33	0
MICHIGAN STATE UNIV	46	5	0	1	1	0	39	0	2	0	0	0	0	0	2	0
MONMOUTH UNIV	17	0	0	0	1	0	15	2	0	0	0	0	0	0	0	0
NEW MEXICO STATE	19	0	1	0	1	1	12	4	3	1	0	1	0	0	1	0

116

TABLE 404

Ethnic Characteristics of Full-time and Part-time Graduate Faculty

Program	At Least 50 Percent in Social Work Program								Less Than 50 Percent in Social Work Program							
	Total	African American	Amerian Indian	Asian American	Chic/Mex American	Puerto Rican	White	Other	Total	African American	Amerian Indian	Asian American	Chic/Mex American	Puerto Rican	White	Other
NEW YORK UNIV	60	6	0	1	1	2	45	5	120	4	0	1	0	4	110	1
OHIO STATE UNIV	31	7	0	2	0	1	20	1	0	0	0	0	0	0	0	0
OHIO UNIV	12	0	0	1	0	0	11	0	4	0	0	0	0	0	4	0
OUR LADY OF LAKE	11	1	0	1	3	0	6	0	9	1	0	0	1	0	7	0
PORTLAND STATE UNIV	30	3	1	0	1	0	25	0	15	0	1	0	0	0	13	1
RADFORD UNIV	32	3	0	0	0	0	28	1	0	0	0	0	0	0	0	0
RHODE ISLAND COLL	19	2	0	1	0	0	16	0	17	1	0	0	0	0	16	0
RUTGERS UNIV/NB	30	7	0	0	0	1	22	0	44	4	0	0	0	1	39	0
SALEM STATE COLL	17	2	0	0	0	0	15	0	0	0	0	0	0	0	0	0
SAN FRANCISCO STATE	19	3	0	4	0	2	10	0	11	2	0	2	0	1	6	0
SAVANNAH STATE UNIV	9	4	0	0	0	0	2	3	5	4	0	0	0	0	1	0
SHIPPENSBURG UNIV	2	1	0	0	0	0	1	0	2	0	0	0	0	2	0	0
SIMMONS COLL	25	6	0	0	0	0	18	0	57	2	0	1	2	2	50	0
SMITH COLL	15	4	0	0	0	0	11	0	0	0	0	0	0	0	0	0
SOUTHERN CONNECTICUT	18	1	0	0	0	1	13	3	0	0	0	0	0	0	0	0
SOUTHERN ILL/EDW	10	2	0	0	0	0	8	0	0	2	0	0	0	0	0	0
SOUTHERN UNIV	24	16	0	0	0	0	8	0	12	11	0	0	0	0	1	0
SOUTHWEST MISSOURI	6	1	0	0	0	0	5	0	3	1	0	0	0	0	2	0
SOUTHWEST TEXAS	14	2	0	0	2	0	10	0	7	2	0	0	2	0	3	0
SPALDING UNIV	10	0	0	0	1	0	9	0	3	0	0	0	0	0	3	0
ST AMBROSE UNIV	7	0	0	0	0	0	7	0	0	0	0	0	0	0	0	0
STEPHEN F AUSTIN	13	5	0	0	1	0	7	0	2	0	0	0	0	0	2	0
SUNY/ALBANY	29	3	2	0	0	0	24	0	0	0	0	0	0	0	0	0
TEMPLE UNIV	24	7	0	0	0	0	17	0	0	0	0	0	0	0	0	0
TEXAS A&M UNIV/COM	10	2	0	0	0	0	8	0	0	0	0	0	0	0	0	0
TULANE UNIV	18	4	0	0	1	0	13	0	31	3	0	0	0	0	28	0
U OF ALABAMA	28	4	0	0	0	0	24	0	14	4	0	0	0	0	10	0
U OF ALASKA/ANK	9	0	0	0	0	0	9	0	5	0	0	0	0	0	5	0
U OF ARKANSAS/LR	15	1	0	0	2	0	12	0	0	0	0	0	0	0	0	0
U OF CENTRAL FLORIDA	17	3	0	0	0	2	11	1	10	1	0	1	0	1	7	0
U OF CHICAGO	29	4	0	0	0	0	25	0	1	0	0	0	0	0	1	0
U OF CONNECTICUT	30	2	0	2	0	3	22	1	36	6	0	0	0	1	29	0
U OF DENVER	33	2	2	0	2	0	26	1	29	2	0	0	1	1	25	0
U OF GEORGIA	29	6	0	1	1	0	21	0	0	0	0	0	0	0	0	0
U OF HAWAII	34	0	0	13	0	0	17	4	1	0	0	0	0	0	1	0
U OF ILLINOIS/CHI	33	9	0	1	0	1	22	0	0	0	0	0	0	0	0	0
U OF ILLINOIS/URB	19	1	0	2	0	0	16	0	0	0	0	0	0	0	0	0
U OF IOWA	17	2	0	0	0	0	15	0	14	3	0	0	0	0	11	0
U OF KENTUCKY	44	1	1	1	0	0	42	0	27	0	0	2	0	0	25	0
U OF LOUISVILLE	20	2	0	1	0	0	17	0	42	3	0	1	0	0	37	1
U OF MARYLAND	86	18	2	1	0	0	63	2	1	0	0	0	0	0	1	0
U OF MICHIGAN	44	7	0	3	1	0	32	1	3	0	0	0	1	0	2	0
U OF MINNESOTA/DUL	9	0	3	0	0	0	6	0	7	0	2	0	0	0	5	0
U OF MISSOURI/COL	25	2	0	0	0	0	23	0	10	2	0	0	0	0	8	0

TABLE 404

Ethnic Characteristics of Full-time and Part-time Graduate Faculty

Program	At Least 50 Percent in Social Work Program								Less Than 50 Percent in Social Work Program							
	Total	African American	Amerian Indian	Asian American	Chic/Mex American	Puerto Rican	White	Other	Total	African American	Amerian Indian	Asian American	Chic/Mex American	Puerto Rican	White	Other
U OF MISSOURI/KC	5	1	0	0	0	0	4	0	0	0	0	0	0	0	0	0
U OF MISSOURI/STL	17	2	0	1	0	0	14	0	0	0	0	0	0	0	0	0
U OF NEBRASKA/OMA	15	2	0	2	1	0	10	0	1	0	0	0	0	0	1	0
U OF NEVADA/LV	15	4	0	2	0	0	9	0	4	0	0	0	0	0	4	0
U OF NEVADA/REN	9	0	0	0	0	0	9	0	0	0	0	0	0	0	0	0
U OF NEW HAMPSHIRE	14	0	0	0	0	1	13	0	8	0	0	0	0	0	8	0
U OF NORTH CAR/CH	80	14	0	0	0	0	66	0	2	0	0	0	0	0	2	0
U OF NORTH CAR/CHT	8	2	0	0	0	0	6	0	4	1	0	0	0	0	3	0
U OF NORTH CAR/GRB	10	3	0	0	0	0	7	0	0	0	0	0	0	0	0	0
U OF NORTH DAKOTA	12	0	1	0	0	0	11	0	2	0	0	0	0	0	2	0
U OF NORTHERN IOWA	13	1	0	0	0	0	12	0	3	1	0	0	0	0	3	0
U OF PENNSYLVANIA	34	9	0	2	0	0	23	0	26	1	0	1	0	0	24	0
U OF PITTSBURGH	33	8	0	1	0	0	24	0	48	6	0	0	0	0	41	1
U OF PUERTO RICO/RP	18	0	0	0	0	18	0	0	0	0	0	0	0	0	0	0
U OF SACRED HEART	3	0	0	0	0	3	0	0	0	0	0	0	0	0	0	0
U OF SOUTH CAROLINA	39	4	0	3	0	0	32	0	10	2	0	0	0	0	8	0
U OF SOUTH FLORIDA	18	1	0	0	0	0	17	0	1	0	0	0	0	0	1	0
U OF SOUTHERN IND	15	1	0	0	0	0	14	0	2	0	0	0	0	0	2	0
U OF TENNESSEE/KNX	36	2	1	1	0	0	31	1	0	0	0	0	0	0	0	0
U OF TEXAS/AUS	47	6	1	0	5	0	35	0	19	1	0	0	4	0	14	0
U OF TEXAS/PAN	9	0	0	0	7	0	2	0	0	0	0	0	0	0	0	0
U OF UTAH	24	0	0	1	0	1	21	1	0	0	0	0	0	0	0	0
U OF WASHINGTON	50	3	1	6	0	1	39	0	9	1	0	0	0	0	8	0
U OF WISCONSIN/MAD	24	0	0	0	0	1	23	0	17	0	3	0	1	0	14	0
U OF WISCONSIN/MIL	29	3	1	1	0	1	23	0	30	1	0	0	1	0	28	0
U OF WYOMING	4	1	0	0	0	0	3	0	1	0	0	0	0	0	1	0
VALDOSTA STATE UNIV	7	1	0	0	0	0	6	0	0	0	0	0	0	0	0	0
VIRGINIA COMMONWEAL	37	5	0	0	0	0	32	0	23	2	0	0	0	0	21	0
WALLA WALLA COLL	21	1	0	0	0	0	19	1	0	0	0	0	0	0	0	0
WAYNE STATE UNIV	37	11	1	0	1	1	23	0	48	14	0	0	0	1	34	0
WEST CHESTER UNIV	7	2	0	0	0	0	5	0	0	0	0	0	0	0	0	0
WEST VIRGINIA UNIV	15	0	0	2	0	0	13	0	3	0	0	0	0	0	3	0
WESTERN MICHIGAN	19	2	0	0	0	0	17	0	30	2	1	0	0	0	27	0
WICHITA STATE UNIV	9	1	0	0	1	0	7	0	0	0	0	0	0	0	0	0
YESHIVA UNIV	43	3	0	0	0	1	39	0	17	0	0	0	0	0	17	0

118

APPENDIX B

Colleges and Universities with Baccalaureate Social Work Degree Programs Accredited by the Council on Social Work Education 1999-2000*

Alabama

Alabama A & M University
Alabama State University
Auburn University
Jacksonville State University
Miles College
Oakwood College
Talladega College
Troy State University
Tuskegee University
University of Alabama
University of Alabama at Birmingham
University of Montevallo
University of North Alabama

Alaska

University of Alaska Fairbanks
University of Alaska, Anchorage

Arizona

Arizona State University
Arizona State University West
Northern Arizona University

Arkansas

Arkansas State University
Harding University
University of Arkansas at Pine Bluff
University of Arkansas, Fayetteville

California

Azusa Pacific University
California State University, Chico
California State University, Fresno
California State University, Long Beach
California State University, Los Angeles
California State University, Sacramento
Humboldt State University
La Sierra University
Pacific Union College
San Diego State University
San Francisco State University
San Jose State University
Whittier College

Colorado

Colorado State University
Metropolitan State College of Denver
University of Southern Colorado

Connecticut

Central Connecticut State University
Sacred Heart University
Saint Joseph College
Southern Connecticut State University
Western Connecticut State University

Delaware

Delaware State University

District of Columbia

Catholic University of America
Gallaudet University
University of the District of Columbia

Florida

Florida Agriculture and Mechanical University
Florida Atlantic University
Florida International University
Florida State University
Saint Leo University
University of Central Florida
University of South Florida
University of West Florida

Georgia

Clark Atlanta University
Georgia State University
Savannah State University
University of Georgia

Hawaii

Brigham Young University, Hawai'i Campus
University of Hawai'i at Manoa

Idaho

Boise State University
Idaho State University
Lewis-Clark State College
Northwest Nazarene University

Illinois

Aurora University
Governors State University
Illinois State University
Loyola University of Chicago
MacMurray College
Northeastern Illinois University
Olivet Nazarene University
Southern Illinois University at Carbondale
Southern Illinois University at Edwardsville
University of Illinois at Chicago
University of Illinois at Springfield
University of Saint Francis
Western Illinois University

Indiana

Anderson University
Ball State University
Goshen College
Indiana State University
Indiana University
Indiana Wesleyan University
Manchester College
Saint Mary's College
Taylor University
University of Indianapolis
University of Saint Francis
University of Southern Indiana
Valparaiso University

Iowa

Briar Cliff College
Buena Vista University
Dordt College
Loras College/Clarke College
Luther College
Marycrest International University
Mount Mercy College
Northwestern College
University of Iowa
University of Northern Iowa
Wartburg College

Kansas

Bethany College
Bethel College
Fort Hays State University
Kansas State University
Pittsburg State University
University of Kansas

Washburn University
Wichita State University

Kentucky

Brescia University
Eastern Kentucky University
Kentucky Christian College
Kentucky State University
Morehead State University
Murray State University
Northern Kentucky University
Spalding University
University of Kentucky
Western Kentucky University

Louisiana

Grambling State University
Louisiana College
Northwestern State University of Louisiana
Southeastern Louisiana University
Southern University and A & M College
Southern University at New Orleans
University of Louisiana at Monroe

Maine

University of Maine
University of Maine at Presque Isle
University of Southern Maine

Maryland

Bowie State University
Coppin State College
Frostburg State University
Hood College
Morgan State University
Salisbury State University
University of Maryland
Western Maryland College

Massachusetts

Anna Maria College
Atlantic Union College
Bridgewater State College
Eastern Nazarene College
Elms College
Gordon College
Regis College
Salem State College
Western New England College
Wheelock College

Michigan

Andrews University
Calvin College
Eastern Michigan University
Ferris State University
Grand Valley State University
Hope College
Madonna University
Marygrove College
Michigan State University
Northern Michigan University
Saginaw Valley State University
Spring Arbor College
University of Detroit Mercy
University of Michigan-Flint
Wayne State University
Western Michigan University

Minnesota

Augsburg College
Bemidji State University
Bethel College
College of Saint Benedict/Saint John's University
College of Saint Catherine/University of Saint Thomas
College of Saint Scholastica
Concordia College
Metropolitan State University
Minnesota State University Moorhead
Minnesota State University, Mankato
Southwest State University
St. Cloud State University
St. Olaf College
Winona State University

Mississippi

Delta State University
Jackson State University
Mississippi College
Mississippi State University
Mississippi Valley State University
University of Mississippi
University of Southern Mississippi

Missouri

Avila College
Central Missouri State University
Columbia College
Evangel University
Missouri Western State College
Saint Louis University

Southeast Missouri State University
Southwest Missouri State University
University of Missouri-Columbia
University of Missouri-St. Louis
William Woods University

Montana

Carroll College
University of Montana

Nebraska

Chadron State College
Creighton University
Dana College
Nebraska Wesleyan University/Union College
University of Nebraska at Kearney
University of Nebraska at Omaha

Nevada

University of Nevada, Las Vegas
University of Nevada, Reno

New Hampshire

Plymouth State College
University of New Hampshire

New Jersey

Georgian Court College
Kean University
Monmouth University
Ramapo College
Richard Stockton College of New Jersey
Rutgers University - The State University of New Je
Rutgers University - The State University of New Je
Seton Hall University

New Mexico

New Mexico Highlands University
New Mexico State University
Western New Mexico University

New York

Adelphi University
Buffalo State College
College of New Rochelle
Concordia College
Cornell University
D'Youville College
Daemen College
Dominican College of Blauvet
Iona College

Keuka College
Lehman College, City University of New York
Long Island University-C.W. Post
Marist College
Marymount College
Mercy College
Molloy College
Nazareth College of Rochester
New York University
Niagara University
Roberts Wesleyan College
Rochester Institute of Technology
Siena College
Skidmore College
State University of New York at Stony Brook
State University of New York, College at Brockport
State University of New York, University at Albany
Syracuse University
York College of the City University of New York

North Carolina

Appalachian State University
Barton College
Bennett College
Campbell University
East Carolina University
Mars Hill College
Meredith College
Methodist College
North Carolina A & T State University
North Carolina Central University
North Carolina State University
University of North Carolina at Charlotte
University of North Carolina at Greensboro
University of North Carolina at Pembroke
Warren Wilson College
Western Carolina University

North Dakota

Minot State University
University of Mary
University of North Dakota

Ohio

Ashland University
Bluffton College
Bowling Green State University
Capital University
Cedarville College
Cleveland State University

College of Mount Saint Joseph
Defiance College
Lourdes College
Malone College
Miami University
Ohio State University
Ohio University
University of Akron
University of Cincinnati
University of Findlay
University of Rio Grande
University of Toledo
Ursuline College
Wright State University
Xavier University
Youngstown State University

Oklahoma

East Central University
Northeastern State University
Oral Roberts University
University of Oklahoma

Pennsylvania

Alvernia College
Bloomsburg University
Cabrini College
California University of Pennsylvania
Carlow College
Cedar Crest College
College Misericordia
Eastern College
Edinboro University of Pennsylvania
Elizabethtown College
Gannon University
Juniata College
Kutztown University
La Salle University
Lock Haven University of Pennsylvania
Mansfield University of Pennsylvania
Marywood University
Mercyhurst College
Messiah College
Millersville University of Pennsylvania
Philadelphia College of Bible
Saint Francis College
Shippensburg University
Slippery Rock University
Temple University
University of Pittsburgh

West Chester University
Widener University

Puerto Rico

Pontificia Universidad Catolica de Puerto Rico
Universidad Interamericana de Puerto Rico, Recinto de Arecibo
Universidad Interamericana de Puerto Rico, Recinto Metropolitano
University of Puerto Rico at Humacao
University of Puerto Rico, Rio Piedras Campus
University of the Sacred Heart

Rhode Island

Providence College
Rhode Island College
Salve Regina University

South Carolina

Benedict College
Columbia College
South Carolina State University
Winthrop University

South Dakota

Augustana College/University of Sioux Falls
Presentation College
University of South Dakota

Tennessee

Austin Peay State University
Belmont University
David Lipscomb University
East Tennessee State University
Freed-Hardeman University
Middle Tennessee State University
Southern Adventist University
Tennessee State University
University of Memphis
University of Tennessee
University of Tennessee, Chattanooga
University of Tennessee, Martin

Texas

Abilene Christian University
Baylor University
Hardin-Simmons University
Howard Payne University
Lamar University
Lubbock Christian University
Midwestern State University

Our Lady of the Lake University
Prairie View A & M University
Southwest Texas State University
Southwestern Adventist University
St. Edward's University
Stephen F. Austin State University
Tarleton University System Center - Central Texas
Texas A&M University - Commerce
Texas Christian University
Texas Lutheran University
Texas Southern University
Texas Tech University
Texas Woman's University
University of Mary Hardin-Baylor
University of North Texas
University of Texas at Arlington
University of Texas at Austin
University of Texas at El Paso
University of Texas-Pan American
West Texas A & M University

Utah

Brigham Young University
Utah State University
Weber State University

Vermont

Castleton State College
Trinity College
University of Vermont

Virginia

Christopher Newport University
Eastern Mennonite University
Ferrum College
George Mason University
James Madison University
Longwood College
Norfolk State University
Radford University
Virginia Commonwealth University
Virginia Intermont College
Virginia State University
Virginia Union University

Washington

Eastern Washington University
Heritage College
Pacific Lutheran University
University of Washington
Walla Walla College

West Virginia

Bethany College
Concord College
Marshall University
Shepherd College
West Virginia State College
West Virginia University

Wisconsin

Carroll College
Carthage College
Concordia University Wisconsin
Marian College of Fond du Lac
Marquette University
Mount Mary College
Mount Senario College
University of Wisconsin-Eau Claire
University of Wisconsin-Green Bay
University of Wisconsin-Madison
University of Wisconsin-Milwaukee
University of Wisconsin-Oshkosh
University of Wisconsin-River Falls
University of Wisconsin-Superior
University of Wisconsin-Whitewater

Wyoming

University of Wyoming

* Status in June 2000

Colleges and Universities with Baccalaureate Social Work Degree Programs in Candidacy for Accreditation 1999-2000*

Arkansas

Philander Smith College
Southern Arkansas University
University of Arkansas at Little Rock
University of Arkansas at Monticello

Connecticut

Eastern Connecticut State University

Georgia

Albany State University
Thomas University

Guam

University of Guam

Hawaii

Hawaii Pacific University

Illinois

Bradley University

Indiana

Grace College

Kentucky

Campbellsville University

Massachusetts

Westfield State College

Mississippi

Mississippi State University-Meridian
Rust College

New York

College of Saint Rose
College of Staten Island
Fordham University
Long Island University-Brooklyn Campus
State University of New York at Plattsburgh
State University of New York, College at Fredonia

North Carolina

Johnson C. Smith University
University of North Carolina at Wilmington

Oklahoma

Southwestern Oklahoma State University

Oregon

George Fox University

Pennsylvania

Seton Hill College

South Carolina

Limestone College

Tennessee

Lincoln Memorial University
Union University

Texas

Texas A&M University, Kingsville

West Virginia

College of West Virginia

Wisconsin

Viterbo University

* Status in June 2000

125

APPENDIX C

Colleges and Universities with Graduate Social Work Degree Programs Accredited by the Council on Social Work Education 1999-2000*

Alabama

Alabama A & M University
University of Alabama

Alaska

University of Alaska, Anchorage

Arizona

Arizona State University

Arkansas

University of Arkansas at Little Rock

California

California State University, Fresno
California State University, Long Beach
California State University, Los Angeles
California State University, Sacramento
California State University, San Bernardino
California State University, Stanislaus
Loma Linda University
San Diego State University
San Francisco State University
San Jose State University
University of California at Berkeley
University of California at Los Angeles
University of Southern California

Colorado

Colorado State University
University of Denver

Connecticut

Southern Connecticut State University
University of Connecticut

Delaware

Delaware State University

District of Columbia

Catholic University of America
Gallaudet University
Howard University

Florida

Barry University
Florida International University
Florida State University
University of Central Florida
University of South Florida

Georgia

Clark Atlanta University
Savannah State University
University of Georgia
Valdosta State University

Hawaii

University of Hawai'i at Manoa

Idaho

Boise State University

Illinois

Aurora University
Loyola University of Chicago
Southern Illinois University at Carbondale
University of Chicago
University of Illinois at Chicago
University of Illinois at Urbana-Champaign

Indiana

Indiana University
University of Southern Indiana

Iowa

St. Ambrose University
University of Iowa

Kansas

University of Kansas
Washburn University

Kentucky

University of Kentucky
University of Louisville

Louisiana

Grambling State University

Louisiana State University
Southern University at New Orleans
Tulane University

Maine

University of Maine
University of New England

Maryland

University of Maryland

Massachusetts

Boston College
Boston University
Salem State College
Simmons College
Smith College
Springfield College

Michigan

Andrews University
Eastern Michigan University
Grand Valley State University
Michigan State University
University of Michigan
Wayne State University
Western Michigan University

Minnesota

Augsburg College
College of Saint Catherine/University of Saint Thomas
University of Minnesota-Duluth
University of Minnesota-Twin Cities

Mississippi

Jackson State University
University of Southern Mississippi

Missouri

Saint Louis University
Southwest Missouri State University
University of Missouri-Columbia
Washington University

Nebraska

University of Nebraska at Omaha

Nevada

University of Nevada, Las Vegas
University of Nevada, Reno

New Hampshire

University of New Hampshire

New Jersey

Kean University
Rutgers University - The State University of New Je

New Mexico

New Mexico Highlands University
New Mexico State University

New York

Adelphi University
Columbia University
Fordham University
Hunter College of the City University of New York
New York University
Roberts Wesleyan College
State University of New York at Stony Brook
State University of New York, University at Albany
State University of New York, University at Buffalo
Syracuse University
Yeshiva University

North Carolina

East Carolina University
University of North Carolina at Chapel Hill
University of North Carolina at Greensboro/North Carolina A & T State University

North Dakota

University of North Dakota

Ohio

Case Western Reserve University
Cleveland State University/University of Akron
Ohio State University
University of Cincinnati

Oklahoma

University of Oklahoma

Oregon

Portland State University

Pennsylvania

Bryn Mawr College
Marywood University
Temple University
University of Pennsylvania
University of Pittsburgh
Widener University

Puerto Rico

Universidad Interamericana de Puerto Rico, Recinto Metropolitano
University of Puerto Rico, Rio Piedras Campus

Rhode Island

Rhode Island College

South Carolina

University of South Carolina

Tennessee

University of Tennessee

Texas

Our Lady of the Lake University
Southwest Texas State University
University of Houston
University of Texas at Arlington
University of Texas at Austin

Utah

Brigham Young University
University of Utah

Vermont

University of Vermont

Virginia

Norfolk State University
Radford University
Virginia Commonwealth University

Washington

Eastern Washington University
University of Washington
Walla Walla College

West Virginia

West Virginia University

Wisconsin

University of Wisconsin-Madison
University of Wisconsin-Milwaukee

Wyoming

University of Wyoming

* Status in June 2000

Colleges and Universities with Graduate Social Work Degree Programs in Candidacy for Accreditation 1999-2000*

Arizona

Arizona State University West

California

California State University, Bakersfield

Florida

Florida Gulf Coast University

Georgia

Georgia State University

Illinois

Illinois State University
Southern Illinois University at Edwardsville

Kansas

Newman University
Wichita State University

Kentucky

Spalding University

Missouri

University of Missouri-Kansas City
University of Missouri-St. Louis

New Jersey

Monmouth University

New York

Greater Rochester Collaborative MSW Program

Ohio

Ohio University

Pennsylvania

California University of Pennsylvania
West Chester University

Texas

Baylor University
Stephen F. Austin State University
University of Texas-Pan American

* Status in June 2000